Maryland Environmental Law Handbook

Maryland Environmental Law Handbook

Fifth Edition

Theda Braddock

Bernan Press

Lanham • Boulder • New York • London

Published by Bernan Press
An imprint of The Rowman & Littlefield Publishing Group, Inc.
4501 Forbes Boulevard, Suite 200, Lanham, Maryland 20706
www.rowman.com
800-462-6420

6 Tinworth Street, London SE11 5AL, United Kingdom

ISBN: 978-1-64143-378-5
E-ISBN: 978-1-64143-379-2

Contents

Chapter 1

Introduction to Environmental Law

This *Handbook* surveys Maryland environmental law. It includes both discussions of major federal statutes as they are enforced in Maryland (noting what modifications and adjustments have been made at the state level) and discussions of regulatory programs peculiar to Maryland, such as the Chesapeake Bay Critical Area Protection Program. Particular emphasis is placed upon the laws that are most likely to affect the day-to-day transactions of business and industry.

FEDERAL ENVIRONMENTAL LAW

In 1969, Congress enacted the National Environmental Policy Act (NEPA),[1] which requires federal agencies to prepare environmental assessments of their proposed spending and regulatory actions. If an assessment reveals that the proposed action will have "significant" effects on "the quality of the human environment," then an environmental impact statement must be prepared.[2]

In 1970, the United States Environmental Protection Agency (EPA) was created. In that same year, the Clean Air Act was enacted. Through the 1970s, 1980s, and into the 1990s, Congress enacted many other major environmental statutes, including: (1) the Clean Water Act, enacted in 1972 with major amendments in 1977 and 1987; (2) the Resource Conservation and Recovery Act (RCRA) (regulating hazardous waste) enacted in 1976 with major amendments in 1980 and 1984; (3) the Comprehensive Environmental Response, Compensation, and Liability Act (CERCLA or Superfund), enacted in 1980 and reauthorized in 1986 by the Superfund Amendments and Reauthorization Act (SARA); and (4) the Toxic Substances Control Act (TSCA) (regulating the manufacture and import of toxic substances), enacted in 1976, amended in 1981, 1984, and 1986. Additionally, in 1990, Congress passed major amendments to the Clean Air Act of 1970.[3]

---

[1] 42 U.S.C. §§4331 to 4370f.
[2] 42 U.S.C. §4332.
[3] 42 U.S.C. §§7401–7671q.

The major federal statutes listed above set forth regulatory approaches based on minimum standards of compliance and national permit programs. The minimum compliance standards prevent states from competing for industrial development by offering standards less strict than the national minimum. States, however, may impose more stringent requirements. The federal government allows states the opportunity to establish their own programs of environmental enforcement through an authorization process, so long as the states meet the minimum standards. To become authorized, states must submit a full description of the proposed program to EPA. If the state program is approved, EPA suspends the federal program and allows the state to administer enforcement. However, EPA retains the power to resume control and to veto any state-issued permits.

MARYLAND DEPARTMENT OF THE ENVIRONMENT

Maryland's Department of the Environment (MDE) was created on July 1, 1987, to consolidate all environmental regulatory functions into one cabinet-level agency. The purpose of this consolidation was to strengthen the state's enforcement capability and to streamline its fulfillment of other environmental responsibilities.

The Office of the Secretary includes the Office of Pollution Prevention & Sustainability, the Commission on Climate Change, the Maryland Water Quality Trading Advisory Committee, the Office of Budget & Infrastructure Financing (including the Maryland Water Quality Financing Administration), the Emergency Preparedness & Planning Program, and the Office of Environmental Information, as well as a number of other offices tasked with legal and administrative matters.

There are three divisions responsible for environmental implementation and enforcement.

1. The Air and Radiation Administration, which covers air quality permits, air quality planning (including the Climate Change Division), air quality compliance (including asbestos), air quality monitoring, mobile source control, radiological health, and operational and administrative services.
2. The Land and Materials Administration, which covers lead poisoning prevention, solid waste, land restoration, oil control, mining, resource management, and technical services and operations.
3. The Water and Science Administration, which handles compliance; wastewater permits; wetlands and waterways; water supply; sediment, stormwater, and dam safety; total maximum daily load (TMDL) technical development and implementation; environmental assessment and standards; water quality restoration and protection; and field services.

Detailed information on the environmental permit and approval process is available at https://perma.cc/P7KC-4FZG.

The Office of the Attorney General operates as legal counsel to MDE, providing all necessary legal advice and representation. Assistant Attorneys General advise the different administrations, represent the department in civil and administrative proceedings, and prosecute the more serious cases within the Environmental Crimes Unit.

REGULATORY PROCESS

Promulgation of Regulations

The Secretary of MDE has the general authority to promulgate regulations within MDE's subject matter jurisdiction.[4] In doing so, the Secretary must comply with both the general requirements of the Maryland Administrative Procedure Act[5] and any additional specific requirements applicable to the particular environmental program. Regulations are developed by MDE's technical staff, and the process of their development follows a pattern of proposal, comments, consideration, and re-proposal.

To promulgate or revise a regulation, the Secretary must first submit the proposed regulation to the Joint Committee on Administrative, Executive, and Legislative Review (AELR) for review. The Secretary then publishes the proposed regulation or change in the Maryland Register. The proposed regulation must include an economic impact statement and a statement of the impact on small businesses. This publication must either provide a telephone number and address where comments on the regulations can be directed or schedule a public hearing at which oral or written comments may be submitted.[6] The proposed regulation or revision may not be formally adopted and implemented until forty-five days after its publication in the Maryland Register. This forty-five-day delay can be avoided if emergency adoption is necessary, a fiscal impact statement is developed, and AELR gives approval.[7]

Before adopting the final regulation, the agency must publish a notice of final action in the Maryland Register, citing the proposed regulation and noting any changes from the formerly published version.[8] The effective date of the regulation is the tenth calendar day after notice of adoption is published, unless a later date is specified in the enabling statute.[9] After adoption, regulations are published in the Code of Maryland Regulations (COMAR), Maryland's analog to the Code of Federal Regulations (CFR).

Periodic Review of Existing Regulations

Regulations are reviewed every eight years under the Regulatory Review and Evaluation Act.[10] The purpose of the review is to determine whether the regulations:

1. continue to be necessary for the public interest;
2. continue to be supported by statutory authority and judicial opinions; and
3. are obsolete and otherwise appropriate for amendment or repeal.[11]

---

[4] MD. CODE, ENVIR. §1-404.
[5] MD. CODE, STATE GOV'T. §§10-101 to 305.
[6] MD. CODE, STATE GOV'T. §10-112.
[7] MD. CODE, STATE GOV'T. §10-111.
[8] MD. CODE, STATE GOV'T. §10-114.
[9] MD. CODE, STATE GOV'T. §10-117.
[10] MD. CODE, STATE GOV'T. §§10-130 to 139.
[11] MD. CODE, STATE GOV'T. §10-132.

At least one year prior to the commencement of review of regulations, the agency or administrative unit must prepare a work plan and submit the plan to the Governor.[12] The work plan must include a description of methods used by the unit, which may include procedures for inviting public comment, ensuring the participation of stakeholders, ensuring participation by other units affected by the regulations, and gathering information. Under the new statute, the unit's evaluation report must include a list of any stakeholders or affected units invited to comment, any notices published, summaries of comments received and the unit's responses, summaries of any interunit conflicts, and summaries of any relevant information.

Regulatory Challenges

In addition to the public comment opportunity for proposed regulations and revisions (except emergency regulations), interested persons (including businesses) may also petition MDE for adoption of a regulation or challenge the validity of any regulation in court.[13] If a petition for adoption of a regulation is submitted, MDE must either initiate procedures for adoption of the proposed regulation or, within sixty days, deny the petition and state the reasons for the denial.[14] To challenge the validity of a regulation promulgated by MDE, a petition for declaratory judgment must be filed in the circuit court for the county where the petitioner resides or has a principal place of business.[15] The circuit court may invalidate the regulation if it violates the United States or Maryland Constitutions, exceeds statutory authority, or was adopted in violation of statutory procedural requirements.[16]

THE PERMITTING PROCESS

Many of the environmental statutory schemes require facilities to obtain permits. A permit application submitted to MDE first will be evaluated for completeness. If material or information is missing, the reviewer will notify the applicant so that the application can be completed.

In cases involving permits for certain air pollution sources, water discharges, landfills, incinerators, sewage sludge storage or distribution structures, hazardous materials and low-level nuclear waste facilities, heightened public participation in the overall permitting process is required.[17] Upon a facility's application for a permit and before technical review by MDE, public notice is required and any person can request a public informational meeting. After review of the application and publication of a draft permit by MDE, the usual 30-day period for public comment ensues, with a public information hearing available upon request. Upon a final determination

[12] MD. CODE, STATE GOV'T. §10-134.
[13] MD. CODE, STATE GOV'T. §10-123.
[14] *Id.*
[15] MD. CODE, STATE GOV'T. §10-125.
[16] *Id.*
[17] MD. CODE, ENVIR. §§1-601 to 607.

by MDE, a party seeking a contested case hearing must request adjudication within 30 days of publication of the final determination.[18] A party may contest the determination by requesting a trial-like contested case hearing so long as the party states factual allegations with sufficient particularity to demonstrate that:

1. the party is aggrieved by the final determination, and
2. the final determination is legally inconsistent with applicable law or is based upon an incorrect determination of relevant and material fact.

Following the adjudicatory hearing, the administrative law judge at the Office of Administrative Hearings recommends a decision to the Secretary of MDE. There is then an opportunity for the losing party to file exceptions. The Secretary or his designee considers the recommended decision and exceptions and renders a final decision.[19] At that point a final permit is issued or denied. The losing party may appeal to the circuit court if aggrievement can be demonstrated.[20]

If no adverse comments are received on a draft permit, MDE usually will issue a final permit and impose a permit fee. If a permit application is denied, the applicant may request a contested case hearing. If the administrative process described above affirms the permit denial, the applicant may appeal to the circuit court.

A permit is a type of license,[21] and as such it is entitled to certain protections. As long as a renewal application is sought at least two calendar weeks before the expiration date, the permittee is protected from expiration of the permit until:

1. final action is taken on the application; and
2. either:
   (a) the time for taking judicial review expires; or
   (b) any judicial stay of MDE's final action expires.[22]

Furthermore, a permit may not be suspended or revoked unless certain procedural safeguards are met. Generally, this means the permittee is entitled to written notice of the facts which give rise to the suspension or revocation and an opportunity to present its point of view.[23]

Occasionally an emergency may warrant immediate suspension. This is only allowable if MDE finds that public health, safety, or welfare imperatively requires emergency action and promptly gives the permittee written notice of the suspension and the facts, and again, an opportunity to be heard.[24] If the emergency revocation is upheld at the required hearing, then the permittee may appeal to the circuit court as with any other disputed MDE decision.

---

[18] MD. CODE, ENVIR. §1-605(b).
[19] MD. CODE ANN., STATE GOV'T. §10-221.
[20] MD. CODE, STATE GOV'T. §10-222.
[21] MD. CODE, STATE GOV'T. §10-226(a)(2).
[22] MD. CODE, STATE GOV'T. §10-226(b).
[23] MD. CODE, STATE GOV'T. §10-226(c).
[24] *Id.*

MDE Inspections

MDE relies on regular inspections to ensure permitted facilities are complying with the law. MDE personnel have a right of entry to business premises at any reasonable hour if it is necessary to carry out a statutory duty.[25]

Permits often contain a consent to an inspection. In the case of wastewater discharge permits, the issuance is contingent upon the grant to MDE by the permit holder of a right of entry on the permit site at any reasonable time to inspect and investigate for violation of any permit condition.[26] Although exceptions to the warrant requirements have not yet been applied to environmental statutes, warrants may not be required when: (1) there is a substantial federal interest in regulation; (2) Congress has expressly dispensed with warrant requirements; or (3) the regulatory scheme is old enough or broad enough to give adequate notice of possible inspection.[27] Warrants are not required for "open-field" inspections (i.e., where the facility is not entered and the inspector remains in a public area).[28]

With each inspection, the MDE representative typically will complete an inspection report and give a copy of the report to the facility owner or operator. The report usually is a checklist upon which the inspector marks the appropriate box and then adds comments on the space provided. Inspectors may seek a broad range of information, including the facility background, inspection reports, records and files, waste control systems data, regulatory compliance reports, and enforcement reports.

Businesses should prepare in advance for inspections, particularly if notice of the inspection has been given. The following inspection guidelines may be useful:

- records required to be kept by the various environmental statutes, regulations, and permits should be compiled;
- records of environmental information that are not required by law should be stored separately in an effort to protect confidentiality;
- perform a housekeeping check for compliance, inform the employees that an inspection will take place, and ensure that the person or persons directing the inspection will be present the entire time;
- for unannounced inspections, facility guards and receptionists should notify the appropriate personnel and contact legal counsel to ensure the inspection is within the agency's statutory authority;
- employees should be cooperative but should try to define the limits of the inspection so that it does not become a "fishing expedition";
- upon completion, an exit conference should be requested to discuss what the inspection has revealed; and
- a confirming memorandum of the discussion after the conference should be made and a copy of the final inspection report should be requested if it has not already been given.

---

[25] MD. CODE, ENVIR. §1-404(k)(l).
[26] MD. CODE, ENVIR. §9-326(b).
[27] *Illinois v. Krull*, 480 U.S. 340 (1987).
[28] *State v. Sampson*, 362 Md. 438 (2001).

ENFORCEMENT OF ENVIRONMENTAL LAWS

Sources of Enforcement Actions

Enforcement actions begin in a variety of ways. Common sources are complaints from neighbors, past and present employees, or environmental organizations. When complaints are made, MDE often conducts compliance investigations.

MDE's periodic review of required reports is another source of enforcement action. Manifests for shipment of hazardous wastes and discharge monitoring reports required by point source water pollution discharge permits may reveal failures to follow regulations or excessive levels of pollutants in the discharge. Periodic site inspections by MDE inspectors, county health inspectors, and local fire officials may also alert MDE to infractions of environmental laws and regulations.

Many municipal governments have adopted ordinances granting them concurrent jurisdiction over environmental issues and inspection rights. For example, most county health departments maintain authority over septic tank permitting. Concurrent inspection authority may also result in joint enforcement actions by these agencies.

The Maryland Attorney General's Office has the responsibility of representing MDE in all legal proceedings.[29] This means that whenever the state brings an administrative or judicial proceeding against an alleged violator, an assistant attorney general will prosecute the lawsuit for MDE. The Attorney General's Office may bring civil and/or criminal actions, as allowed by statute in each regulatory area, or assist in negotiating a consent order to settle the problem.

Some federal environmental statutes also allow private citizens to bring enforcement suits. These statutes generally require the citizen to give 60 days' prior notice to the EPA, the state enforcement agency, and the alleged violator. However, such statutes bar citizen action if the state or federal agency is diligently prosecuting a civil or criminal action in a court proceeding. Maryland has a general Environmental Standing Act, which, although less broad than the federal version, allows persons with standing to bring an action for mandamus or equitable relief for any failure of a state agency or officer to perform a nondiscretionary function under an environmental quality standard.[30] Under the Maryland Environmental Standing Act, a plaintiff must provide the state at least 30 days' notice.[31]

Procedures for State Enforcement

The procedures followed by MDE for enforcement of its rules, regulations, or orders are governed by the statutes relating to each regulatory program and by the Maryland Administrative Procedure Act.[32]

Typically, the first step is for an MDE site inspector to prepare a written record of the site inspection. At some point after the inspection, an MDE supervisor reviews the inspector's finding to determine if the facility is in compliance. If the review

---

[29] MD. CODE, ENVIR. §1-407.
[30] MD. CODE, NAT. RES. §§1-501 to 508.
[31] MD. CODE, NAT. RES. §1-505(b).
[32] MD. CODE, STATE GOV'T. §§10-101 to 10-305.

identifies any violations, MDE makes a determination as to the seriousness of the violation. In most cases, MDE serves a report of violation on the facility. The report of violation describes any violations alleged and may also list remedial actions that would ensure compliance. The report of violation may simply be the written record of inspection or a separate document. These reports may not direct that action be taken or impose any penalties. The legal effect of these documents is to give notice to operators that violations are alleged. This notice is important because civil penalty assessments are often based upon the extent to which the existence of the violation was known but uncorrected and the extent to which the violator exercised reasonable care. Thus, a failure to remedy an alleged violation or to prevent a recurrence may result in a larger penalty.[33] An operator may contest the allegations by sending a letter to the enforcement chief of the appropriate regulatory program describing why the allegations are incorrect.

Legal proceedings are initiated for recurring or more serious violations. MDE has the option at this point to bring administrative or civil proceedings, to seek injunctive relief, to suspend or revoke issued licenses, or, if the violations are sufficiently egregious under the applicable statute, to bring criminal proceedings.

Responding to the State's Enforcement Action

The most influential responsive action is fast, thorough, and complete remediation of any violation and its consequences as soon as notice is received. A company's willingness to work with the state in addressing environmental issues enhances the possibility of resolution. The involvement of upper management at an early point in the process will demonstrate a company's recognition of the importance of environmental issues.

An acknowledgment of environmental problems often facilitates a resolution with MDE and EPA. It also may help protect the business from the expense and publicity of citizen suit litigation. On the other hand, admissions or violations may lead to other legal actions or consequences. Therefore, choosing the appropriate strategy is a very serious and often complex matter for which counsel should be consulted.

ADMINISTRATIVE ENFORCEMENT PROCEEDINGS

Because administrative proceedings are relatively inexpensive, quick, and efficient, they are the most common enforcement option used. Under most of the environmental statutes, the Maryland General Assembly has granted MDE the power to make initial determinations of environmental violations. MDE employs the administrative process to determine whether a violation occurred and, if so, whether a penalty or permit revocation is appropriate.

The process begins when MDE issues and serves a complaint and order on the site operator. The complaint and order specify the provisions alleged to have been

---

[33] See, e.g., MD. CODE, ENVIR. §7-266(b)(2)(ii)(1).

violated. The order may direct that corrective action be taken, that a written report be filed, or that the violator appear for a hearing.[34]

Administrative Penalties

In administrative proceedings, only fines may be imposed, the amounts of which vary among the regulatory programs. The amount of the penalty is based on an evaluation of the willfulness of the violation, environmental harm, cleanup cost, overall harm and potential for greater harm, the feasibility of preventing the harm, the hazardous nature of the materials, and whether there was a pattern of violations.[35] Although MDE will consider all of the factors, they may assess a maximum penalty in cases where specific factors are applicable. Penalty credit is considered for voluntary efforts that exceed legal requirements or create environmental benefits beyond mere remediation.

Contested Case Procedure

If a person decides to request a contested case hearing, that person must send a written request to MDE with a brief statement of the factual and legal basis for the request.[36] The parties may request the issuance of subpoenas requiring the attendance of witnesses and the production of any evidence at the hearing.[37] The request may be made *not later than* five working days before the scheduled hearing date. Discovery is only permitted for relevant and non-privileged files, memoranda, correspondence, documents, objects, or tangible things, unless the parties agree to further discovery.[38]

MDE is not required to provide an opportunity for any person other than the applicant for a contested case hearing, except for the permits listed below:

1. air quality control permits to construct (subject to MD Code, Environment §2-404);
2. permits to install, materially alter, or materially extend landfill systems, incinerators for public use, or rubble landfills (subject to MD Code, Environment §9-209);
3. permits to discharge pollutants to waters of the state (subject to MD Code, Environment §9 323);
4. permits to install, materially alter, or materially extend a structure used for the storage or distribution of any type of sewage sludge issued, renewed, or amended (subject to MD Code, Environment §9-234-1 or 9-238);
5. permits to own, operate, establish, or maintain a controlled hazardous substance facility or a hazardous material facility (subject to MD Code, Environment §7-103 or §7-232); and
6. permits to own, operate, or maintain a low-level nuclear waste facility (subject to MD Code, Environment §7-233).

---

[34] See MD. CODE, ENVIR. §§7-258, 7-259 (Controlled Hazardous Substances); §§9-334, 9-335 (Water Pollution); §§2-603, 2-604 (Air Pollution); and §4-412(a) (Oil Control).

[35] MD. CODE, ENVIR. §§7-266, 9-342.

[36] COMAR 26.01.02.06.

[37] COMAR 26.01.02.18. The Rules of Procedure for the Office of Administrative Hearings are found at COMAR 28.02.01. These rules supersede MDE's rules pursuant to COMAR 26.01.02, except where there is a conflict between the rules, in which event MDE's rules control.

[38] COMAR 28.02.01.13.

Administrative hearings are conducted before an administrative law judge. The administrative law judge may conduct a pre-hearing conference to discuss settlement, enter stipulations, or narrow the issues to be litigated.[39] Hearings follow a mini-trial format, giving both sides the opportunity to call witnesses, offer evidence and rebuttal evidence, cross-examine opposing witnesses, and present closing arguments.[40] The hearings do not follow the strict courtroom rules of evidence and are less formal in general.

The decision of the administrative law judge may not be made final until a proposed decision has been served on the parties and an opportunity has been afforded to file exceptions. Any party adversely affected by the proposed decision may file exceptions within 21 days after receiving the decision.[41] Failure to file exceptions constitutes a failure to exhaust administrative remedies and bars future appeal rights.[42] The Secretary must grant a hearing on the exceptions if the adversely affected party requests one. However, additional evidence and testimony may not be introduced; all hearings and reviews must be conducted on the basis of the record. The Secretary then must make a final decision.

Although requests for reconsideration are available in all cases, they are not a prerequisite to judicial review.[43] Even if exceptions are not filed, the Secretary still has the power to review the administrative law judge's findings. If the Secretary concludes that he or she cannot approve the proposed decision, the parties are notified and given the opportunity to be heard on the issues that are being reconsidered before a final decision is delivered.[44]

Administrative Hearing Decisions

Any person aggrieved by MDE's final decision in a contested case may take a direct judicial appeal to the circuit court where any party resides or has a principal place of business. The reviewing court conducts the proceeding without a jury and bases its decision on the record before the agency, although the court may order the agency to consider additional evidence in very limited circumstances.[45] Any party that is aggrieved by the circuit court's decision, including MDE, may appeal to the Court of Special Appeals.[46]

---

39 COMAR 28.02.01.17.
40 COMAR 28.02.01.20.
41 COMAR 26.01.02.35C.
42 COMAR 26.01.02.35B.
43 COMAR 26.01.02.38A.
44 COMAR 26.01.02.34.
45 MD Code, ENVIR. §§7-264 (Controlled Hazardous Substances), 9-340 (Water Pollution), 2-607 (Air Pollution), and 4-412(b) (Oil Control); MD CODE, STATE GOV'T. §10-222.
46 MD CODE, STATE GOV'T. §10-223.

Chapter 2

Regulation of Air Pollution

The Clean Air Act Amendments of 1970[1] (CAAA) established the current framework for federal and state enforcement of air pollution control laws. The Act authorizes the federal government, through the U.S. Environmental Protection Agency (EPA), to set standards for the control of air pollution and directs the states to work toward achievement of these national standards. As a result of the 1990 Amendments to the CAA,[2] regulation of air quality is managed through a combination of ambient air quality standards, emission standards, state planning processes, and construction and operating permits. Existing sources are subject to different regulatory strategies than are modified or new sources of air pollution. Targeted problem areas, such as non-attainment areas, hazardous air pollutants, acid rain, and accidental emissions are provided special levels of protection.

In Maryland, regulations are proposed for promulgation by the Maryland Department of the Environment's (MDE) Air and Radiation Administration and submitted for review to the Air Quality Control Advisory Council or the Radiation Control Advisory Board, as applicable. The Air Quality Control Advisory Council is limited to 15 members, chosen by MDE's Secretary, from engineers, manufacturers, physicians, local governments, labor organizations, universities, and the general public.[3] The Council's role is purely advisory and, within thirty days of MDE's submitting a proposed regulation to the Council for its review, the Council recommends adoption, rejection, or modification.[4] The Radiation Control Advisory Board consists of 12 members appointed by the Secretary of ten members have been recognized as knowledgeable on the subject of radiation, and two members of the community at large.[5]

---

[1] 42 U.S.C. §§7401-7671q.
[2] *Id.*
[3] MD. CODE ANN., ENVIR. §2-202.
[4] MD. CODE ANN., ENVIR. §2-206.
[5] MD. CODE ANN., ENVIR. §8-202.

AIR QUALITY STANDARDS

There are two types of air pollutant standards: ambient and emission. Ambient standards, as the name suggests, seek to establish maximum limits of acceptable pollution levels in the outdoor air in general, without regard to their cause or source or the eventual cost of control. EPA promulgates National Ambient Air Quality Standards (NAAQS) on a pollutant-by-pollutant basis, after determining that the pollutant "may reasonably be anticipated to endanger public health or welfare."[6] EPA must show a reasonable basis for its determination that there is a risk of harm, but evidence of actual harm is not required. In contrast, emission standards set limitations on pollutants emitted from an identifiable source. EPA has established emission standards for particular hazardous pollutants and for particular sources.

Ambient Air Quality Standards

EPA has developed National Ambient Air Quality Standards (NAAQS), which establish maximum allowable levels of certain commonly found pollutants in the air, regardless of source.[7] The NAAQS are ceiling levels that may not be exceeded anywhere in the United States. Areas that are not in compliance with these standards (non-attainment areas) may face severe sanctions including construction bans and cut-offs of federal funding.[8] The Maryland General Assembly has directed MDE to: "set ambient air quality standards for pollutants that are identical to the standards for pollutants for which national primary or secondary ambient air quality standards have been set by the federal government."[9]

The primary standard is the maximum amount of pollutant that can exist in the air before the public health would be endangered and is set without regard to technical considerations or economic feasibility; it uses public health protection as its only test.[10] The secondary standard may be more stringent. When setting a secondary standard, EPA considers issues of "public welfare" (i.e., protection from any known or anticipated adverse effect associated with the presence of an air pollutant in the ambient air).[11]

Maryland has adopted EPA's national ambient air quality standards that limit the following pollutants: particulate matter (PM-10), sulfur oxides, carbon monoxide, 1-hour ozone, nitrogen dioxide, and lead.[12] The state also has adopted a state ambient air quality standard for fluorides.[13]

---

[6] 42 U.S.C. §7408.
[7] 42 U.S.C. §7409.
[8] 42 U.S.C. §§7409(b), 7506.
[9] MD. CODE ANN., ENVIR. §2-302(c) (1996).
[10] 42 U.S.C. §7409(b)(l).
[11] 42 U.S.C. §7409(b)(2).
[12] COMAR 26.11.04.04-.09.
[13] COMAR 26.11.04.01.

National Emission Standards for Hazardous Air Pollutants (NESHAPs)

The 1970 Amendments to the Clean Air Act established a special program for the regulation of certain hazardous air pollutants, which Maryland has incorporated in its program. A hazardous air pollutant under that program is one for which no ambient air quality standard is applicable and that may cause or contribute to air pollution in a manner reasonably anticipated to result in an increase in mortality or serious illness.[14]

EPA had designated eight pollutants as hazardous under this program: asbestos, benzene, beryllium, coke oven emissions, inorganic arsenic, mercury, radionuclides, and vinyl chloride.[15] Maryland has adopted most of EPA's designations for NESHAP sources by reference; the NESHAP for sources of radionuclides is a notable exception.[16]

Hazardous Air Pollutants

Title III of the 1990 CAAA significantly changed the approach to controlling hazardous air pollutants (HAPs). Unlike the NESHAP program, where emission standards are health-based, Title III utilizes a technology-based standard. The Act now lists 189 HAPs that EPA must regulate[17] and stipulates that EPA must revise the list as necessary.[18]

EPA has categorized and subcategorized a list of affected HAP sources. Major sources are defined as all sources with the potential to emit 10 tpy of any listed HAP or 25 tpy of any combination of HAPs, while area sources are those that emit less than that.[19]

STATE IMPLEMENTATION PLANS

The Clean Air Act gives the states primary authority and responsibility to carry out the air programs with EPA oversight. Maryland and EPA have worked closely since the early 1970s to develop the required State Implementation Plan (SIP), a statewide air quality management program. The result is a regulatory and permitting scheme that reflects some of the state's priorities but remains within a federal framework.

The SIP consists of state regulations, orders, permits, etc., which limit the emissions of specific individual sources and categories of sources to prevent the total emissions of a pollutant in the state from exceeding the NAAQS. The state is given large measures of flexibility in determining which businesses to regulate and the manner of regulation, but the overall plan must be properly adopted, with public notice and

---

14 42 U.S.C. §7412(a)(6) and 42 U.S.C. §7412(b).
15 40 C.F.R. §61.01(a).
16 COMAR 26.1 l.0l.01B(21).
17 42 U.S.C. §7412(b)(1).
18 42 U.S.C. §7412(b)(2).
19 42 U.S.C. §7412(a)(1) and (2).

hearings, and approved by EPA as capable of attaining each NAAQS.[20] Both the state and EPA may seek enforcement of the SIP.

Attainment Areas/Prevention of Significant Deterioration

Any area that is in compliance with the ambient air quality standard for a particular pollutant is called an "attainment area."[21] To prevent air degradation in those "clean air" areas, Maryland and federal regulations impose a Prevention of Significant Deterioration Program (PSD), which limits the amount of increased pollutants that may be emitted in those areas and ensures compliance with the NAAQS.

REGULATION OF "EXISTING" SOURCES

EPA has promulgated regulations outlining the minimum requirements for a state operating permit program pursuant to Title V of the 1990 Clean Air Act Amendments. MDE has promulgated regulations implementing the new Title V operating permit program (the "Part 70" permit program), which applies primarily to major sources but may also apply to other sources, including area sources, subject to a standard, limitation, or other requirement for new stationary sources of pollutants in the state.[22]

Pursuant to Maryland's long-standing regulatory scheme, many existing categories of sources are specifically listed as requiring a permit to operate.[23] Even if an existing facility is not required to be permitted, however, it is still required to be registered if it is within the description of facilities that would require a permit to construct when new.[24] Registration terminates upon change of ownership. New owners of existing facilities must therefore re-register within thirty days of change in ownership. Similarly, re-registration is required any other time MDE's information becomes inaccurate.

In general, existing sources are expected to comply with whatever emissions requirements are applicable for existing sources in their air quality control region, with the concomitant emissions testing, monitoring, record keeping, reporting, and air pollution control equipment operation standards. Existing major sources of NOx and VOCs in both attainment and non-attainment areas for ozone, however, must adopt "reasonably available control technology" (RACT) to reduce emissions.[25]

Emission Standards for Existing Sources

The emission standards for existing sources vary among air quality control regions; the date dividing existing from new facilities also varies.[26] MDE currently has

---

20 Maryland's SIP is described in 40 C.F.R. §52.1070 *et seq.*
21 Maryland's Attainment Status Designations are set forth in 40 C.F.R. §81.321.
22 COMAR 26.11.03.01A.
23 COMAR 26.11.02.13 (listing 65 sources, including "any other source that the Department determines has the potential to have a significant impact on air quality").
24 COMAR 26.11.02.02.
25 COMAR 26.11.09.08; COMAR 26.11.19.02.
26 COMAR 26.11.06.

standards governing one or more region's emissions of the following pollutants: visible emissions,[27] particulate matter,[28] carbon monoxide,[29] sulfur compounds from other than fuel-burning equipment,[30] volatile organic compounds,[31] fluorides,[32] nuisances,[33] odors,[34] and unpermitted refuse burning.[35]

Emissions Testing, Monitoring, and Record Keeping

MDE may require any person to conduct testing or have testing conducted to determine compliance; it may witness or even conduct the tests.[36] All installations constructed after January 4, 1971, must have, in the exhaust gas duct work, stack or chimney openings that allow sample collection.[37] MDE may also require monitoring.[38] MDE may require that monitoring records be kept and that MDE must be given access to those records and information at a reasonable time.[39] Any contrivance that circumvents testing equipment or otherwise conceals the fact that emissions violate any applicable air pollution control regulation is prohibited.[40]

PERMITTING OF NEW AND MODIFIED SOURCES

The following discussion regarding permitting is divided into two parts. The first part deals with state permits to construct and operate and state approvals, Maryland's long-standing permitting scheme. The second part deals with the new operating permit program, referred to as the Title V Part 70 permit program, required by the CAAA.

Permits Required

Maryland regulations prohibit a person from constructing any of the following sources or installations without first obtaining, and maintaining current, certain permits to construct and approvals: New Source Review (NSR) Source, Prevention of Significant Deterioration (PSD) Source, New Source Performance Standard (NSPS) Source, National Emission Standards for Hazardous Air Pollutants (NESHAPs) Source, stationary sources of lead that discharge one ton per year or more of lead or lead compounds measured as elemental lead, and all sources, including installations and

[27] COMAR 26.11.06.02.
[28] COMAR 26.11.06.03.
[29] COMAR 26.11.06.04.
[30] COMAR 26.11.06.05.
[31] COMAR 26.11.06.06.
[32] COMAR 26.11.06.07.
[33] COMAR 26.11.06.08.
[34] COMAR 26.11.06.09.
[35] COMAR 26.11.06.10.
[36] COMAR 26.11.01.04A.
[37] COMAR 26.11.01.04A.
[38] COMAR 26.11.01.04B.
[39] COMAR 26.11.01.04B.
[40] COMAR 26.11.01.06.

air pollution control.[41] These permits may include conditions that limit emissions from a source.[42]

MDE also requires permits to operate for 61 specific types of installations and other sources that the Department determines have the potential to have a significant impact on air quality.[43]

Duration of Permits

Permits to construct and approvals expire if the planned work does not commence within eighteen months or if there is more than an 18-month hiatus between discontinued work and its recommencement.[44] Permits to construct and approvals also expire if the work is not completed within a reasonable time after issuance.[45] Permits to operate expire five years after the date of issuance, pursuant to the 1990 Amendments.[46] A renewal application for a permit to operate must be submitted 60 days before the current permit expires.[47]

Procedure for Obtaining Permits

MDE provides application forms for permits to construct, approvals, and permits to operate.[48] There are differences in the information to be submitted by the applicant, but the action taken by MDE follows a patterned course. Furthermore, all permit and approval applications, under the regulations, must contain a certification of truth by a responsible official.[49]

The permit process varies depending on the type of permit sought. While certain permits (such as applications for state permits to operate, permits to construct air pollution control equipment, and other limited permits to construct) are not subject to public notice, informational hearings, or other public participation procedures,[50] most sources must abide by a fairly extensive application process.

Once obtained, a permit must be maintained upon the premises and made available to the Department immediately upon request. Permits may not be transferred between people, facilities, or even different installations at the same facility, except as approved by the Department.[51]

Procedure If a Permit Is Denied, Revoked, or Reopened

A denial of a permit or approval is served upon the applicant in person or by certified mail.[52] The applicant may request a hearing within 15 days of service; otherwise, the

---

41 COMAR 26.11.02.09.
42 COMAR 26.11.02.03.
43 COMAR 26.11.02.13.
44 COMAR 26.11.02.04.
45 *Id.*
46 *Id.*
47 COMAR 26.11.02.14D.
48 MDE downloadable permit forms and required information are available at https://perma.cc/8BVU-HAVC.
49 COMAR 26.1 1.02.02F.
50 COMAR 26.11.02.14E.
51 COMAR 26.11.02.02E and COMAR 26.11.03.15.
52 COMAR 26.11.02.07A.

denial becomes final. Hearings are held in accordance with the contested case hearing provisions.[53]

An order revoking or reopening a state permit to operate or the state-only enforceable provisions of a Part 70 permit is served upon the applicant in person or by certified mail. The applicant may request a hearing within 15 days; otherwise, the order becomes final.[54] Hearings are held in accordance with the contested case hearing provisions.[55]

Title V (Part 70) Operating Permits

Under Title V of the CAAA, all major sources of air emissions will be required to have an operating permit.[56] The development of state operating permit programs in Title V represents a significant shift away from the use of State Implementation Plans as the main tool for implementing and enforcing the Act. EPA has promulgated regulations establishing the minimum requirements for a state permit program under Title V.[57] For the most part, EPA regulations represent only EPA's minimum requirements—the states are free to impose stricter standards.

Scope

The operating permit program is intended initially to cover all major sources of air pollutants. Pursuant to EPA's regulations, states may exempt non-major sources until EPA makes a determination as to how to regulate them.[58] However, the state does reserve the right to require non-major sources to obtain an operating permit.

Permit Applications

Federal law requires that permit applications be submitted by affected sources within a maximum of one year after EPA approval of the state operating permit plan.[59] Maryland's regulations are the same.[60] New sources are required to submit Part 70 permit applications within 12 months after commencing operations or becoming subject to Part 70.[61]

Permit applications must be on a standard form and must contain certain minimum information in order to be complete for review by the state. This information includes:

1. identification of the affected source and a description of all relevant processes and products;

---

53 *Id.*
54 COMAR 26.11.02.07C.
55 COMAR 26.11.02.07C.
56 See https://perma.cc/B6HW-JYSM.
57 40 CFR part 70.
58 40 C.F.R. §70.3(b).
59 40 C.F.R. §70.5(a).
60 COMAR 26.11.03.02.
61 COMAR 26.11.03.02B(4).

2. current emissions data to demonstrate compliance, a description of existing control equipment, limits on source operation, a future compliance schedule, and a compliance certification; and
3. a certification of truth by a responsible official.[62]

A source cannot operate after the deadline for submission of an application unless it has submitted a complete and timely application consistent with these guidelines. Within 60 days after a source has submitted a Part 70 permit application, MDE must notify the source whether the criteria for a complete application have been met.[63]

Permit Issuance

Before the state can issue an operating permit, the application must be complete, there must be adequate public participation, the state must notify all affected states, the permit must provide for measures of compliance with all applicable requirements of the Act.[64]

Operating Permits

Standard permits must contain emissions limitations, operational requirements, and the legal/regulatory origin of both. Permits will be in effect for a period of no more than five years, except for municipal waste combustors, which may have a term not to exceed 12 years. They must also specify periodic emissions monitoring procedures and aver the state's right to enter and inspect all facilities and records to ensure compliance with the permit terms.[65]

EPA's standards also require the source to perform extensive record keeping of its monitoring activities and to retain such records for at least five years. Furthermore, at least quarterly, each source must submit to the state reports of monitoring activities and deviations from permit requirements.[66] Semiannual progress reports detailing compliance are also required, containing among other things certifications of whether compliance has been intermittent or continuous.

General Permits

Where numerous similar sources apply for operating permits, the state may issue a general permit covering them all. General permits may deviate from the standard permit requirements so long as the general permit terms are consistent with Title V, but each source must nonetheless file permit applications satisfying the standard application requirements.[67]

---

[62] 40 C.F.R. §70.5(c), COMAR 26.11.03.03B.
[63] 40 C.F.R. §70.7(a), COMAR 26.11.03.02C.
[64] 40 C.F.R. §70.7(a), COMAR 26.11.03.06G, .07, .08, and .09.
[65] 40 C.F.R. §70.6(a) and (c), COMAR 26.11.03.05 and .06.
[66] COMAR 26.11.03.06C(7).
[67] 40 C.F.R. §70.6(d). Maryland's regulations provide that general permits may be issued covering numerous similar sources or emissions units, after notice and opportunity for public comment and hearing. COMAR

Permit Shield

The state may elect to include in its permits a "permit shield," which is a clause stating that compliance with the permit conditions represents compliance with all applicable requirements of the CAA. However, before the permit shield can be effective, the applicable requirements of the CAA must be included in the permit or the state must find that all other underlying CAA requirements do not relate to the applicant source.[68] Furthermore, EPA has adopted a narrow reading of the permit shield provision—a shield provision will not relieve the source from the duty to comply with standards and requirements promulgated after the operating permit is issued.[69]

Enforceability

EPA retains the right to enforce the terms and conditions contained within the permit. However, the state may elect to designate some of the terms as not federally enforceable so long as those terms are not required by the Act or no other applicable federal requirements underlie them. Maryland's regulations provide that a Part 70 permit may include provisions that are "state-only enforceable" if they are based upon applicable requirements of state air pollution control laws that are not federally enforceable.[70]

Minor Permit Modification

Minor permit modifications are appropriate where the modification sought results in no violation of the Act's applicable requirements and where no significant changes to existing monitoring or record keeping are being made.[71] The applicant can make the desired change while the modification request is pending so long as the change does not require a permit to construct, but it must adhere to the revised terms as proposed.[72]

The state, upon complete review, can approve the modification, deny the modification, determine that the modification is significant and should be processed as such, or revise the draft permit modification and send a copy to EPA.[73]

Operational Flexibility

A crucial provision of the CAA and EPA criteria mandates that sources be allowed a certain measure of operational flexibility.[74] In addition to mandatory emissions trading and alternative operating scenario allowances, sources can execute certain facility changes and contravene certain express permit terms provided the changes made do not result in emissions that exceed the permit's stated limits or any SIP or CAA provisions. Nor can the changes contravene permit terms involving monitoring,

---

26.11.03.21.

68 40 C.F.R. §70.6(f) and COMAR 26.11.03.23.

69 40 C.F.R. part 70.

70 40 C.F.R. §70.6(b) and COMAR 26.11.03.05E.

71 40 C.F.R. §70.7(e) and COMAR 26.11.03.15B.

72 40 C.F.R. §70.7(e)(2) and COMAR 26.11.03.16G.

73 40 C.F.R. §70.7(e) and COMAR 26.11.03.16F.

74 40 C.F.R. §70.4(b)(12).

reporting, or compliance certification.[75] Of course, the utility of such a provision is in question since it is severely limited by the emissions terms of the permit and the federal requirements.

Another important provision is an assurance that sources can make changes not addressed or prohibited by the permit.[76] For instance, a source may be required to seek permit revisions for increases in some pollutants, but a change that results in the emission of a new pollutant not regulated in the permit, the SIP, or the CAA may not require permit revision.

Significant Modification Procedures

The state is empowered to create a mechanism for determining whether a source's proposed modification of an existing permit provision is significant. At a minimum, EPA stipulates that every significant change in monitoring and every relaxation of reporting or record keeping standards be considered a "significant" modification for review purposes.[77]

Reopening for Cause

Each permit must list the reasons a state may reopen a permit prior to expiration.[78] They include cases where any new requirements become applicable to the source with more than three years left on its permit, where EPA or state finds a material mistake or inaccuracy in the permit standards, or where the permit must be revoked to comply with applicable CAA requirements.[79]

EPA may also terminate, revoke, or modify the permit, providing that it does so with procedures that are fair and reasonable and proper notice is given to the source.[80]

Public Participation

Public participation is required for all permit procedures except minor modifications or administrative changes.[81] However, several groups have petitioned or sued EPA, challenging EPA's decision not to require public notice or participation when minor permit modifications are sought; the issue remains to be resolved.

Permit Fees

The state has set permit fees for the permit program.[82]

---

[75] 40 C.F.R. §70.4(b)(12); COMAR 26.11.03.18.
[76] 40 C.F.R. §70.4(b)(14) and COMAR 26.11.03.19.
[77] 40 C.F.R. §70.7(e)(4) and COMAR 26.11.03.17.
[78] 40 C.F.R. §70.7(f); COMAR 26.11.03.20.
[79] *Id.*
[80] 40 C.F.R. §70.7(g); COMAR 26.11.03.20B.
[81] 40 C.F.R. §70.7(h); COMAR 26.11.03.17.
[82] COMAR 26.11.02.17, .18, and .19.

New Source Performance Standards (NSPS)

NSPSs are emission limitations based on the pollution control technology available to each particular category of new sources.[83] The categories identify types of industry, such as cement plants or copper smelters. The standards seek to reflect the degree of emission reduction achievable through the application of the best system of continuous emission reduction if such a system were installed on the new source of pollution.[84]

A new source includes any facility or installation, the construction or modification of which was commenced after publication of a proposed regulation that is ultimately promulgated prescribing an applicable performance standard.[85] A modification of a source occurs when there is either a physical change or a change in the method of operation that results in new or increased emissions of any pollutant.[86]

New Source Review Sources

In order to ensure that major new sources do not adversely affect Maryland's air quality, MDE, driven by the CAAA, has promulgated extensive requirements for major new sources of VOC, NOx, and CO located in areas regulated as non-attainment.[87] Under the regulations, major sources and major modifications will only receive a permit if the new source or modification will meet the lowest achievable emissions rate (LAER) for VOC, NOx, or CO, and if the source has attained certain emissions offsets of the relevant pollutant from other sources, preferably in the same non-attainment area.[88]

Major new sources are defined pursuant to the Title I non-attainment classifications. Major modifications are significant changes in emissions rates of major sources resulting in an increase in emissions of 25 tpy of VOC or NOx in severe and serious ozone non-attainment regions (Metropolitan Baltimore and Washington areas), 40 tpy of VOCs or NOx in the rest of the state, and 100 tpy of CO in a CO non-attainment area.[89]

The emissions offsets required for new VOC or NOx sources seeking permits are 1.3 to 1 for sources in Baltimore City or Anne Arundel, Baltimore, Calvert, Carroll, Cecil, Frederick, Harford, Montgomery, or Prince George's counties, and 1.15 to 1 in Allegany, Caroline, Dorchester, Garrett, Kent, Queen Anne's, Somerset, St. Mary's, Talbot, Washington, Wicomico, or Worcester counties.[90] An offset means that before startup, an NSR source must ensure that another source in the region lowers its emissions of VOCs or NOx by the same amount as the new source's anticipated emissions, plus another fraction of that amount to yield a positive net air quality benefit. For example, a new source in Baltimore City, which is subject to a 1.3 to 1 offset, seeking to emit 1,000 lbs. per day of VOCs, must secure a reduction of 1,300 lbs. per day of

---

[83] COMAR 26.11.01.01(23); 40 C.F.R. Part 60.
[84] 42 U.S.C. §7411(a)(l).
[85] 42 U.S.C. §7411(a)(2).
[86] 42 U.S.C. §7411(a)(4).
[87] COMAR 26.11.17.02.
[88] COMAR 26.11.17.03B(15).
[89] COMAR 26.11.17.01B.
[90] COMAR 26. 1 1.17.03B.

VOCs from other sources in the area. Air quality is thus bettered by 300 lbs. per day of VOCs.

Emissions credits could be approved by MDE for control that exceeds the levels mandated by the regulations[91] or that result from the shutdown of another source. MDE has not promulgated a fully developed regulation for banking and trading credits that could be used to meet the offset requirements.

EPA has developed an emissions trading policy. This policy establishes the general principles EPA will use to evaluate emissions trades under the Clean Air Act.

PREVENTING SIGNIFICANT DETERIORATION

The program for Prevention of Significant Deterioration (PSD) is designed to ensure that air quality will not significantly deteriorate in areas where the ambient standards are being met, primarily by controlling construction of new sources in those areas. Maryland has adopted the federal PSD provisions.[92]

Structure of the PSD Program

The PSD program requires review, approval, and permits for construction or modification of any major source of an applicable pollutant in an attainment area. In this context, major sources are listed by category and emit or have the potential to emit 100 tons or more per year of any air pollutant regulated under the Act.[93] Additionally, any source with the potential to emit 250 tons per year of any criteria air pollutant is covered, even if not included in the listed categories.[94] Modifications to existing sources may need PSD review if there is a significant "net emissions increase" of a criteria pollutant.[95]

AIR TOXICS

The Maryland air toxics regulations divide toxic pollutants into two categories. Class I toxic air pollutants (TAPs) are broadly classified as carcinogens; the list includes about 260 substances that have been identified as known, probable, or potential human carcinogens by either the National Toxicology Program or the International Agency for Research on Cancer. Class II TAPs are generally "health hazards" as defined by the U.S. Occupational Safety and Health Administration.[96]

---

[91] COMAR 26.11.17.04A.
[92] COMAR 26.11.06.14.
[93] COMAR 26.11.01.01B(37); 40 C.F.R. §52.21.
[94] COMAR 26.11.01.01B(37).
[95] 40 C.F.R. §52.21(b)(23).
[96] COMAR 26.11.15.01B(4) and (5), and COMAR 26.11.16.06 and .07B.

Some substances are specifically exempted from the program: simple asphyxiants,[97] substances for which there are ambient air quality standards, and "nuisance particulates."[98]

There are six types of sources targeted by the air toxics program: new sources, existing sources, facilities that burn refuse-derived fuel, hazardous waste incinerators required to have a hazardous waste facility permit, sources subject to MACT standards under 40 CFR Part 63, and any source that could unreasonably endanger health.[99]

Requirements of Air Toxics Regulations

The regulations are based on "allowable" emissions, the maximum emissions that the facility is capable of discharging, rather than those actually discharged. The regulations have three general requirements: to quantify emissions, to impose best available control technology (T-BACT) on new sources of TAPs, and to avoid unreasonable endangerment of human health.[100]

The first requirement, quantifying emissions, requires the industries to list the pollutants and quantity of each one discharged.[101]

The T-BACT requirement applies to all new and reconstructed sources, as well as some existing sources that comply with the ambient impact requirement by using dispersion techniques.[102] T-BACT is determined through a case-by-case analysis that considers the cost and feasibility of controls and the potency or toxicity of the discharged substances.

The requirement to demonstrate that emissions do not unreasonably endanger human health, called the ambient impact requirement, is set with a margin of safety to protect the public.[103] Industries must show that emissions do not result in unacceptable concentrations of emitted substances off their property.

Demonstrating Compliance

A facility may demonstrate compliance with the ambient impact requirements in several ways. The first is to show that emissions meet levels listed in the regulations. Alternatively, a source may demonstrate that emissions do not result in ambient concentrations that are greater than health-protective "screening levels." The procedures for determining screening levels are established in the regulations. If a facility cannot use a screening level to demonstrate compliance, a second-tier analysis may be used. In a second-tier analysis, a more refined assessment of actual exposure levels and health effects may be conducted.[104]

---

97 COMAR 26.11.15.01B(17).
98 COMAR 26.11.15.01B(11).
99 COMAR 26.11.15.03.
100 COMAR 26.11.15.04, .05, and .06.
101 COMAR 26.11.15.04.
102 COMAR 26.11.15.05.
103 COMAR 26.11.15.06.
104 COMAR 26.11.15.07.

ACCIDENTAL RELEASE PROTECTION PROGRAMS

The CAA requires that EPA develop regulations to prevent accidental releases of regulated substances and to minimize the severity of those releases.[105] The decision to list a substance is to be based on: (1) the severity of any acute adverse health effects associated with accidental releases, (2) the likelihood of accidental releases, and (3) the potential magnitude of human exposure to accidental releases of the substance.

EPA has promulgated regulations establishing risk management programs to prevent accidental releases of extremely hazardous substances from stationary sources.[106]

The Amendments also provide for the establishment of a five-member Chemical Safety and Hazard Investigation Board to investigate chemical accidents.

ENFORCEMENT

The Maryland regulations make some allowances for malfunctions. Although directed to consider as a violation every emission that exceeds the applicable standard, MDE, in determining whether or not to bring an enforcement action, will consider whether the excess was caused by a "malfunction."[107] "Malfunction" is defined as a sudden and unavoidable failure of an installation to operate in its normal and usual manner.[108] It specifically excludes failures caused, wholly or in part, by inadequate design, poor maintenance, careless operation, and preventable upset conditions or preventable equipment breakdown.

Any excess emission that exceeds one hour's duration must be reported to MDE by telephone.[109] MDE may request a written report discussing: the identity of the installation; the nature, time, onset, and duration of the emission; the quantity of excess emissions and methods by which the quantity was calculated; the cause of the occurrence and whether a malfunction is alleged; corrections undertaken; previous excesses in the past year; the maintenance plan for the installation and documentation that it was both appropriate to and carried out in the installation; and finally, the steps taken to prevent reoccurrence.[110]

Penalties

The Department may seek civil penalties in state circuit court up to $25,000 per day for violations of the air pollution laws, regulations, or orders.[111] Each day is considered to be "a separate violation."[112] Civil penalty claims may be compromised and settled and, if the violation has been eliminated within 36 months of settlement, the person

---

105 42 U.S.C. §7412(r).
106 40 C.F.R part 68.
107 COMAR 26. 11.01.07B.
108 COMAR 26.11.01.07A(2).
109 COMAR 26.11.01.07C.
110 COMAR 26.11.01.07D.
111 MD CODE ANN., ENVIR. §2-610 (1996).
112 *Id.*

charged with a violation may seek remittance of a portion of the penalty paid in settlement. The remittance is limited to a return of 75 percent or less.[113] There are state criminal penalties, imposed for "knowing" violations of the air regulations, which include fines of up to $25,000 per day of violation and/or one year imprisonment and up to $50,000 per day of violation and/or two years' imprisonment for repeat offenders.[114] Knowing falsification of reports and tampering with monitoring devices can result in fines of $10,000 per day and/or six months' imprisonment.[115]

Penalties may also be assessed in an administrative hearing at which MDE may impose a $2,500 fine for each violation.[116] These administrative penalties are limited to a total of $50,000.[117] Penalty assessment factors include the violator's willfulness, the harm caused by the violation, and whether the event causing the violation was controllable.[118] Failure to pay a penalty may result in a lien on personal or real property in the amount of the fine, plus interest and costs.[119]

MOBILE SOURCES

Vehicle Emissions Inspection Program

Maryland requires that owners of gasoline-powered passenger vehicles have the vehicle's tailpipe emissions tested once every two years.[120]

Diesel Smoke Testing Program

Diesel vehicles over 10,000 pounds, such as trucks and buses, are subject to testing for excessive smoke emissions emitted from the vehicle's exhaust.[121] Regulations to implement the Diesel Vehicle Control Program have been adopted.[122] Vehicles are prohibited from exceeding the following smoke opacity levels: 70 percent for model year engines 1973 and older; 55 percent for model year engines 1974 to 1990; and 40 percent for model year engines 1991 and newer.

Any owner whose Maryland-registered vehicle fails the emissions test is issued a Safety Equipment Repair Order (SERO) and is required to get the vehicle repaired and retested to show that the vehicle has been brought into compliance with the emissions standards.[123]

---

[113] MD CODE ANN., ENVIR. §2-610 (1996).
[114] MD CODE ANN., ENVIR. §2-609.1 (1996).
[115] *Id.*
[116] MD CODE ANN., ENVIR. §2-610.1 (1996).
[117] *Id.*
[118] *Id.*
[119] *Id.*
[120] COMAR 11.14.08.05.
[121] MD CODE ANN., TRANS., §23-401 to 23-404 (2001).
[122] COMAR 11.21.02.
[123] COMAR 11.21.02.09A(2).

Chapter 3

Regulation of Water Quality

The federal Clean Water Act (CWA) is the framework for federal and state enforcement of water pollution control laws. The objective of the CWA is to "restore and maintain the chemical, physical, and biological integrity of the nation's waters."[1] Similar in structure to the Clean Air Act, it authorizes the federal government, through the EPA, to set standards for the control of water pollution and enables Maryland and other states to work toward achievement of these standards.

MARYLAND WATER QUALITY STANDARDS

The Clean Water Act requires states to set water quality standards by designating uses and water quality criteria for water bodies across the state. In making its designated use evaluation, the Maryland Department of Environment (MDE) considers whether the waters are used for water contact recreation; fishing; propagation of fish, other aquatic life, and wildlife; and agricultural and industrial water supply.[2] MDE sets water quality criteria to protect the designated uses.[3] The water quality criteria consist of general criteria, as well as more specific numerical criteria for particular physical, chemical, or biological characteristics of water.

General Criteria

The general criteria provide that state waters may not be polluted by substances or materials attributable to sewage, industrial waste, or other waste in amounts that are unsightly, malodorous, a nuisance, or interfere in any way with the water's designated use.[4] The general criteria also prohibit high temperature and corrosive or toxic

1 33 U.S.C. §1251(a).
2 COMAR 26.08.02.01B(2).
3 COMAR 26.08.02.01, .02.
4 COMAR 26.08.02.03B.

substances to the extent that they interfere directly or indirectly with designated uses or are harmful to human, animal, plant, or aquatic life.[5]

Specific Numerical Criteria

The numerical criteria are set according to the pollutant and the body of water.[6] The 1987 Clean Water Act amendments put new emphasis on the achievement of water quality standards for toxic pollutants. In 1989, pursuant to §304(1), MDE submitted to EPA a final list of waters impaired by point source discharges of toxic pollutants as a predicate to developing individual control strategies to bring the impaired waters into compliance by the statutory deadline.

In 1993, MDE finalized its water toxics regulations.[7] These regulations were innovative in many ways and served as a model for other states. For example, they allowed permit writers to adjust effluent discharge limits after taking into account mixing zones.[8]

Anti-Degradation Policy and Federal Permit or License

The water quality laws also establish an anti-degradation policy so that those waters that surpass their required standards will not become more polluted than their current level.[9] The quality of these waters must be maintained unless it is determined by MDE that a change is justifiable because of necessary economic or social development, and the change will not diminish the existing or presently possible uses. Downgrading of use will only be considered if:

1) the designated use is not attained because of natural causes,
2) the designated use is not attainable because of irreversible man-made conditions, or
3) controls more stringent than the federal effluent limitations and national performance standards would result in substantial and widespread economic and social impact.[10]

In Maryland, so-called "Tier II" waters are those waters that have an existing water quality that is significantly better than the minimum requirements.[11] They are designated based on biological community scores for benthic macroinvertebrates and fish using procedures dictated by Maryland Biological Stream Survey developed by the Maryland Department of Natural Resources.[12]

---

[5] COMAR 26.08.02.03B(3).
[6] COMAR 26.08.02.03-1 to .03-2.
[7] COMAR 26.08.02, .03, .04.
[8] *See* COMAR 26.08.02.05 and COMAR 26.08.04.02-lD.
[9] COMAR 26.08.02.04, 40 C.F.R.§131.12.
[10] COMAR 26.08.02.04D.
[11] A map of these Tier II waters is available at https://perma.cc/28E9-5FH9.
[12] See https://perma.cc/HEA6-PFWQ.

Total Maximum Daily Loads

Under Section 303 of the federal Clean Water Act, states are required to compile a list of state waters that do not meet water quality standards notwithstanding the imposition of technology-based discharge limitations.[13] These impaired waters are prioritized based on the severity of the pollution and other factors. The list of impaired waters is known as the 303(d) list, reflecting the section of the Clean Water Act that mandates the list's development. The 303(d) list is subject to EPA approval and must be updated every two years. For each of the waters identified as impaired, the states are required to calculate the total maximum daily loads (TMDLs) of the impairing pollutants that are necessary to meet the applicable water quality standards.[14] Over 70 of Maryland's TMDLs have been approved by EPA.[15]

When listing waters on the 303(d) list and developing TMDLs for specific water bodies, MDE uses available monitoring data to identify the impairment and its sources. Additional data may be gathered in some circumstances. Using the applicable water quality criteria as a quantitative goal or target end point for the water body, MDE calculates the maximum additional loading of the problem pollutant that the water body can assimilate. The loading may be adjusted to account for uncertainties (e.g., the statutorily required "margin of safety") and, in some instances, a portion of the available loading may be reserved for future allocation based on projected growth. MDE allocates the total maximum daily load among point and nonpoint sources of the impairing pollutant.[16]

After a TMDL has been approved by EPA, state and local water management plans are required to be updated and control measures implemented.[17] NPDES permits for discharges to impaired waters may contain more stringent effluent limitations based on the TMDLs.[18] Nonpoint source controls may be implemented by using best management practices through applicable voluntary or mandatory programs in order to meet the TMDL.[19]

MDE has adopted a watershed cycling strategy for developing TMDLs and incorporating the resultant limitations into permits. The goal of this strategy is to coordinate permitting activities within the same watershed. MDE has divided the state into five watershed regions and intends to rotate the regions annually in a five-year cycle to allow for concentrated research, assessment, and definition of each region's water quality problems. MDE will also use the watershed cycling strategy to put all NPDES permits in a watershed on a coordinated schedule for renewal. This cycling approach is supported by the EPA and has been used by other states.

---

13 33 U.S.C. §1313(d)(l).
14 33 U.S.C. §1313(d)(l)(D). Federal TMDL regulations are found at 40 C.F.R. §130.7.
15 Maryland's 2017 EPA-approved 303(d) list is available at https://perma.cc/DB8V-9T92.
16 Additional data about TMDL loads, allocations, and GIS files are available at https://perma.cc/7KAW-M8BH.
17 33 U.S.C. §1313(d)(2); 40 C.F.R. §130.6(c)(6).
18 40 C.F.R. §130.7(a).
19 See generally 33 U.S.C. §1329.

Certification Process

The Clean Water Act prohibits the issuance of a federal permit or license to conduct any activity that might result in a discharge to navigable waters unless there is state certification that the activity does not violate water quality standards. Therefore, a certification program is also part of the water quality regulations.[20] General water quality certification, meaning that the activity is generally allowable so long as regulatory guidelines are followed, is granted for four activities: marsh creation projects, installation of utility lines, construction of bulkheads, and placement of rip rap for shore protection.[21] All other projects must receive certification on a case-by-case basis.[22]

POINT SOURCES, NPDES, AND THE STATE DISCHARGE PERMIT SYSTEM

The National Pollutant Discharge Elimination System (NPDES) is a CWA permit program to enforce nationwide standards for wastewater discharges into water. The CWA allows for delegation of the NPDES program to a state if the state's program is approved by EPA. Maryland commenced its own approved NPDES program in September 1974; it received final approval in 1985 when it added a pretreatment program to comply with later CWA amendments.[23] Thus, Maryland's permit program, administered by the MDE, ordinarily operates in lieu of the federal CWA permit program.

Maryland prohibits any discharge without a permit and defines a discharge as "(1) [t]he addition, introduction, leaking, spilling, or emitting of a pollutant into the waters of this State; or (2) [t]he placing of a pollutant in a location where the pollutant is likely to pollute."[24] This definition makes Maryland's NPDES program more stringent than the federal law. Federal law only prohibits discharges from "point sources" (i.e., a discrete, confined conveyance, pipe, or outlet) into navigable waters.[25]

Discharges That Require Permits

Maryland regulations define "pollutant" as any waste or wastewater discharged from any publicly owned treatment works or industrial source and all other substances that will pollute any waters of the state.[26] The regulation's definition of pollution is lengthy, but it may be summarized as any alteration that adversely affects the water's beneficial uses.

---

20 COMAR 26.08.02.10.
21 COMAR26.08.02.11, .12, .13.
22 COMAR 26.08.02.10.
23 33 U.S.C. §1342(i); COMAR 26.08.01–26.08.04 and 26.08.08.
24 MD. CODE, ENVIR. §9-101(b).
25 EPA's regulations define "waters of the United States" very broadly to include interstate waters, intrastate waters affected by interstate commerce (also broadly defined), tributaries of such waters, and wetlands adjacent to such waters or their tributaries. 40 C.F.R. §122.2. "Waters of the State," in contrast, includes groundwater. COMAR 26.08.01.01B(103).
26 COMAR 26.08.01.01B(66).

The federal statutes and regulations further divide pollutants into three basic categories: conventional, non-conventional, and toxic. These divisions are important because one aspect of the permitting process, the granting of variances, has not been delegated to the state, and the availability of certain variances sometimes depends upon the category of the pollutant. Conventional pollutants include pH, fecal coliform bacteria, total suspended solids (TSS), biochemical oxygen demand (BOD), and oil and grease.[27] Non-conventional pollutants are any pollutants that are not listed as either toxic or conventional and include heat (thermal discharge), chlorine, and iron.[28] Toxic pollutants are those specified by either the CWA or the EPA.[29]

Maryland regulations specifically require a permit for the following discharges into State waters and related activities:

1. The discharge of any waters in excess of 10,000 gallons per day, as a monthly average (with the exception of stormwater runoff not regulated by the CWA);
2. The discharge of any waste or wastewaters regardless of volume (with the exception of groundwater discharges associated with specified permitted waste disposal systems);
3. The construction, installation, modification, extension, alteration, or operation of any system that disposes of or may result in the discharge of waste or wastewater, regardless of quality or volume (with the exception of stormwater runoff not regulated by the CWA);
4. Changes in volume, temperature, or concentration of any waste or wastewater in excess of the discharges authorized by an existing discharge permit;
5. The construction, installation, or operation of any industrial, commercial, or other establishment that would increase the waste or wastewater discharge or alter the physical, chemical, or biological properties of Maryland waters.[30]

Stormwater Discharges

Recognizing that stormwater discharges contribute significantly to water pollution, Congress amended the CWA in 1987 to require a phased NPDES program for stormwater discharges.[31] Pursuant to this congressional mandate, EPA published regulations in 1990 requiring NPDES permits for stormwater discharges associated with industrial activity and discharges from municipal separate storm sewer systems serving a population of 100,000 or more (Phase I).[32] In 1999, EPA finalized rules for other stormwater discharges (Phase II), including small municipal separate storm sewer systems and construction activities disturbing from one to five acres.[33]

---

[27] 40 C.F.R. §401.16.
[28] 33 U.S.C. §1311(g)(l).
[29] 33 U.S.C. §1317(a)(l).
[30] *See* COMAR 26.08.04.01B.
[31] 33 U.S.C. §1342(p).
[32] 40 C.F.R. §122.26.
[33] 40 C.F.R. §122.

Stormwater Discharges Associated with Industrial Activity

Phase I of the federal stormwater program required stormwater permits for construction activities disturbing five acres or more, for many manufacturing and storage facilities, as well as for landfills and other areas where hazardous substances are present. EPA exempted smaller construction sites and light industries where designated activities are not exposed to stormwater from the Phase I permitting requirements but included these categories in the Phase II stormwater permitting program described below.

In Maryland, stormwater discharges associated with industrial activities are permitted under general permits or individual permits. Most stormwater permitting is accomplished through general discharge permits.[34] Maryland has issued three general stormwater discharge permits. These general permits cover: stormwater discharges associated with industrial activity, municipal separate storm sewer systems, and stormwater discharges associated with construction activity.[35] Dischargers who wish to be covered by a general permit must submit a notice of intent (NOI) to comply with the requirements specified in the state-issued general permit.[36]

Certain stormwater discharges are not eligible for the general permits, including facilities with effluent limitation guidelines for stormwater; those that MDE expects to contribute to a violation of a water quality standard; inactive mining or inactive oil and gas operations occurring on federal lands; and facilities whose NPDES permit has expired, been terminated, or denied or for which MDE requires an individual permit or alternative general permit. Dischargers who do not qualify for the general permit must apply for an individual permit.

MDE also reserves the right to require any facility to file an individual permit application whether or not it would normally qualify for a general permit. Facilities with existing NPDES permits for their industrial wastewater discharges should expect MDE to incorporate individual stormwater discharge requirements into those permits when they are renewed.

Applying for an individual stormwater permit can be resource intensive and cumbersome. The application procedures for obtaining individual stormwater permits are explained below along with the procedures for receiving other individual permits.

Municipal Separate Storm Sewer Systems

Large and medium municipal separate storm sewer systems (MS4s) must have their own permits under Phase I.[37] A large MS4 is one located in an incorporated place or in designated counties with unincorporated urbanized populations of 250,000 or more. Medium MS4s are located in incorporated places or in counties with unincorporated

---

[34] *See* COMAR 26.08.04.08.09.

[35] Stormwater discharges from specific industrial operations may also be covered under general discharge permits issued for wastewater discharges for that industry (e.g., for surface coal mines and related activities; seafood processors; mineral mines, concrete plants, and asphalt plants; certain tanks and other containment structures; and marinas). See COMAR 26.08.04.09.

[36] COMAR 26.08.04.09-1B(2).

[37] 40 C.F.R. §§122.26(d)(l)–(2).

urbanized areas with populations between 100,000 and 249,999. Others may be designated large or medium provided certain conditions are met.[38]

These permits may be system- or jurisdiction-wide. Permittees must reduce the discharge of pollutants to the maximum extent practicable, adhere to water quality–based controls where applicable, prohibit discharges other than stormwater into sewers, and monitor pollutants from industrial facilities whose stormwater is discharged through the MS4.[39] Part I of the application required MS4s to provide information regarding existing stormwater programs and control measures. It also required a field screening analysis of outfalls to detect illicit discharges. A second part of the application required information on proposed plans for the control of stormwater discharges.

Phase II Permits

Phase II of the stormwater permitting program is intended to address all other stormwater discharges not covered under the Phase I program.[40] The Phase II program requires NPDES permits for small municipal separate storm sewer systems ("small MS4s") in urban areas, as defined by the last Census, and construction activities disturbing between one and five acres of land.[41] The permit application deadline for these discharges was March 10, 2003.

The operators of small municipal separate storm sewer systems and small construction activities (between one and five acres of land disturbance) are automatically designated for coverage under Phase IL Permitting authorities may waive this automatic designation if the regulated dischargers meet certain criteria demonstrating that their discharges do not cause or have potential to cause water quality impairment.[42]

A small MS4 that serves a population of fewer than 1,000 people can obtain a waiver if

> (1) the system is not contributing substantially to the pollutant loadings of any physically interconnected municipal sewer system which is required to have a stormwater permit, and (2) an applicable TMDL does not require stormwater controls to implement the waste load allocation.[43] A small MS4 serving fewer than 10,000 people can obtain a waiver if an evaluation of all receiving waters shows that stormwater controls are not needed based on waste load allocations or established TMDLs and MDE determines that future discharges do not have the potential to result in exceedances of water quality standards or other significant water quality impacts.[44]

Under the Phase II rule, a waiver for construction activities disturbing between one and five acres of land may be obtained if the operators are able to make certain certifications or if a determination is made that stormwater controls are not necessary based on either a TMDL for the pollutants of concern or an equivalent analysis that

---

[38] 40 C.F.R. §§122.26(b)(4) and (7).
[39] 40 C.F.R. §§122.26(d)(2)(iv)(A)–(D).
[40] 33 U.S.C. §1342.
[41] 40 C.F.R. §§122.32, 122.26(a)(9).
[42] 40 C.F.R. §122.26.
[43] 40 C.F.R. §122.32(d).
[44] 40 C.F.R. §122.32(e).

determines that allocations are not needed to protect water quality.[45] After December 21, 2020, operator certifications must be submitted electronically.[46]

Under the Phase II final rule, small MS4 operations must develop, implement, and enforce a stormwater management program that reduces the discharge of pollutants from the small MS4 to the maximum extent practicable to protect water quality and to satisfy water quality requirements of the Clean Water Act. The MS4 stormwater management program must include public education and outreach, public participation and involvement, illicit discharge detection and elimination, construction site runoff control, post-construction runoff control, and pollution prevention and good housekeeping.[47] The regulated small MS4 operator must identify its selection of best management practices and measurable goals for each measure on its permit application.

For small construction activity, the specific requirements for stormwater controls will be defined by the NPDES permitting authority on a state-by-state basis. EPA expects that NPDES permitting authorities will use their existing Phase I general permits as a guide for their Phase II permits for small construction activity. Maryland's General Permit for Construction Activity requires the permittee to have an approved erosion and sediment control plan and an approved stormwater management plan before beginning construction.

Under the schedule for the Phase II final rule, an NPDES permitting authority was required to issue general permits for Phase II designated small MS4s and small construction activity by March 10, 2003.[48] Operators of small MS4s designated for coverage under Phase II and small construction activity must obtain permit coverage within 90 days of permit issuance. The NPDES permitting authority may phase in coverage for other small MS4s. Operators of the regulated small MS4s must fully implement their stormwater management programs by the end of the first permit term, typically a five-year period. Since Maryland's regulation directly tracks and incorporates the scope of federally regulated activities, MDE had immediate regulatory authority to develop its Phase II program.

Application Process for All Individual Permits

Discharge permits (which in Maryland are generally combined state/NPDES permits) must be obtained before pollutants are discharged into water. For traditional NPDES permits, a complete application must be filed 180 days before commencing discharges and in sufficient time to ensure compliance with the law.[49]

Who Must Apply

Any individual, corporation, or government entity may apply for a discharge permit by completing a form issued by MDE. The applicant must submit information

[45] 40 C.F.R. §122.26(b)(15)(i)(B).
[46] 40 C.F.R. §122.26(b)(15)(i)(C).
[47] 40 C.F.R. §122.34(b).
[48] 40 C.F.R. §122.26(e)(8)–(9).
[49] COMAR 26.08.04.01-1.

regarding the names of any affiliates, any presently held discharge permits, and any previous administrative complaints or orders. Maryland prohibits the discharge of pollutants into any state water, including groundwater. Therefore, the location of all storage and disposal sites for liquid and solid wastes on the site of the facility must also be included in the discharge permit application. A new facility must submit preliminary plans sufficient for evaluation of the facility's proposed pollution control measures and may be required to submit additional reports or specifications if deemed necessary. The application must be signed by the proper responsible official[50] and be accompanied by an application fee.[51]

Generally, the public has access to the information disclosed in the application and to other material provided to the state or BPA. For this reason, the applicant may seek to keep confidential methods or processes entitled to protection as trade secrets.[52]

Administrative Process

MDE publishes notice when it receives a discharge permit application. An informational meeting may be held to discuss the application if requested by the public or otherwise scheduled by MDE.[53] After evaluating the application, MDE prepares a tentative permit determination, establishing proposed effluent limitations and a schedule of compliance addressing any special conditions that significantly affect the discharge.[54] This draft permit is provided to the applicant and is available for public inspection. For major facilities, MDE also prepares an accompanying fact sheet, which is likewise available to the public.[55] Notice of the tentative determination and the opportunity to request a hearing is published in the area where the proposed discharge is to be located.[56]

Public Hearing and Notice

Upon request or at MDE's discretion, MDE will schedule a public hearing.[57] Notice must be published at least 30 days before the hearing, and written comments may be submitted in the five days following the hearing.

If no comments adverse to the tentative determination are submitted and there are no substantive changes, the tentative determination becomes a final decision and the permit may be issued. Otherwise, MDE issues a final determination.[58] Parties aggrieved by the final determination can institute an administrative appeal by

[50] COMAR 26.08.04.01-1B(5). In the case of corporations, the responsible corporate official must be a president, secretary, treasurer, or vice president of the corporation in charge of a principal business function, or any other person who performs similar corporate functions.
[51] MD. CODE, ENVIR. §§9-324, 325; COMAR 26.08.04.11(C).
[52] COMAR 26.08.04.01-IE.
[53] COMAR 26.08.04.01-2A.
[54] MD. CODE, ENVIR. §1-604(a), COMAR 26.08.04.01-2B.
[55] COMAR 26.08.04.01-2B.
[56] COMAR 26.08.04.01-2B(2).
[57] MD. COD., ENVIR. §l-604(a), COMAR 26.08.04.01-2B(5), (6).
[58] MD. CODE, ENVIR. §1-604(b), COMAR 26.08.04.01-3A.

requesting a contested case hearing, which is a trial-like, adjudicatory hearing.[59] Contested case hearings are subject to judicial review, which extends considerably the time it takes to obtain a discharge permit.

Discharge Permit Requirements

A permitted discharge must comply with all applicable effluent limitations, receiving water quality standards, and federal and state laws and regulations. Permits generally specify two quantitative limits on the amount of regulated substances that can be present in wastewater: an average and a maximum daily limit.[60] These limits are expressed in terms of concentration or weight, except where inappropriate, as in the case of pH. Permits are also contingent upon the permit holder granting MDE a right of entry to the permitted site at reasonable times for inspection.[61]

Variances

Under narrow circumstances, an applicant can obtain a variance from a technology-based limitation on the discharge level of a pollutant, except for new source performance standards. The applicant must demonstrate that its equipment, facility, or process is fundamentally different from what the EPA considered when developing the national effluent limitation guidelines (ELG).[62] Mere differences in cost do not meet this test.[63] There are strict requirements for the timeframe of a variance request and for participation in the ELG process.

Variances for technology-based limitations are theoretically available for discharges of nonconventional pollutants in other circumstances, but they are rarely granted. The CWA provides for a variance if the discharger can demonstrate: (1) that the modified requirements represent the discharger's maximum use of technology within the discharger's economic capability; and (2) that there will be reasonable future progress toward the elimination of pollutant discharge.[64]

Variances from limitations based on best available technology for nonconventional pollutants may also be sought if the discharger is able to demonstrate that the modifications still meet minimum standards, do not result in additional control requirements for other pollution sources, and do not hinder the attainment or maintenance of water quality goals.[65]

An applicant seeking a variance or modification from technology-based limitations must submit a request for the variance or modification to MDE. MDE will then forward the request to EPA together with one of three recommendations for action: approval, denial, or no recommendation. If MDE recommends denial, EPA invariably follows the recommendation.

---

[59] MD. CODE, ENVIR. §1-605(a), COMAR 26.08.04.01-3C.
[60] COMAR 26.08.04.02-1.
[61] MD. CODE, ENVIR. §9-326(b).
[62] 33 U.S.C. §1311(m)(1); 40 C.F.R. §122.21(m)(1).
[63] 40 C.F.R. §125.31.
[64] 33 U.S.C. §1311(c).
[65] 33 U.S.C. §1311(g).

Monitoring, Record Keeping, and Reporting

The permitted discharger has three duties involving information: monitoring, record keeping, and reporting. The permit outlines the frequency and type of sampling and analysis according to MDE's requirements.[66]

The permittee must retain all records for a minimum of three years. The records must include the exact date, place, time, and method of sampling, and the complete analyses. Reporting must be completed on the state discharge form at a frequency set forth in the permits, which will be at least once a year.[67] Discharge monitoring reports must generally be submitted to MDE and EPA Region ID on a monthly basis.

Duration of Permits

Permits are issued for a period not to exceed five years. This term may be reduced if the permit is amended, suspended, or revoked. Expiration dates must be specified in each permit. Renewal should be sought at least 180 days before expiration.[68]

MDE's watershed cycling strategy should result in all permits within a watershed being renewed in the same year. During the transition period, some permits may be issued for fewer than five years. Likewise, some permits may be administratively extended for a period necessary to bring the permits within the appropriate cycle.

Review, Modification, Suspension, and Revocation of Permits

MDE may review any permit it has issued in order to verify that the permit's conditions have been followed and to determine whether a permit should be modified, suspended, or revoked.[69] Minor modifications can be made without public participation. Major modifications must follow the procedures for permit issuance.

MDE may suspend or revoke a permit under the circumstances set out in the regulations. Revocation is permitted if there is false or inaccurate information in the application, if a violation of permit conditions has occurred or is about to occur, or if there is a substantial deviation from plans. Other reasons include a refusal to recognize the Department's right of entry, a change in conditions that requires discharge reduction or limitations, a threat to violate any water quality or effluent standard, or any other good cause.[70]

INDIRECT DISCHARGES: PRETREATMENT

Indirect discharges are those that travel through sewer systems to POTWs before reaching a body of water. To the extent that indirect discharges contain certain pollutants,

---

66 COMAR 26.08.04.03.
67 *Id.*
68 MD. CODE, ENVIR. §9-328; COMAR 26.08.04.01-lA.
69 COMAR 26.08.04.10B.
70 MD. CODE, ENVIR. §9-330, COMAR 26.08.04.10-1.

they may make it more difficult for POTWs to meet the effluent limitations in their NPDES permits. Some pollutants could pass through the POTW untreated. Thus, indirect discharges may ultimately affect the body of water into which the POTW discharges. In addition, the indirect discharges may contain toxic constituents that could render unusable the sludge produced by POTWs. In order to avoid these results, pretreatment standards are imposed upon industrial wastewater discharges into sewers.

Administration of the Pretreatment Program

MDE has promulgated regulations, approved by EPA, which delegate to municipalities, counties, and towns that operate POTWs the authority to regulate, along with the state, indirect discharges to POTWs. POTW owners must implement a pretreatment program if their plants handle more than five million gallons per day and if industrial users discharge pollutants that either pass through untreated, cause interference with the POTW, or are otherwise subject to pretreatment standards.[71] POTW owners that implement pretreatment programs must conform to standard administrative procedures, including public notice, opportunity for a public hearing, and appeal of final determinations.[72] Typically these requirements are set out in a local ordinance or by agreement if an industrial discharger is outside a municipality's geographic limits.

Pretreatment Standards and Prohibitions

Maryland prohibits a person from introducing industrial waste into a POTW except in compliance with pretreatment requirements, where applicable. Preventing or interfering with the inspection and sampling of users subject to those requirements is also prohibited.

Maryland applies the pretreatment standards developed by the EPA. Pretreatment standards fall into two categories: (1) general pretreatment standards that prohibit certain discharges (a flat-out ban); and (2) categorical standards based on the industrial classification of the indirect discharger. The following discharges are prohibited under the general pretreatment standards:

1. pollutants that create a fire or explosion hazard in the collection system of the POTW;
2. pollutants that are corrosive, including any discharge with a pH lower than 5.0, unless the POTW is specifically designed to handle such discharges;
3. solid or viscous pollutants in amounts that will obstruct the flow in the collection system and treatment plant, resulting in interference with operations;
4. any pollutant discharged in quantities sufficient to interfere with POTW operations;
5. discharges with temperatures above 104° F (40° C) when they reach the treatment plant, or hot enough to interfere with biological treatment processes at the sewage treatment plant;

---

[71] COMAR 26.08.08.03A, B.
[72] COMAR 26.08.08.02, .03E.

6. petroleum oil, nonbiodegradable cutting oil, or products of mineral oil origin in amounts that will cause interference or pass through;
7. pollutants that result in the presence of toxic gases, vapors, or fumes within the POTW in a quantity that may cause acute worker health and safety problems; and
8. any trucked or hauled pollutants, except at discharge points designated by the POTW.[73]

The categorical pretreatment standards regulate any pollutant that might interfere with the operation of the POTW, that might pass through the POTW, or that might contaminate the POTW's sludge. Examples of categories of industry to which pretreatment standards apply include: dairy product processing, grain mills, textile mills, and cement manufacturing. The other industrial categories are found in 40 C.F.R. §§405-471.

Variances

Categorical standards may be adjusted in three circumstances. They are:

1. a net/gross calculation—this allows the facility to adjust a pollutant level to reflect credits for pollutants in the intake water, provided the intake water is drawn from the same body of water as that into which the POTW discharges;
2. removal credit—this allows a facility to discharge a greater amount of a particular pollutant if the POTW serving it is removing that pollutant effectively; and
3. fundamentally different factors variance—this is similar to the NPDES fundamentally different factors variance discussed above. A facility must show that because of "fundamental differences" (i.e., unique processing methods), it should not really be included in the EPA classification. There are strict time limits on using this basis for a variance.[74]

An applicant seeking a variance from a pretreatment requirement must submit a request for the variance to MDE. MDE will then forward the request to EPA with a recommendation for action. Again, recommendations of MDE that the request be denied are invariably followed by EPA.

NONPOINT SOURCES

Nonpoint sources, as defined in the Clean Water Act, include all sources of pollution not defined as point sources.[75] Examples of nonpoint sources of pollution include agricultural runoff and pesticide and nutrient releases from existing developments. The following sections describe various programs developed to address nonpoint sources.

---

[73] 40 C.F.R. §403.5.
[74] 40 C.F.R. §§403.7, 403.13, 403.15.
[75] 33 U.S.C. §1329.

Section 319 Programs

Section 319 of the Clean Water Act established a program for states to control dispersed sources of pollution, or discharges not defined as point sources.[76] States are to submit to EPA an assessment of state water bodies, noting those water bodies that without additional nonpoint source controls cannot be expected to maintain applicable water quality standards. The Act also requires that plans be developed to control nonpoint sources, so as to attain water quality standards. For participating states, EPA makes available some funds for the implementation of nonpoint source projects, and also provides technical assistance. Section 319 reports are to be submitted every two years.

Specifically, the Section 319 report must:

1. identify those navigable waters which, without additional action to control nonpoint sources of pollution, cannot reasonably be expected to attain or maintain applicable water quality standards;
2. identify nonpoint sources that add significant pollution to each portion of the navigable waters identified above;
3. describe the process for identifying best management practices and measures to control nonpoint sources; and
4. identify the state and local programs for controlling nonpoint source pollution to each such portion of the navigable waters.

Maryland participates in the §319 program. In conjunction with the state's promulgation of TMDLs, Maryland is utilizing the §319 program as a method for implementing maximum daily loads from nonpoint sources entering Maryland waterways that are not meeting the designated water quality standards.

Coastal Zone Management

The 1990 reauthorization of the Coastal Zone Act (CZARA) also addresses the control of nonpoint pollution.[77] As a prerequisite to obtaining Coastal Zone grants, the Act requires that states develop a management program for their coastal zones. The purpose of the management programs is to "achieve wise use of the land and water resources of the coastal zone giving full consideration to ecological, cultural, historic, and esthetic values as well as the needs for compatible economic development." The requirements of the Act represent a major initiative to control nonpoint sources of pollution, such as pollution caused by silvicultural and agricultural practices.

Maryland's Coastal Zone Management Program (CZMP) is a network of state laws and policies designed to protect the coastal and marine resources of the state. The coastal zone is designated as 16 counties and Baltimore City—approximately two-thirds of the state.[78] Under Maryland's CZMP Section 309 strategy, the initial

---

[76] 33 U.S.C. §1329.

[77] 16 U.S.C. §1451–1464

[78] The counties in the coastal zone include Anne Arundel, Baltimore, Calvert, Caroline, Charles, Cecil, Dorchester, Harford, Kent, Prince George's, Queen Anne's, Somerset, St. Mary's, Talbot, Wicomico, and Worcester.

voluntary grants program focused on cumulative and secondary impacts, including watershed restoration action strategies. Beginning in 2001 and continuing through 2005, the focus of Maryland's Section 309 strategy had shifted to include coastal hazards such as shore erosion, hazard mitigation planning, and sea level rise, in addition to the cumulative and secondary impacts in the original program. Maryland's Department of Natural Resources (DNR) is the agency managing the CZMP. The agency is responsible for ensuring that federal programs and activities within the coastal zone are consistent with state policies and the CZMP. If the activity is conducted by or on behalf of the federal government agency; requires a federal license or permit; receives federal funding; or is a plan for exploration, development, or production of any area leased under the Outer Continental Shelf Lands Act, the activity is subject to federal consistency review by DNR.[79]

Agricultural Sediment Pollution Control

In 1994, the General Assembly enacted legislation prohibiting farmers from releasing sediment into waters of the state, unless they were implementing an approved soil conservation and water quality plan (SCWQP).[80] SCWQP is a land use plan for an entire farm prepared and approved by the local soil conservation district in accordance with specified technical references.[81] Penalties for sediment discharges may not be imposed on farmers with an approved plan, unless:

1. the agricultural practices in use on the site where a violation is alleged are not included in the plan,
2. the plan is not being properly implemented, or
3. agricultural practices are being implemented on-site that are causing the approved practices to fail.[82]

Process for Responding to Reported Agricultural Sediment Violations

The Maryland Department of Agriculture (MDA) is required to investigate any report to determine if violations have occurred. MDA may respond to a request for investigation by notifying the alleged violator of the report and requesting voluntary cooperation with the local soil conservation district or by investigating the site.[83] Once the violation is observed and documented, MDA may issue a written complaint or may decide to issue an order for the farmer to correct the conditions and to obtain and implement a corrective action water quality plan (CAWQP). CAWQPs are plans designed to address a specific sediment pollution violation.[84] These plans must be approved by local conservation district staff within 30 days of the order, the

Baltimore City is also included within the zone.

79 16 U.S.C. §1456C.

80 MD. CODE, ENVIR. §4-413(b).

81 COMAR 26.17.03.02B(10).

82 COMAR 26.17.03.03.

83 COMAR 26.17.03.05A(2).

84 COMAR 26.17.03.02B(2).

farmer must also submit a district-approved schedule for obtaining a SCWQP for the whole farm. Both types of plans must include the specific elements described in the regulations.[85]

Agricultural Nutrient Management

In 1998, the Maryland General Assembly passed legislation to protect the state's waterways by establishing short- and long-term strategies for reducing nutrient levels from agricultural operations.[86] Under the Water Quality Improvement Act, every farm or agricultural operation with a gross income greater than $2,500 or a livestock operation with over eight animal units (animal unit = 1,000 lbs. of live animal weight) is required to have a nutrient management plan.[87] A nutrient management plan, which must be prepared by a certified nutrient management consultant, is designed to manage the amount, placement, timing, and application of animal waste, commercial fertilizers, sludge, or other plant nutrients.[88] Each nutrient management plan is to consider the following factors: levels of bioavailable nitrogen and phosphorous in the soil; levels of bioavailable nitrogen and phosphorous in fertilizer materials; the amount of nitrogen and phosphorous necessary to achieve crop yield; soil erodibility and nutrient retention capacity; the best reasonable scientific methods; and existing best management practices. Each nutrient management plan is to be filed with the Department of Agriculture when it is developed and each time it is updated.[89]

The program includes a staggered implementation schedule. On December 31, 2002, farms using chemical fertilizers were required to comply with the nutrient management plan for nitrogen and phosphorous. By that same time period, a person operating a farm using sludge or animal manure was required to comply with the nutrient management plan for nitrogen. By July 1, 2005, a person operating a farm using sludge or animal manure had to be in compliance with the nutrient management plan for both nitrogen and phosphorous.[90]

The Department of Agriculture (MDA) has promulgated regulations for the certification of nutrient management consultants.[91] MDA also requires educational programs for nutrient applicators who apply nutrients to 10 acres or more of land each year and for persons who apply nutrients for hire.[92]

ENFORCEMENT

Enforcement actions may be instituted by EPA or MDE for violations of NPDES permit requirements and by those agencies or a local POTW owner for violations of

[85] COMAR 26.17.03.06–07.
[86] MD CODE, AGR. §8-801.1–8-807.
[87] MD CODE, AGR. §8-803.1.
[88] MD. CODE, AGR. §8-801.
[89] MD. CODE, AGR. §8-801.l(b).
[90] MD. CODE, AGR. §8-803.l(f).
[91] COMAR §15.20.04.
[92] MD. CODE, AGR. §8-803.2.

pretreatment requirements. Typically, the enforcement action is proven using a discharger's own monitoring reports to demonstrate that one or more permit parameters have been exceeded.

Methods of Enforcement

EPA may issue a compliance order and impose penalties under a two-tiered system through its own administrative process. This system imposes Class I penalties of up to $10,000 per violation with a $25,000 maximum and Class II penalties of up to $10,000 per day of violation with a $125,000 maximum.[93] The EPA may also commence a civil action in United States District Court, where a violator is subject to a penalty of up to $25,000 per day of violation.[94]

If the EPA seeks criminal prosecution by the Department of Justice, willful or negligent violators may be punished with a fine of not less than $2,500 nor more than $25,000 per day of violation and/or imprisonment of up to one year. If the violator knowingly places another person in imminent danger, the penalty may rise to a $250,000 fine and a 15-year imprisonment for an individual's first offense, and $1 million for a corporation's first offense. The penalties are doubled for repeat offenders.[95]

State and Local Government Enforcement Procedures

MDE may issue an administrative complaint when it has reasonable grounds to believe that there has been a violation of a water pollution control law, regulation, permit, or order.[96] Concurrently or thereafter, MDE issues a notice or order directing the responsible party either to take corrective action or to file a report about the alleged violation. MDE may also require the party to appear before the agency at a hearing.[97] If an order is issued, the responsible party may contest it by filing a timely hearing request.[98] After the opportunity for a hearing, MDE may also assess administrative penalties against violators.[99] The penalties may be as much as $10,000 per day of violation, but may not exceed $100,000 in total. The assessment reflects several factors, including willfulness, actual harm, cost of cleanup, the available technology and economic reasonableness to control the violation, and other factors.

In addition to administrative actions, MDE may also bring actions in court for injunctive relief, civil penalties, and/or criminal penalties. Civil penalties are available up to $10,000 per day of violation.[100] Criminal penalties are even more severe. A first offense may be punished by a fine of up to $25,000 and/or one year of imprisonment. Repeat offenders may be punished by a fine of up to $50,000 for each day of violation

---

[93] 33 U.S.C. §1319(g); 40 C.F.R. §19.4.
[94] 33 U.S.C. §1319(d); 40 C.F.R. §19.4.
[95] 33 U.S.C. §1319(c).
[96] MD. CODE, ENVIR. §9-334.
[97] MD. CODE, ENVIR. §9-335.
[98] MD. CODE, ENVIR. §9-337.
[99] MD. CODE, ENVIR. §9-342(b).
[100] MD. CODE, ENVIR. §9-342(a).

and/or two years of imprisonment. Falsifying required documents is a misdemeanor for which the violator is subject to a fine of up to $50,000 and/or two years in prison.[101]

All fees and penalties collected by MDE under its water pollution law are paid into the Maryland Clean Water Fund. The Fund is used for the study and regulation of discharged effluent, with a particular emphasis on the quality of the Chesapeake Bay.[102]

The scope of local government enforcement actions for pretreatment violations varies depending on the local ordinance.

CITIZEN SUITS

The CWA provides that citizens may sue for violations of NPDES permits, pretreatment requirements, and the dredge and fill permit provisions under certain circumstances. Citizen suits must be filed in the United States District Court.[103] Maryland does not have an analogous provision.

The Supreme Court has held that citizen suits may be brought only when there is a good faith basis for alleging that the permittee is currently in violation and not for wholly past violations.[104] In addition, certain other requirements must be met. Citizens must demonstrate that they have standing. This is accomplished by showing a direct injury to the citizen, which might include, for example, loss to the citizen of recreational or aesthetic resources. There is a requirement that citizens inform the violator and the involved state and federal agencies of the intent to sue 60 days before the suit is filed. Finally, the suit may not be brought if there is diligent government prosecution of the case.[105]

The state's records and the company's own records, such as discharge monitoring reports, which are submitted to the state, are publicly available. Environmental groups and other citizens who review these reports may use them as the basis for a legal action.[106]

Defenses

Beyond those defenses applicable to any CWA violation, defendants in a citizen suit may also argue that an enforcement action brought by either the EPA or the state precludes a citizen suit.[107] Because a citizen suit may not be filed if there is a pending government action, a potential defendant may agree with the state or federal authorities to enter into a court-approved consent decree regarding a violation so as to preclude a citizen suit. However, the citizen may intervene in court proceedings to review the consent decree.

---

[101] MD. CODE, ENVIR. §9-343.
[102] MD. CODE, ENVIR. §9-342(b)(6).
[103] 33 U.S.C. §1365.
[104] *Chesapeake Bay Foundation & NRDC v. Gwaltney of Smithfield Ltd.*, 484 U.S. 49 (1987).
[105] 33 U.S.C. §1365.
[106] *See,* e.g., *Sierra Club v. Union Oil Co.*, 813 F.2d 1480 (9th Cir. 1987).
[107] 33 U.S.C. §1365.

Chapter 4

Environmental Laws Relating to Land Use

CHESAPEAKE BAY AND ATLANTIC COASTAL BAYS CRITICAL AREAS

The goal of the Critical Area Program[1] is to protect the natural resources of the Bay by controlling the intensity of human activities within the Bay's watershed. Rapid development and certain agricultural practices cause particular concern because they strip the protective vegetation that inhibits pollutants such as sediment and nutrients from washing into the Bay and its tributaries. The program also seeks to conserve fish, wildlife, and plant habitats.[2]

The "Initial Planning Area" for determination of the "Chesapeake Bay Critical Area" is defined as:

1. all waters of and lands under the Chesapeake Bay and its tributaries to the head of tide as indicated on the state wetland maps, and all state and private wetlands designated under the Wetland and Riparian Rights Act (Title 16 of the Environment Article);
2. all land and water areas within 1,000 feet beyond the landward boundaries of state or private wetlands and the heads of tides designated under the Wetland and Riparian Rights Act; and
3. all land and water areas within 1,000 feet beyond the landward boundaries of the resources identified above.[3]

The Initial Planning Area for determination of the "Atlantic Coastal Bays Critical Area" is defined as:

1. all waters of and lands under the coastal bays and their tributaries to the head of tide;

---

[1] MD. CODE, NAT. RES. §§8-1801–1817.
[2] MD. CODE, NAT. RES. §8-1808.
[3] MD. CODE, NAT. RES. §8-1807(a).

2. all state and private wetlands designated under Title 16 of the Environment Article; and
3. all land and water areas within 1,000 feet beyond the landward boundaries of the resources identified above.[4]

Certain portions of the above areas may be excluded from the critical area designation by the local jurisdictions with Critical Area Commission approval, if specific requirements are met. These excludable portions must be either heavily developed urban areas where imposition of the Critical Area Program would not substantially improve conservation efforts, or areas that are separated from open water by wetlands of at least 1,000 feet that will protect the tidal environment from adverse impact.[5] The "Initial Planning Area" may be supplemented with approval of the Critical Area Commission by the local jurisdictions. The area remaining after approved exclusions or inclusions is the "Critical Area."

Local Program Development

Local governments must develop a Critical Area Program, which includes a comprehensive zoning map and an overall plan for the areas within the critical area. The zoning maps must designate lands within the critical area as Intensely Developed Areas (IDAs), Limited Development Areas (LDAs), or Resource Conservation Areas (RCAs).[6] The degree to which development is restricted varies with the designation of the area.

Public Approval Requirements

Before the local jurisdiction may implement its program, the Critical Area Commission must review and approve it.[7] Once the program is submitted, a public hearing is held. The Commission then either approves or disapproves the program. If approved, the local jurisdiction holds hearings and adopts the program as a local ordinance. If disapproved, changes are made and the whole cycle begins again. Any change in an approved program must also be submitted to the Commission for approval. The local jurisdictions are required to review the programs at least once every four years to see if amendments are needed.[8]

Each step of the approval cycle must occur within a specific time period. For example, the Commission has 90 days after it receives a proposed program to either approve the proposal or notify the local jurisdiction of specific changes that are necessary. If the Commission fails to meet its 90-day review deadline, the program is automatically approved.[9] If a local jurisdiction fails to develop a program within the

---

[4] MD. CODE, NAT. RES. §8-1807(b)
[5] MD. CODE, NAT. RES. §8-1807(c).
[6] COMAR 27.01.02.02.
[7] MD. CODE, NAT. RES. §8-1809(e).
[8] *Id.*
[9] *Id.*

prescribed time period, the Commission will impose a program on the jurisdiction, which the local jurisdiction must enforce until it develops an approved program of its own.[10]

Development Criteria

The "Criteria" are state regulations, developed by the Critical Area Commission to guide the formation of local critical area programs. Once formulated and approved, these local programs serve to regulate development activities at the local level.

Intensely Developed Areas (IDAs) are those areas where residential, commercial, institutional, and/or industrially developed land uses predominate with little natural habitat.[11] When occurring within a critical area, new intense development must be in or near pre-existing IDAs, reduce or offset the runoff pollution it creates, conserve "Habitat Protection Areas,"[12] and not encroach upon Resource Conservation Areas (RCAs). New development must also demonstrate the capability to manage stormwater runoff properly, minimize forest destruction, and utilize cluster development wherever possible.[13]

Limited Development Areas (LDAs) are those with low- or moderate-intensity development.[14] Further development is permitted if it does not increase the overall intensity of development beyond the level already established, does not change the prevailing character of the area, maintains the quality of runoff and groundwater entering the tidal waters, and maintains existing areas of natural habitat. New low or moderate intensity development must also minimize forest destruction, limit the amount of impervious surfaces and development on steep slopes, and observe existing laws on soil erosion and stormwater management.[15] Developers are required to replace cleared forest cover at a ratio from 1:1 to 1:1.5.[16]

RCAs are those areas characterized by nature-dominated environments (including wetlands and forests) and resource-utilization activities (including farming and fisheries activities). New development is allowed in RCAs if it is primarily residential in nature and the resulting overall density does not exceed one dwelling unit per 20 acres.[17] Limited intrafamily transfers are also allowed in RCAs, even if they cause subdivision, if the local jurisdiction has established conditions that ensure that each transfer is a bona fide intrafamily occurrence.[18]

Re-designation to allow the IDAs and LDAs to expand and change RCA designation is allowed, but it is limited to an area equal to 5 percent of the portion of the jurisdiction's RCA that is neither tidal wetlands nor federally owned.[19] Where and by what percentage the expansion may occur is set forth in the Criteria. New IDAs should

---

10 MD. CODE, NAT. RES. §8-1810.
11 COMAR 27.01.02.03.
12 MD. CODE, Nat. RES. §8-1906; COMAR 27.01.09.
13 COMAR 27.01.02.03.
14 COMAR 27.01.02.04.
15 COMAR 27.01.02.04.
16 COMAR 27.01.02.04(C)(3).
17 COMAR 27.01.02.05.
18 MD. CODE, NAT. RES. §8-1808.2.
19 COMAR 27.01.02.06.

be located within existing LDAs or adjacent to existing IDAs. New LDAs must be adjacent to existing IDAs or LDAs. In several of the less-developed counties on the Eastern Shore and in Southern Maryland, the location criteria may be relaxed for half of the allowable expansion if the above criteria cannot be met and any growth in an RCA is clustered to protect the maximum amount of undeveloped area.[20]

Any necessary amendments to current local zoning, subdivision, or enforcement regulations must be put into effect. The local jurisdiction must then develop provisions that accomplish the following minimum goals, which are derived from the statute and detailed in the Criteria:

1. require project approvals to be based upon consistency with the goals of the Critical Areas program;
2. limit the amount of impervious surface (i.e., roads and parking lots);[21]
3. encourage cluster development;
4. establish buffer areas that limit permitted agriculture to operations that utilize "best management practices" to minimize pollutant run-off;
5. designate minimum setbacks for shoreline septic fields and structures;
6. designate which shoreline is suitable for recreational use or marine industry use;
7. control the harvesting of timber in critical areas; and
8. allow exceptions from pollutant run-off control requirements where the natural topography sufficiently controls pollutant runoff.

Local jurisdictions can choose to adopt stricter requirements. It is important to review carefully the programs of each county when planning development in a Critical Area.

Other Development Criteria

The Critical Areas regulations set forth criteria for water dependent facilities, shore erosion protection works, forest protection, agriculture, surface mining, natural parks, and the "Habitat Protection Areas" mentioned earlier.[22]

The Habitat Protection Area requirements have significant impact on all development in the Critical Area because they impose, *inter alia*, at least a 100-foot buffer strip along all tidal waters, tributary streams, and tidal wetlands.[23] The buffer is to be maintained as inviolate as possible; even water-dependent facilities must minimize its disturbance by placing as much of the facility as possible outside the buffer.[24] The Habitat Protection Area requirements also provide for the protection of nontidal wetlands, the habitats of species that are endangered, threatened, or in need of conservation, and protection of certain other plants, wildlife, and fish.[25]

---

20 MD. CODE, NAT. RES. §8-1808.1.
21 MD. CODE, NAT. RES. §8-1808-3.
22 COMAR 27.01.09.
23 COMAR 27.01.09.01E(3)–(7).
24 COMAR 27.01.03.03A(4).
25 COMAR 27.01.09.02–05.

The 2014 Chesapeake Watershed Agreement

The 2014 Chesapeake Watershed Agreement[26] renewed a multijurisdictional agreement between Maryland, Virginia, Pennsylvania, the District of Columbia, Delaware, New York, West Virginia, the EPA, and the Chesapeake Bay Commission to restore the Chesapeake Bay. Once EPA had issued its enforceable pollution limits for nitrogen, phosphorus, and sediment (the Bay TMDLs or Total Maximum Daily Loads) in 2010, the six Bay states and the District of Columbia released their plans (Watershed Implementation Plans or WIPs) to meet those limits by 2025. The WIPs are collectively known as the Clean Water Blueprint. In addition, the Agreement identified five themes:

1. Abundant Life: to ensure sustainable populations of finfish, shellfish, and other living creatures as well as to restore their habitats and create a balanced ecosystem network;
2. Clean Water: to reduce nutrient pollution to achieve water quality that can support aquatic life, to free the Bay and its tributaries from the effects of toxic pollutants, and to sustain healthy sub-watersheds;
3. Climate Change: to increase the resiliency of the Bay and tributaries to withstand changing weather and the impacts it will bring;
4. Conserved Lands: to conserve working forests, farms, maritime communities, and lands with cultural and other values; and
5. Engaged Communities: to increase public involvement in Bay stewardship, expand public access to the Bay, and enable environmentally literate students to graduate from high school.

WETLANDS REGULATION

Activity in wetlands is governed in Maryland principally by two overlapping regulatory programs: (1) the federal Clean Water Act (CWA) Section 404 dredge-and-fill permit program administered by the U.S. Army Corps of Engineers (the "Corps") under EPA supervision, which covers both tidal and nontidal wetlands; and (2) the state's wetlands permitting program administered by the Maryland Department of the Environment (MDE)[27] under (a) the Maryland Nontidal Wetlands Protection Act of 1989,[28] and (b) the Maryland Wetlands Act of 1970.[29] This chapter provides an overview of both the federal and state wetland regulatory programs.

Federal Authority

The primary federal statutory protection for both tidal and nontidal wetlands is found in Section 404 of the CWA, which requires that a permit be obtained from the Corps

[26] Available at https://perma.cc/RS9X-G2FT.
[27] MDE's program is implemented by the Department's Water Management Administration, Wetlands and Waterways Program.
[28] MD. CODE, ENVIR. §§5-901-5-911.
[29] MD. CODE, ENVIR. §§16-101 *et seq.*

prior to the discharge of dredged or fill material into the navigable waters of the United States.[30] Section 404(b)(1) requires that the decision on the issuance of a permit be based on guidelines developed jointly by the Corps and the EPA, and Section 404(c) gives the EPA veto authority over the issuance of any permit.[31] As a practical matter, however, the EPA rarely vetoes a permitting decision, leaving the Corps as the principal federal agency administering the wetlands program nationwide.

Areas and Activities Subject to Federal Wetlands Regulation

To understand the scope of federal wetlands jurisdiction it is useful to ask the following three questions: (1) what is a wetland; (2) is a particular wetland within the jurisdiction of the CWA; and (3) is work proposed on the property a regulated activity? This section will discuss the jurisdictional implications of each of these questions.

The question of what constitutes a federally regulated wetland is one of the most complicated and contentious issues in wetlands law. The Corps defines "wetlands" as:

> [A]reas that are inundated or saturated by surface or ground water at a frequency and duration sufficient to support, and that under normal circumstances do support, a prevalence of vegetation typically adapted for life in saturated soil conditions.[32]

Using this definition as a starting point, federal regulators have developed methods and guidance for identifying or "delineating" wetlands. In 1987, the Corps published a wetlands delineation manual that continues, with regional supplements, to be the generally accepted technical guidance for identifying wetlands.[33] Maryland also makes wetlands delineations using the 1987 Corps Manual.

Is a Wetland within the Jurisdiction of the Federal Clean Water Act?

Not all properties that meet the definition of "wetlands" are regulated by federal law. The Corps and EPA have jurisdiction over certain wetlands pursuant to authority granted to them to regulate activity in "waters of the United States."[34] Although Section 404 specifically applies to "navigable waters," the term is defined as "waters of the United States"—a term with much broader implications than waters that are navigable in fact.[35] Because the CWA does not define "waters of the United States," the Corps and EPA have issued regulations that define the scope of federal jurisdiction over wetlands under the Clean Water Act. However, a 2001 decision by the United States Supreme Court limits the Corps' jurisdiction over "isolated" wetlands. See *Solid Waste Agency of Northern Cook County (SWANCC) v. Corps of Engineers*, 531 U.S. 159 (2001).

---

30 33 U.S.C. §1344(f)(2).
31 33 U.S.C. §1344(b)(l) and (c).
32 33 C.F.R. §328.3(b). A site-by-site technical assessment is required for each wetland.
33 U.S. Army Corps of Engineers, Corps of Engineers Wetlands Delineation Manual (1987) (hereinafter "1987 Corps Manual").
34 33 U.S.C. §1344(a) and 1362(7).
35 33 C.F.R. §328.3.

Under Trump administration proposed rulemaking, wetlands may require a surface water connection in order to be jurisdictional under federal law. The practical impact of the Trump administration rulemaking in Maryland is less significant. MDE's jurisdiction to regulate isolated nontidal wetlands is governed by Maryland law, which is much broader than the federal scheme. Thus, while the *SWANCC* decision may limit the need for a federal dredge-and-fill permit for activity affecting isolated wetlands in Maryland, a state permit is still required.

Is the Work Proposed on a Wetland a "Regulated Activity"?

Not all activities that impact jurisdictional wetlands are regulated under federal law. The Clean Water Act authorized the Corps to regulate the *discharge of dredge and fill material*.[36] Thus, only activity that causes a "discharge" of dredged or fill material requires a federal wetlands permit. There has been much controversy over the scope of activities that constitute a "discharge" for the purpose of the federal Clean Water Act.

The controversy over the scope of activity in wetlands subject to federal permitting requirements does not affect the need to obtain a state nontidal wetlands permit. Maryland regulates almost any activity in and around wetlands that might have a negative impact. Thus, while development activity that may have an indirect impact on wetlands may not require a federal wetlands permit, such activity may require a state wetlands permit.

Permitting Procedures

There are two categories of Corps dredge-and-fill permits: Individual Permits and General Permits. Individual Permits are issued by the Corps on a case-by-case basis to one permittee for a particular site. General permits (which may be issued with nationwide, regional, or specific state coverage) establish generally applicable requirements for specific low-impact activities.

The application process to obtain an individual permit is coordinated with the Maryland program through a joint application procedure.[37] A joint federal and state application form for any work in a nontidal or tidal wetland is submitted to MDE, which in turn forwards a copy of the application to the Corps's District Engineer. The application requires a delineation of the wetland area, a description of the proposed project, its location and purpose, proposed mitigation of any wetland loss, and other information.[38] The joint application is intended to streamline the review and permit process.

Individual Permits

If the Corps determines to proceed by the individual permit process, then it will issue a public notice of the application, soliciting comments and information necessary

---

[36] 33 U.S.C. §1344(a).

[37] A copy of the joint application may be downloaded at https://perma.cc/4XP2-XHE4.

[38] *Id.*

to evaluate the probable impact on the public interest.[39] The District Engineer will also evaluate the application to determine the need for a public hearing. In deciding whether to issue the individual permit, the Corps considers, among other things, impacts of the proposed activity on the public interest, effects on wetlands, effects on fish and wildlife, effects on water quality standards and effluent limitations, and mitigation of resource losses.[40]

General Permits

Section 404 of the Clean Water Act allows the Corps to issue general permits on a state, regional, and nationwide basis for any category of activities where the activities are "substantially similar in nature and cause only minimal individual and cumulative environmental impacts."[41] Any activity covered by a general permit can be conducted without obtaining an individual permit as long as the permittee satisfies all of the required conditions for the authorized activity. Although an individual Corps permit is not required, a permittee still must obtain other state and federal approvals.

Federal Wetlands Enforcement and Penalties

Section 404 provides the Corps with broad enforcement powers, including the authority to issue cease-and-desist orders and to seek injunctive relief in federal court. In addition, civil penalties of up to $25,000 per day may be imposed for permit violations.[42] These civil penalties may be imposed for each day from the date of the alleged discharge until the offending material is removed or some other remedial action is taken. Knowing violations, which are felonies, carry even tougher penalties of up to $50,000 per day and three years' imprisonment.

Maryland Nontidal Wetlands Regulations

Nontidal wetlands are inland, freshwater wetlands that are not subject to tidal influence. Maryland's nontidal wetlands program[43] is intended to attain no net overall loss in nontidal wetland acreage and function, strive for a net resource gain over then-existing conditions, and prevent further degradation and losses of wetlands wherever possible.[44] In furtherance of these aims, the program establishes a state permit requirement for certain activities in nontidal wetlands. MDE has authority to administer the program but may delegate its authority to a county that enacts a nontidal wetlands protection program that meets all the state law requirements.[45]

The scope of Maryland regulations governing nontidal wetlands is more expansive than the federal regulations described above, both in terms of geography and

---

39 33 C.F.R. §325.2.
40 33 C.F.R. §320.4.
41 33 C.F.R. §323.2(h)(1).
42 33 U.S.C. §1344(s)(4).
43 MD. CODE, ENVIR. §5-901 to 911.
44 *Id.* §5-902(b) and (c).
45 *Id.* §5-904.

regulated activity. The geographic reach of Maryland's nontidal wetland program is more expansive than the federal Clean Water Act § 404 permit program in two key respects: (1) the state program regulates "isolated" wetlands, regardless of a "commerce clause" connection; and (2) Maryland law prohibits, without a permit, certain regulated activities within a nontidal wetland, within a 25-foot buffer of the wetland, and within an expanded buffer not to exceed 100 feet for "nontidal wetlands of special state concern."[46] Otherwise, the definition of a nontidal wetland is virtually the same as the federal definition of wetlands and is to be determined according to the 1987 Corps Manual. Areas excluded from state permitting requirements include minimal impact activities, such as repair and maintenance of existing structures, and activities in isolated nontidal wetlands of less than one acre that have no significant plant or wildlife value.[47]

Activities affecting nontidal wetlands regulated under Maryland law are also broader than those regulated under federal law. The state-regulated activities affecting nontidal wetlands in Maryland include:

1. the removal, excavation, or dredging of soil, sand, gravel, minerals, organic matter, or materials of any kind;
2. the changing of existing drainage characteristics, sedimentation patterns, flow patterns, or flood retention characteristics;
3. the disturbance of the water level or water table by drainage, impoundment, or other means;
4. the dumping, discharging of material, or filling with material, including the driving of piles and placing of obstructions;
5. the grading or removal of material that would alter existing topography; and
6. the destruction or removal of plant life that would alter the character of a nontidal wetland.[48]

Certain agricultural and forestry activities are exempted specifically from regulation in Maryland.[49]

Nontidal Wetlands Permitting Standards

MDE may not issue a permit for a regulated activity unless the applicant has satisfied a multi-part test modeled closely after federal 404(b)(l) guidelines. First, if the activity is water-dependent, then it must require access to the nontidal wetland as a central element. If the activity is not water-dependent, then there must be no practicable alternative to disturbing the wetland.[50]

In either instance, the applicant also must prove that the activity will not cause or contribute to a degradation of groundwaters or surface waters, is consistent with any

---

46 *Id.* §5-906(i).
47 *Id.* § 5-906(a)(l) and (2).
48 MD. CODE, ENVIR. §5-901(n).
49 *Id.* §5-905(a).
50 *Id.* §5-907; COMAR 26.23.02.04.

comprehensive watershed management plan developed or approved by MDE, and will minimize alteration or impairment of the nontidal wetland.[51]

Additionally, all applicants must demonstrate that alternative locations and activities have been analyzed and that the regulated activity has no practicable alternative.[52] In making this demonstration, the applicant needs to show that the project's purpose cannot reasonably be accomplished on one or more other sites in the same general area with less adverse impact to nontidal wetlands.[53] The search for alternative sites must be made during the activity's "initial planning stage" or other dates specified in the regulations.[54] The applicant must document its efforts and identify the alternatives considered. In evaluating practicable alternatives, MDE also will balance the economic value of the proposed activity in meeting a demonstrated public need in the area against the ecological value of the nontidal wetland.[55]

An applicant must also demonstrate to the Department's satisfaction that all necessary steps have been taken to first avoid and then minimize the adverse impact of the activity on the nontidal wetland.[56] This may require a reduction in density of proposed development or change in the project's design. MDE will only permit losses of nontidal wetlands when adverse impacts are necessary and unavoidable.[57]

If the applicant demonstrates to the Department's satisfaction that losses of nontidal wetlands are unavoidable and necessary, the Department will require the permittee to develop and implement mitigation measures.[58] The mitigation requirement is based on the wetlands regulations' overall goal of no net loss of wetlands. Therefore, where permitted losses occur, these losses must be offset where practicable through the creation, restoration, or enhancement of nontidal wetlands. The statute establishes specific acreage replacement ratios, which provide at the low end a ratio of 1 to 1 for emergent nontidal wetlands and at the high end a replacement ratio of 4.5 to 1 for forested wetlands designated as being of special state concern.[59] Where mitigation is not feasible, monetary compensation may be allowed.[60]

Mitigation involves substantial monitoring and financial obligations. The permittee must implement the required mitigation and must submit annual monitoring reports to the Department for five years following the completion of construction of the mitigation project.[61] In addition, the permittee must file a performance bond with the Department before the mitigation begins.[62] The amount of the bond is set at $20,000 per acre of required nontidal wetland mitigation. The bond is released to the permittee after mitigation requirements have been fulfilled.[63]

---

[51] *Id.*
[52] *Id.*
[53] *Id.*
[54] *Id.*; see also COMAR 26.23.02.05A.
[55] COMAR 26.23.02.04D.
[56] COMAR 26.23.02.05B.
[57] *Id.*
[58] MD. CODE, ENVIR. §5-909; COMAR 26.23.04.02.
[59] COMAR 26.23.04.03C.
[60] MD. CODE ANN., ENVIR. §5-909(b)(2).
[61] COMAR 26.23.04.04.
[62] COMAR 26.23.04.04B.
[63] *Id.*

Nontidal Permit Application Procedures

To obtain a permit, one must submit the joint federal/state application to MDE with a delineation of the affected nontidal wetlands.[64] MDE has 45 days to notify the applicant whether the application is complete and the delineation is correct.[65] If the Department fails to notify the applicant within the required time, the application is considered complete and the delineation correct.[66]

After receipt of a complete application, MDE must issue a public notice soliciting written comments on the application and giving an opportunity to request a public informational meeting.[67] If requested, a public informational meeting must be held within 45 days.[68] MDE must render a decision on the permit within 45 days of a meeting or within 60 days of the receipt of a completed application if no meeting is requested.[69]

Any person with standing who has been adversely affected by MDE's decision may appeal.[70] The appeal is in the form of an administrative contested case hearing before an independent administrative law judge and must be requested within 30 days of the decision.[71] Further appeals must be taken to the Circuit Court.[72]

MDE may issue a Letter of Authorization (a more streamlined review process) for certain low-impact projects that are not located in the critical area.[73] Letters of Authorization are available for activities impacting fewer than 5,000 square feet of nontidal wetlands or less than one acre of isolated nontidal wetlands.[74] This streamlined process requires no alternative site analysis, no public informational meeting and comment period, and no opportunity for appeal.[75]

Enforcement and Penalties

MDE may revoke a permit for cause, including violation of permit conditions, obtaining a permit by misrepresentation, or a change in condition.[76] MDE may also issue stop work orders to any person violating the statute or an individual permit.[77]

MDE may bring a civil action to enforce the wetlands law, which subjects the violator to a penalty up to $10,000 for each day of violation.[78] The court may also issue an injunction to cease the violation and restore the area unlawfully disturbed.[79] Citizen suit provisions are not included in the law.

---

64 MD. CODE, ENVIR. §5-906 (c); COMAR 26.23.02.01.
65 MD. CODE, ENVIR. §5-906(d).
66 *Id.*
67 MD. CODE, ENVIR. §5-906(e).
68 *Id.*
69 COMAR 26.23.02.03A.
70 COMAR 26.23.02.03B(1)
71 COMAR 26.23.02.03B(2).
72 COMAR 26.23.02.03B(5).
73 COMAR 26.23.03.01.
74 *Id.*
75 *Id.*
76 MD. CODE, ENVIR. §5-911.
77 *Id.*
78 *Id.*
79 *Id.*

Finally, the Department has the option to seek criminal penalties against a violator. Violations are a misdemeanor offense and carry a maximum fine of $10,000 for a first offense, and $25,000 for a second or subsequent offense.[80]

Maryland Tidal Wetlands Regulations

Tidal wetlands in the State of Maryland are those swamps, marshes, and other low-lying areas that border the Chesapeake Bay, its tributaries, and the state's coastal bays. Tidal wetlands are subject to state regulation pursuant to the Maryland Wetlands Act.[81] Enacted in 1970, the Wetlands Act is intended to preserve tidal wetlands and prevent their despoliation and destruction while taking into account varying ecological, economic, developmental, recreational, and aesthetic values.[82]

The Tidal Wetlands Act divides tidal wetlands into two categories: state and private wetlands. "State wetlands" are defined as: "[A]ny land under the navigable waters of the State below the mean high tide, affected by the regular rise and fall of the tide."[83] "Private wetlands" are defined as: "[A]ny land not considered 'state wetland' bordering on or lying beneath tidal waters, which is subject to regular or periodic tidal action and supports aquatic growth."[84] Private wetlands include wetlands transferred by the state by valid grant, lease, patent, or grant confirmed by Article 5 of the Maryland Declaration of Rights.[85] The Tidal Wetlands Act requires MDE to map all tidal wetlands.[86] The state's mapping process is subject to a public notice and comment process.[87]

The Tidal Wetlands Act regulates dredge and fill activities on state wetlands, including the removal, displacement, or deposition by any means of soil, sand, gravel, shells, or other material, and the alteration of navigable water levels. The Board of Public Works, with the assistance and recommendation of MDE, issues dredge and fill licenses only if issuance of the license is in the best interest of the state.[88] If the Board issues a license, it may require the licensee to pay a fee to the state.[89] Several activities specifically are exempted from the licensing requirements or public notice requirements, including drainage of agricultural land, in-place repair or replacement of shore erosion control structures, planting of wetlands vegetation, and maintenance and repair of bulkheads.[90]

The Tidal Wetlands Act also establishes a permit program, administered by MDE, for many dredge and fill activities on private wetlands. MDE is granted authority to adopt regulations governing dredging, filling, removing, or otherwise altering or polluting private wetlands.[91]

---

[80] *Id.*
[81] MD. CODE, ENVIR. §§16-101 to 310; COMAR 26.24.0101 to 26.24.05.02.
[82] MD. CODE, ENVIR. §16-102(b).
[83] MD. CODE, ENVIR. §16-101(p).
[84] MD. CODE, ENVIR. §16-101(l).
[85] MD. CODE, ENVIR. §16-101(l)(2).
[86] MD. CODE, ENVIR. §16-301.
[87] *Id.*
[88] MD. CODE, ENVIR. §16-202.
[89] MD. CODE, ENVIR. §16-205.
[90] MD. CODE, ENVIR. §16-202(d).
[91] MD. CODE, ENVIR. §16-307.

Under state regulations, before beginning any work to construct or reconstruct structures in, or to dredge or fill, a state or private tidal wetland, a license (for State wetlands) or permit (for private wetlands) must be obtained.[92] Activities that require permits include: filling wetlands with loam, peat, sand, gravel, or other materials; draining, excavating, or dredging wetlands; or performing any act that would destroy the natural vegetation or existing tidal flow.[93] Certain activities exempted from the permit process include hunting, fishing, and routine maintenance, repair, or replacement of highways, piers, and boathouses.[94] Construction of private piers and boathouses is also exempted from the permit requirements, but only if the specific construction requirements set forth in the regulations are followed.[95] The regulations also allow for general tidal wetlands permits and licenses for installing or maintaining utilities; conserving soil, vegetation, water, fish, and wildlife using best management practices; improving wildlife habitats; and other specified activities.[96]

Tidal Wetlands Permit Criteria

As the basis for a recommendation (with respect to state wetlands) or final decision (with respect to private wetlands), MDE will take into account ecological, economic, developmental, recreational, and aesthetic values of tidal wetlands.[97] As with nontidal wetlands, MDE seeks to preserve tidal wetlands and prevent their loss.[98] MDE considers the extent to which dredging and filling can be avoided or minimized, whether the activity is water-dependent, and how the activity will affect the wetlands, as well as several other considerations.[99]

Mitigation

If alteration of tidal wetlands cannot be avoided, the Department will require mitigation as a condition of a private tidal wetlands permit.[100] Mitigation projects must be connected to existing tidal wetlands or waterways, preferably on-site.[101] Mitigation projects must be designed to replace the values and functions associated with the impacted wetlands.[102] As with nontidal wetlands mitigation, MDE will use acreage replacement ratios for mitigation of tidal wetlands, which will vary depending upon the type of wetlands lost.[103]

---

[92] MD. CODE, ENVIR. §§16-202 and 307; COMAR 26.24.02.01A.
[93] COMAR 26.24.02.01B.
[94] COMAR 26.24.02.01C.
[95] *Id.*
[96] COMAR 26.24.02.04–05.
[97] COMAR 26.24.02.03A.
[98] COMAR 26.24.02.03A.
[99] COMAR 26.24.02.03B.
[100] COMAR 26.24.05.01.
[101] COMAR 26.24.05.01.B.
[102] COMAR 26.24.05.01.B.
[103] COMAR 26.24.05.01.C.

Public Notice Requirements

Applicants may be required to notify adjoining riparian property owners in writing at the time of the permit application.[104] Exceptions to the public notice requirements include certain projects involving construction of shore erosion control structures, projects that qualify under a general license, projects involving the construction of tide gates to protect agricultural ditches, and projects involving the construction of underground utilities if surface wetlands are restored to original condition.[105] In addition, MDE will issue a public notice providing the opportunity to submit written comments or to request that a public informational hearing be held.[106]

Enforcement and Penalties

Any person who violates the permitting provisions of Maryland's tidal wetland regulations regarding state wetlands is guilty of a misdemeanor and subject to a fine of no more than $10,000.[107] Any person who violates the provisions of Maryland's tidal wetland regulations governing the private wetlands permitting process, or violates the terms of any tidal wetlands permit or license issued by the state, is guilty of a misdemeanor and subject to a fine not exceeding $10,000.[108] Fines increase with repeated violations. A person who knowingly violates the regulations may also be liable to the state for restoration of the affected wetlands.[109]

FOREST CONSERVATION

The Forest Conservation Act[110] requires local governments with planning and zoning authorities to establish and implement local forest conservation programs affecting certain land disturbance activities.[111] The requirements include specifications for preconstruction forest inventories, forest conservation plans, reforestation, afforestation, and maintenance and management plans. An approved forest conservation plan is required before the approval of the subdivision, the issuance of a grading permit, or approval of an erosion and sediment control plan, whichever comes first.

Areas and Activities Subject to Forest Conservation Jurisdiction

The forest conservation requirements apply to any activities requiring a subdivision, grading, or sediment control permit on areas of at least 40,000 square feet. State and local land disturbance activities are also regulated. Exemptions[112] include:

---

[104] MD. CODE, ENVIR. §16-202(c) and COMAR 26.24.01.04.
[105] *Id.*
[106] *Id.*
[107] MD. CODE, ENVIR. §16-502.
[108] MD. CODE, ENVIR. §16-501.
[109] *Id.*
[110] MD. CODE, NAT. RES. §§5-1601 *et seq.*
[111] COMAR 8.19.01.01.01.
[112] COMAR 8.19.01.04A.

1. highway construction activities under Natural Resources Article §5-103;
2. areas governed by the Chesapeake Bay Critical Area Protection Law under Natural Resources Article §§8-1801–8-1816;
3. commercial logging and timber harvesting operations that were completed on or after July 1, 1991, that will not be the subject of an application for a grading permit for development within five years after the logging or timber harvesting operation;
4. agricultural activities not resulting in a change in land use category;[113]
5. clearing of public utility rights-of-way or land for electric power–generating stations licensed by the state;
6. routine maintenance or emergency repairs of public utility rights-of-way:
   a) existing before the effective date of the state or local program, or
   b) the initial construction was approved under the approved program;
7. any activity on a single lot that does not result in the cumulative cutting, clearing, or grading of more than 40,000 square feet of forest; does not affect forests regulated under a previous forest conservation plan; and is not the subject of a declaration of intent stating that no regulated activities (forest disturbance) will occur within five years;
8. strip or deep coal mining, or noncoal surface mining activities that are regulated under Environment Article, Title 15;
9. activities associated with housing construction for the land owner, or the heirs of the owner, if the activity does not result in the clearing of 20,000 square feet of forest and is the subject of a declaration of intent stating that no further subdivision or regulated activities will occur within five years of the forest disturbance; or
10. counties that maintain 200,000 or more acres in forest cover and have complied with the exemption request procedure established by the state.[114]

Developing Local Programs

By April 30, 1992, all units of local government with planning and zoning authorities were expected to have submitted proposed forest conservation programs to Maryland DNR for review and approval. The programs were required to include:

1. a policy document and all associated local ordinances relating to the implementation of the regulated activities; and
2. a technical manual outlining the submittal requirements for forest stand delineations, forest conservation plans, and forest conservation criteria and protection techniques.[115]

Failure to submit and adopt local programs results in state assumption of the program. DNR reviews programs every two years.[116] The state approved all of the

[113] Land use changes include agricultural support buildings and other related structures built using accepted best management practices. Agricultural activities that result in the clearing of more than 40,000 sq. ft. per year may not receive an exemption unless the person files a declaration of intent.
[114] COMAR 8.19.01.04A.
[115] MD. CODE, NAT. RES. §5-1603(c)(2).
[116] MD. CODE, NAT. RES. §5-1603(d), (e).

programs for the counties and Baltimore City. All but approximately ten municipal programs were either approved or exempted by the State of Maryland. Specific submittal requirements of the state program are presented below.

Forest Stand Delineation

Any person applying for subdivision, grading, or sediment control permits on areas greater than 40,000 square feet must submit a forest stand delineation (FSD) for the site prepared by a qualified professional.[117] The forest stand delineation is used to determine the most appropriate portions of the site for forest conservation. The program authority, local or state, has 30 days to approve or disapprove the FSD. The FSD must include:

1. a topographic map showing streams and steep slope areas;
2. a soils map depicting various soil limitations, moisture levels, and erosivity;
3. forest stands indicating species, location, tree size, and dominant/codominant species; and
4. any other requirements set out in the program.[118]

Forest Conservation Plan

After receiving approval on the FSD, a Forest Conservation Plan (FCP) developed by a qualified professional must be submitted to the program authority. The plan must reflect the specified priority areas for forest retention,[119] which include vegetation in sensitive areas; preserving large contiguous tracts of forest; rare, endangered, or threatened vegetation species; trees associated with a historical site; or specimen or Champion Trees.[120] The Plan must include:

1. a map of the site at the scale of the site plan;
2. a table listing net tract area, required forest conservation acres, the acreage of forest conserved in the site plan either on-site or off-site;
3. clear graphics showing the forest conservation areas, limits of disturbance, and construction debris and materials stockpile areas;
4. locations of devices to be used to protect forest conservation areas during construction;
5. a binding two-year management agreement for areas designated for reforestation; and
6. any other requirements of the program authority.[121]

---

[117] Defined as a licensed forester, licensed landscape architect, or other qualified professional certified by the state. MD. CODE NAT. RES. §5-1604(a).
[118] MD. CODE, NAT. RES. §5-1604(b).
[119] MD. CODE, NAT. RES. §5-1607(c).
[120] MD. CODE, NAT. RES. §5-1607(c). Trees having a diameter measured 4.5 feet above the ground of 30 inches or more, or 75 percent of the diameter of the State Champion Tree of that species.
[121] MD. CODE, NAT. RES. §5-1605.

Afforestation and Reforestation Requirements

A primary strategy in the Forest Conservation Act is to protect and preserve existing forest cover. For that reason, programs must include a preferred sequence for afforestation and reforestation that discourages the disturbance of existing cover, if possible. Sites without an established threshold value of existing forest cover must be planted or afforested up to that threshold percentage of the net tract area.[122] Agricultural and medium-density residential areas must be afforested to create 20 percent forest cover, while more dense land uses, such as high-density residential, mixed-use, and commercial areas must meet a 15 percent afforestation threshold.[123]

Afforestation must occur within one year or two growing seasons after the completion of the development.[124] If afforestation cannot reasonably be accomplished onsite or offsite, funds can be contributed to the Forest Conservation Fund within 90 days of the completion of the project.[125]

Enforcement and Penalties

The program authority may revoke an approved FCP for cause, including violation of conditions of the plan, misrepresentation, failure to disclose a relevant or material fact, or change in condition. The state must notify the violator in writing and provide an opportunity for hearing. Stop work orders are authorized for violations of the regulation, order, approved plan, or management agreement.

Penalties for violations include a fine of not more than $1,000 per day, with each day that a violation continues considered to be a separate violation. Courts may issue an injunction requiring cessation of activities and may require corrective actions, such as reforestation.[126]

Rural Legacy Program

The Rural Legacy Program is administered by the Maryland Department of Natural Resources.[127] This land preservation program is dedicated to protecting large contiguous tracts of land and other natural resources from urban sprawl and development. The goals of the program are to establish greenbelts of forests and farms around rural communities to preserve their cultural heritage and sense of place; preserve critical habitat for native plant and wildlife species; support natural resource economies such as farming, forestry, tourism, and outdoor recreation; and protect riparian forests, wetlands, and greenways to buffer the Chesapeake Bay and its tributaries from pollutants in stormwater runoff. The Rural Legacy Program encourages local governments and private land trusts to competitively apply for annual funds to complement existing land preservation programs or to create new ones.

---

122 MD. CODE, NAT. RES. §5-1606(a).

123 *Id.*

124 MD. CODE, NAT. RES. §5-1606(f).

125 MD. CODE, NAT. RES. §5-1606(a)(4). The rate of contribution is set at 30 to 36 cents per square foot of required afforestation or reforestation but may be adjusted for inflation. *Id.* at §5-1610(c).

126 MD. CODE, NAT. RES. §5-1612.

127 MD. CODE, NAT. RES. §§5-9A-01 *et seq.*

Chapter 5

Hazardous Waste Regulation

The federal Resource Conservation and Recovery Act of 1976 (RCRA)[1] established a cradle-to-grave hazardous waste management system. EPA has authorized Maryland to administer a state hazardous waste program that generally parallels the federal one.[2] The Maryland enforcement scheme operates in lieu of the federal scheme to the extent of Maryland's authorization, which as yet does not include most of the Hazardous and Solid Waste Amendments of 1984 (HSWA).

HAZARDOUS WASTE IDENTIFICATION

Subtitle C of RCRA regulates the management of hazardous waste. To determine whether a material is regulated as hazardous waste, one must first determine if the material in question is a solid waste. This requires applying both statutory and regulatory definitions. Only if the material is a solid waste will it be necessary to determine whether the waste is hazardous.

Solid Waste Definition

A statutorily defined "solid waste" under federal law includes "any garbage, refuse, sludge . . . and other discarded material including solid, liquid, semi-solid, or contained gaseous material resulting from industrial, commercial, mining and agricultural operations, and community activities," excluding domestic solid sewage, industrial point source discharges, or return flows from irrigation.[3] Maryland statutorily defines solid waste to be any:

---

[1] 42 U.S.C. §6901 *et seq.*
[2] MD. CODE, ENVIR. §§7-101 to 413.
[3] 42 U.S.C. §6903(27).

1. abandoned material or substance that is disposed of, burned, or incinerated or accumulated, stored, or treated before or in lieu of being disposed of, burned, or incinerated;
2. material or substance that is recycled or accumulated, stored or treated before recycling; or
3. material or substance that is considered inherently waste-like.[4]

Maryland regulations further define solid waste to include "any discarded material" that is either:

1. abandoned, by being disposed of, burned, incinerated, or stored prior to or instead of the foregoing;
2. inherently waste-like; or
3. secondary materials (i.e., any spent material, sludge, by-product, listed commercial chemical product or scrap metal) when recycled in any of four ways:
   (a) used in a manner constituting disposal;
   (b) burned for energy recovery, used to produce a fuel or containing a fuel;
   (c) being reclaimed; or
   (d) accumulated speculatively.[5]

The rule of thumb from these definitions is that any substance that is disposed of is a solid waste for purposes of regulatory control.

The statute specifically excludes certain material from the definition of solid waste. Solid waste does not include:

1. domestic sewage that passes through a sewer system to a publicly owned treatment works for treatment;
2. industrial wastewater discharges that are point source discharges permitted under the NPDES discharge permit program;
3. irrigation return flows;
4. materials subjected to in-situ mining techniques that are not removed from the ground as part of the extraction process; or
5. material that is excluded by any rule or regulation adopted under the statute.[6]

Regulations exclude from the definition of solid waste "recycled material" when it is used:

1. as an ingredient in an industrial process to make a product, provided the materials are not reclaimed;
2. as an effective substitute for a commercial product; or
3. in the original process from which it was generated as a substitute for raw material feedstock, when it is returned without first being reclaimed.[7]

---

4 MD. CODE, ENVIR. §7-201(u).
5 COMAR 26.13.02.02.
6 MD. CODE ANN., ENVIR. §7-20l(u)(2); COMAR 26.13.02.04A.
7 COMAR 26.13.02.02E.

If a statute or regulation excludes a material from the definition of solid waste, then the material cannot be a regulated hazardous waste. However, as a practical matter, the statutory and regulatory exclusions are quite narrow. Federal regulations on universal wastes greatly facilitate the collection and management of certain widely generated wastes, such as nickel cadmium and other batteries, pesticides, mercury-containing thermostats, and spent lamps.[8]

Controlled Hazardous Waste Definition

Maryland regulations use the term "controlled hazardous substance" as a synonym for hazardous waste and make exceptions for some recyclable materials.[9] By statute, a controlled hazardous substance (CHS) is any "hazardous substance" identified by MDE as "controlled." Controlled Hazardous Substances also include low-level nuclear waste.[10] Thus to be a CHS or hazardous waste, the material must be a statutory solid waste, meet the criteria of a hazardous substance, and be identified by MDE as controlled.

Maryland defines "hazardous substance" as any substance designated "hazardous" by CERCLA or any substance listed or designated "hazardous" by MDE in Maryland's Code of Regulations.[11]

Numerous materials are Maryland Controlled Hazardous Substances. The Maryland listing regulations divide hazardous wastes into "Hazardous Waste from Non-Specific Sources,"[12] "Hazardous Waste from Specific Sources,"[13] "Hazardous Waste from Specific Sources (State),"[14] and "Discarded Commercial Chemical Products, Off-Specification Species, Containers, and Spill Residues of These."[15]

Even if not on a list, a material may be a regulated hazardous waste or CHS if it demonstrates any one of four characteristics: ignitability, reactivity, toxicity, or corrosivity.[16] Each characteristic is measured using tests incorporated by reference in the regulations. MDE has expanded the list of contaminants considered to exhibit the toxicity characteristic to include volatile compounds whose toxicity is measured by the Toxicity Characteristic Leaching Procedure test (TCLP).[17]

One important difference between the Maryland statute and the federal RCRA is that the Maryland regulatory scheme brings polychlorinated biphenyls (PCBs) under its jurisdiction. Maryland identifies PCBs as acutely hazardous wastes at concentrations above 500 ppm.[18] Maryland regulations identify PCBs in concentrations of 50–500 ppm as Maryland Toxics, which is comparable to an RCRA "U" listing.[19]

---

[8] 60 C.F.R. Part 273.
[9] COMAR 26.13.01.03B(31), adopting by reference COMAR 26.13.02.06.
[10] MD. CODE, ENVIR. §7-201(b).
[11] MD. CODE, ENVIR. §7-201(m).
[12] COMAR 26.13.02.16.
[13] COMAR 26.13.02.17.
[14] COMAR 26.13.02.18.
[15] COMAR 26.13.02.19.
[16] COMAR 26.13.02.10–14.
[17] COMAR 26.13.02.14.
[18] COMAR 26.13.02.19F.
[19] COMAR 26.13.02.19H.

EPA currently does not regulate PCBs under RCRA but does so under the Toxic Substances Control Act (TSCA) and the Clean Water Act.[20]

Mixtures of Hazardous and Non-Hazardous Waste

Mixtures of hazardous and non-hazardous wastes may or may not be statutory hazardous wastes. In general, where a hazardous material that is a "listed" hazardous waste is mixed with other solid wastes, the entire mixture is a hazardous waste.[21] A listed waste may be considered for an exclusion through a petitioning process, which includes public notice requirements.[22] In addition, exemptions are available if the generator can demonstrate that the mixture includes wastewater, the discharge of which is subject to the regulation under §402 or §307(b) of the Clean Water Act, and meets one or more of the specified requirements relating to type of waste and level of usage.[23] Mixtures of characteristic hazardous wastes and a solid waste will be considered hazardous only if the mixture exhibits that hazardous characteristic.[24]

Derived from Hazardous Wastes

As a general rule, wastes that are generated from the treatment, storage, or disposal of a hazardous waste also are considered to be a hazardous waste, unless exempted.[25] Wastes derived from listed wastes are hazardous unless delisted. In contrast, wastes derived from characteristic wastes are not hazardous unless the derived-from waste exhibits that characteristic. Wastes that are reclaimed from solid wastes are not considered to be hazardous wastes unless the reclaimed material is disposed of or used as a fuel.

Contained in Hazardous Wastes

As a general matter, contaminated environmental media (soil, groundwater, surface water, and debris) is not hazardous waste and is not subject to regulation under RCRA. However, EPA considers contaminated media hazardous waste if it "contains" hazardous waste. Media is considered to "contain" hazardous waste: (1) when it exhibits a characteristic of hazardous waste; or, (2) when it is contaminated with concentrations of hazardous constituents from listed hazardous wastes that are above health-based levels. Once contaminated media "contains" hazardous waste, it is subject to all applicable RCRA requirements until it no longer "contains" hazardous waste. However, the LDR treatment standards will continue to apply to contaminated media in certain circumstances, primarily if, after treatment, the media contains hazardous constituents at concentrations above land disposal restriction treatment standards. The contained-in policy has been updated several times since it was first articulated in 1986. A

---

[20] 40 C.F.R. Part 761 and §302.4(a).
[21] COMAR 26.13.02.03A–C.
[22] 40 C.F.R. §260.20(a).
[23] 40 C.F.R. §261.3(a)(2)(iv).
[24] 40 C.F.R. §261.3(a)(2)(i).
[25] 40 C.F.R. §261.4(b).

statement of the policy was provided in the EPA Guidance Manual, *Management of Remediation Waste under RCRA* (October 1999).[26]

GENERATORS AND THEIR RESPONSIBILITIES

Once it is determined that a hazardous waste exists or is being generated, the generator must meet all applicable requirements for identification, record keeping, treatment, storage, transport, and disposal.

Defining Generators

A generator is any person or business whose act or process produces hazardous waste or whose act first causes a hazardous waste to become subject to regulation. It includes a person who imports foreign hazardous waste into the state.[27] "Generator" is a site-specific term, so a business with more than one facility may have more than one set of generator responsibilities.[28]

Small Quantity Generator Exemption

The quantity of hazardous waste generated in a calendar month determines whether a generator is a small quantity generator (SQG). SQGs are exempt from most regulatory requirements.[29] If a generator produces less than 100 kilograms of hazardous waste and less than one kilogram of acutely hazardous waste in a month, then the generator may treat or dispose of the waste in an on-site facility or ensure delivery to an off-site facility. Such a facility must have an RCRA permit or RCRA interim status, have an air quality and limited facility permit, be a utility generating station with a limited facility permit, or be a permitted municipal or industrial solid waste facility.[30] Exceptions to the small quantity generator exemption apply to some wastes.

Responsibility for determining SQG status rests with the generator. The wastes generated may be subject to different regulatory requirements from month to month depending on the quantity produced.

Unlike Maryland, federal RCRA regulates three categories of generators with varying degrees of stringency: (1) conditionally exempt SQGs who produce no more than 100 kilograms of hazardous waste per month; (2) SQGs who produce 100 to 1,000 kilograms of waste per month; and (3) generators who produce more than 1,000 kilograms of waste per month.[31] Anyone who generates more than one kilogram of acutely hazardous waste in any month is fully regulated.

---

[26] Available at https://perma.cc/Q8XG-SLA4.
[27] COMAR 26.13.03.01C.
[28] COMAR 26.13.01.03B(29).
[29] COMAR 26.13.02.05.
[30] *Id.*
[31] *See* 40 C.F.R. §262.44.

There is no procedure to average annual production. The waste of a given month becomes fully regulated if a generator exceeds the small quantity generator limits for either hazardous or acutely hazardous waste production in any one month.

Generator Identification Numbers

A generator may not treat, store, dispose of, transport, or offer for transportation hazardous waste without having received an EPA identification number. A number may be obtained by application to MDE.[32]

Generator's Responsibilities

A generator of a solid waste must determine if the waste is a hazardous waste and, if so, whether disposal or treatment restrictions apply to the waste. The exclusions of solid wastes from regulation should be reviewed to see if any apply. The lists of designated hazardous wastes should also be checked. If the waste is listed, the generator may seek delisting on a demonstration that the waste from the particular site does not warrant hazardous waste regulation.[33] If the waste is not listed, the generator must determine if the waste exhibits any of the hazardous characteristics. This determination may be made by appropriate scientific testing and analysis or by applying knowledge of the hazardous characteristics in light of the materials or processes used.[34] For generators that do not have the expertise to make this determination, a specially permitted hazardous waste transporter can provide assistance. Once a determination is made, the appropriate disposal method must be established.

Packaging and Labeling

The packaging and labeling of hazardous waste for off-site transportation is the responsibility of the generator. The generator must comply with Department of Transportation regulations to ensure safe transportation of the waste prior to ultimate disposal. The waste must be packaged to prevent leakage during normal transport and in potentially dangerous situations, such as vehicle accidents.[35]

Labels on each package or container must indicate the dangers and hazardous characteristics of the waste. Smaller containers (less than 110 gallons) require labeling that identifies the waste as hazardous, gives the generator's name and address and manifest document number, and warns against improper disposal.[36]

Manifests

The regulated generator must ensure that all shipments of hazardous waste off-site are accompanied by a Uniform Hazardous Waste Form.[37] The manifest must give a

---

[32] COMAR 26.13.03.03.
[33] COMAR 26.13.02.09A(3).
[34] COMAR 26.13.03.02.
[35] COMAR 26.13.03.05 (referring to transportation regulations found in 49 C.F.R. §§173, 178, and 179).
[36] COMAR 26.13.03.05C(2), incorporating by reference 49 C.F.R. §172.304.
[37] MD. CODE, ENVIR. §7-209(b).

Department of Transportation description of the waste, identify the number of containers, and calculate the total quantity of the waste being shipped.[38] The manifest must identify the permitted facility designated to receive the waste and may designate on the manifest an alternate facility to be used in the event an emergency prevents delivery of the waste to the primary facility. The generator's name, mailing address, telephone number, and EPA identification number must be included, as well as the name and EPA identification number of each transporter that handles the waste.[39]

The manifest must contain a certification by the generator that a program is in place to reduce the volume (or quantity) and toxicity of hazardous waste generated to the degree the generator determines economically practicable. The generator also must certify that the disposal, treatment, or storage method proposed is the most practicable method currently available to the generator that minimizes present and future threat to human health and the environment.[40]

Land Disposal Restrictions

The generator also must provide one-time written notice of applicable land disposal restrictions under HSWA to the downstream recipients of its waste (i.e., transporters and storage, treatment, and disposal facilities).[41] No further notification is required unless the waste or recipient facility changes.

Accumulation On-Site

A generator may accumulate hazardous waste on-site for 90 days without obtaining a permit, provided the waste is ultimately moved to a permitted facility.[42] The Maryland regulations allow a generator that accumulates less than 500 kilograms of hazardous waste (of which less than 1 kilogram is acutely hazardous waste) an accumulation period of 180 days from the date of initial generation or accumulation.[43] A generator that exceeds either time or quantity limits becomes fully regulated as a permitted storage facility with respect to that waste.

STORING ACCUMULATED HAZARDOUS WASTE

A generator may accumulate the hazardous waste either in containers or in storage tanks. Separate requirements govern each option. The generator must meet requirements addressing either alternative for personnel training, emergency preparedness, and contingency planning.[44]

---

[38] COMAR 26.13.03.04.
[39] *Id.*
[40] 42 U.S.C. §6922(b); COMAR 26.13.03.04F.
[41] 40 C.F.R. §268.7(2).
[42] COMAR 26.13.03.05E(l).
[43] COMAR 26.13.03.05E(2).
[44] COMAR 26.13.03.05E(l).

Containers as Storage

Waste stored in containers must be in containers that will be used for moving the waste off-site, or other containers that meet the Department of Transportation packaging standards. The date upon which accumulation began must be clearly marked and visible for inspection on each container. The appropriate hazard warnings and labels must be applied during accumulation as if the waste were being prepared for transport.[45]

Proper management of the containers requires that they be in good condition, that the accumulated waste and the container be compatible, that the containers be closed, and that they be inspected at least weekly for leaking or deterioration. Ignitable or reactive waste must be stored at least 50 feet from the property line. The storage area must have a containment system, such as a dike, that is capable of collecting and holding spills, leaks, and precipitation.[46]

Used Containers

A hazardous waste container is not "empty," unless it meets the statutory definition. Thus, a container that appears "empty" in layman's terms may still be subject to hazardous waste regulation. A container that held a hazardous waste other than a compressed gas or acutely hazardous waste will be considered empty (and not subject to regulation) if all waste that can possibly be removed has been removed—using the practices common to that type of container—and no more than an inch of residue or no more than three percent by weight of the total capacity of a container that is 110 gallons or less remains on the bottom. If the container is larger than 110 gallons in size, then no more than 0.3 percent by weight of the total capacity may remain. A container that held a compressed gas is empty when the pressure in the container approaches atmospheric. A container or liner that has held an acutely hazardous waste must be triple rinsed with a solvent appropriate for the waste or by some other method that achieves equivalent removal before it is empty.[47]

Personnel Training

Someone trained in hazardous waste management procedures must conduct the personnel training. Employees must receive initial employment training and an annual review thereafter. At a minimum, the training should ensure that facility personnel are able to respond effectively to emergencies. Employees should know procedures for using, inspecting, repairing, and replacing emergency and monitoring equipment at the facility. Personnel should be familiar with appropriate response procedures for fire, explosion, and groundwater contamination incidents. Alarm systems, communications, and appropriate operation shutdown procedures should be part of the training. The facility owner or operator is responsible for ensuring that the training meets regulatory standards.[48]

---

[45] COMAR 26.13.03.05.
[46] COMAR 26.13.05.09.
[47] COMAR 26.13.02.07.
[48] COMAR 26.13.05.02G.

The facility owner or operator must maintain written records identifying each position related to hazardous waste management and the name of the employee filling the position. A written job description for each position must be maintained with a written description of the type of initial and annual training each position shall receive. Records that document the training and job experience of each employee are to be maintained for the duration of employment plus a period of three years, unless the facility is closed.[49]

Emergency Preparedness

The design, construction, maintenance, and operation of the facility must be such as to minimize the possibility of a fire, explosion, or release of a hazardous waste into the environment. A facility must have: an internal communications or alarm system to warn facility personnel in the event of an emergency; an external communications system capable of summoning local emergency response action; and portable spill control and decontamination equipment, as well as portable fire extinguishers.[50]

Where possible, the owner or operator of a facility must make arrangements to familiarize local emergency response teams, including hospital personnel, with the facility and the types of hazardous waste being accumulated and the types of injuries and emergencies that could result. Where state or local authorities decline to enter into these arrangements, the operator must document the efforts undertaken in this regard.[51]

Contingency Planning

Each generator accumulating hazardous waste on-site must develop a contingency plan for the facility designed to minimize hazards to human health or the environment from fires, explosions, or the release of hazardous waste into the environment.[52] The plan provisions must be immediately carried out in the event of an emergency. The generator must maintain copies of the plan at the facility. Local police, fire departments, and hospitals, as well as state and local emergency response teams that may be called upon in an emergency, must also receive copies.

PERMITS: TREATMENT, STORAGE, AND DISPOSAL

Generally, any business that treats, stores, or disposes of hazardous waste must obtain an operating permit from MDE. Generators may contract only with facility permit holders for the treatment, storage, or disposal of a CHS. Alternatively, the generator may contract with a permitted CHS hauler if that hauler has a valid contract with a CHS facility.[53] MDE has adopted performance standards for treatment, storage, and

---

[49] *Id.*
[50] COMAR 26.13.05.03.
[51] COMAR 26.13.05.03H.
[52] COMAR 26.13.05.04.
[53] MD. CODE, ENVIR. §7-253.

disposal facilities (TSDF) which seek to minimize the potential for release of hazardous waste into the environment.[54] Application fees have been set at anywhere from $2,000 to $10,000 depending on the facility, and a permit fee schedule taking into account the facility type, MDE monitoring costs for the facility, and environmental fees has also been created.[55] Furthermore, the permit application process involves significant public participation requirements, including the availability of contested case hearings for parties aggrieved by adverse permit determinations.

Because the Maryland TSDF regulatory details are complex and follow the federal regulatory scheme, they will not be treated in detail here except to provide a brief overview of two federal programs implementing HSWA requirements: corrective action and land disposal restrictions.[56]

Corrective Action

HSWA conditions TSDF permits on compliance with corrective action measures for prior releases of hazardous wastes or constituents from solid waste management units (SWMUs) at that facility.[57] Interim status facilities can also be ordered by EPA to implement corrective action for hazardous waste releases.[58] EPA proposed a comprehensive corrective action regulatory framework in 1990 but has withdrawn these regulations.

Land Disposal Restrictions

HSWA bans all listed and characteristic hazardous waste from land disposal unless proper treatment or recovery is performed. "Land disposal" includes placement of hazardous waste in a landfill, surface impoundment, waste pile, injection well, land treatment facility, salt dome or bed formation, or underground mine or cave.[59]

Storage of hazardous wastes is prohibited unless it is for the purpose of accumulating quantities of waste necessary for proper treatment, recovery, or disposal.[60] Certain wastes may be land disposed if the applicant demonstrates with reasonable certainty that there will be no migration of hazardous constituents from the disposal unit or injection zone for as long as the wastes remain hazardous.[61]

RCRA prescribes that treatment standards must substantially eliminate the toxicity of the waste or the likelihood of migration. EPA has designated treatment standards for hazardous wastes based upon the Best Demonstrated Available Technology (BDAT).[62] Standards may be expressed as numerical values or as specific technologies. In the case of the former, a facility may use any technology so long as analysis

---

[54] See generally COMAR 26.13.05.01, *et seq.*

[55] COMAR 26.13.07.21.

[56] Also, pursuant to HSWA, EPA has established air emissions standards for tanks and containers used for 90-day storage and for treatment, storage, and disposal facilities. *See* C.F.R. §§264.1030–.1065 and 265.1030–.1064.

[57] 42 U.S.C. §6924(u); 40 C.F.R. §264.101.

[58] 42 U.S.C. §6928(h).

[59] 42 U.S.C. §6924(k).

[60] 42 U.S.C. §6924(j).

[61] 42 U.S.C. §6924(g)(5).

[62] 42 U.S.C. §6924(m).

demonstrates that the numerical standard has been achieved; in the case of the latter, the facility must use the specific technology incorporated in the regulation.[63]

Variances from the treatment standards are available by petition in certain cases. For instance, a variance may be granted if the physical or chemical properties of the waste differ substantially from the wastes analyzed when the standard was developed such that the waste cannot be treated to the specified standard.[64] Also, variances may be considered in instances where the treatment technology is inappropriate to the waste.[65] Furthermore, if an applicant demonstrates that adequate treatment, recovery, or disposal capacity cannot be obtained—either through contract with another facility or by construction of a new facility—before the applicable effective date, an extension of up to two years may be granted to allow the applicant sufficient time to iron out the technical and practical difficulties of obtaining such capacity as may be necessary to meet the regulatory requirements.[66] Extensions are renewable twice for up to a year each time.[67]

Hazardous Remediation Waste Rule

In 1998, EPA finalized standards regulating the identification and management of remediation wastes.[68] The provisions apply to the management of "remediation waste" at "remediation waste management sites." "Remediation waste" is defined as "all solid and hazardous wastes and all media (groundwater, surface water, soil, sediment) and debris that contain listed hazardous waste or that exhibit a hazardous characteristic and are managed for implementing cleanup."[69] In turn, "Remediation Waste Management Site" is defined as "a facility where an owner or operator is or will be treating, storing, or disposing of hazardous remediation wastes."[70]

The Hazardous Remediation Waste Rule sets forth significant differences in the permitting of remediation waste sites intended to facilitate remediation of contaminated sites. Most notably, the rule creates a specialized remediation permit (called the Remedial Action Plan (RAP), which provides a streamlined permit that satisfies RCRA requirements but is easier to obtain and provides a heightened degree of certainty.[71] In addition, the rules exempt from RCRA's facility-wide corrective action requirements owners and operators of sites performing remediation work under RAPs.[72] Further, the rules allow facilities undergoing remediation to store waste in a "staging pile," a new waste management unit that provides more flexibility in storing waste during cleanup.[73]

---

[63] 42 U.S.C. §6924(m); 40 C.F.R. §268.40.
[64] 40 C.F.R. §268.44(a).
[65] *Id.*
[66] 40 C.F.R. §268.5(a). See also 40 C.F.R. §268.5(h)(2).
[67] 40 C.F.R. §268.5(e).
[68] Available at https://perma.cc/FX75-R4H9.
[69] 40 C.F.R. §260.10.
[70] *Id.*
[71] 40 C.F.R. §§270.79.
[72] 40 C.F.R. §264.101.
[73] 40 C.F.R. §264.554.

TRANSPORTERS

Maryland restricts transportation of controlled hazardous substances. The state requires a person to obtain three separate certificates to transport any controlled hazardous substance, whether from a Maryland source or to any controlled hazardous substance facility in Maryland. These certificates are:

1. a hauler certificate for the person transporting the substance;
2. a vehicle certificate for the transporting vehicle; and
3. a driver certificate for the vehicle driver.[74]

The scope of the hauler certificate may include conditions such as the use of designated routes, vehicle types, equipment or handling procedures, or other measures to ensure safety.[75] Certified haulers must:

1. maintain a bond sufficient to indemnify the state for abatement of pollution that results from improperly transported or spilled controlled hazardous substances;
2. pay an annual $50 vehicle certificate fee;
3. pass a state vehicle safety inspection;
4. submit proof of liability insurance meeting the requirements of 49 C.F.R. 387;
5. when transporting a controlled hazardous substance:
   (a) carry the manifest and driver certificate in the cab of the vehicle; and
   (b) display the vehicle certificate prominently or affix it to the outside of the cab's left door;
6. ensure all labeling and container requirements are complied with;
7. allow any police officer to stop the vehicle to inspect for any violation;
8. not remove controlled hazardous substances from the vehicle, or treat, store, or mix those substances, except in an emergency, under the MDE's supervision, or upon arrival at the appropriate destination facility; and
9. periodically report the source, nature, volume, and disposal destination of the controlled hazardous substance transported.[76]

Certified drivers must:

1. submit to MDE evidence of adequate training in the handling of controlled hazardous substances;
2. pay an annual $20 driver's fee;
3. submit a copy of both a valid driver's license and driving record;
4. keep a copy of the driver's certificate in the cab of the vehicle used to transport CHS; and
5. comply with all applicable regulations including the hauler's requirements listed at numbers 4 through 7 above.[77]

---

[74] MD. CODE, ENVIR. §7-249.
[75] MD. CODE, ENVIR. §7-251.
[76] MD. CODE, ENVIR. §7-252(a); COMAR 26.13.04.01C
[77] MD. CODE, ENVIR. §7-252(b); COMAR 26.13.04.01F.

Transporters must comply with the hazardous waste manifest system.[78] Waste accepted for shipment must be accompanied by a signed manifest, which the transporter must also sign. Transporters must retain one copy of the signed manifest for three years from the date the hazardous waste was accepted. Special rules apply to transporters shipping hazardous wastes out of the United States, and to those who ship hazardous waste by rail or by water (bulk shipment). The hazardous waste regulations governing transporters supplement Department of Transportation rules concerning the transportation of hazardous materials.

In the event of a discharge of hazardous waste, the transporter must notify MDE and local authorities within one hour of the incident, or within one hour of discovery of the incident, by calling (410) 974-3551.[79] Notification to the National Response Center may also be necessary: (800) 424-8802.[80]

POLLUTION PREVENTION

While the Pollution Prevention Act of 1990 (PPA)[81] affects all environmental statutes, its impact on RCRA-regulated entities is important. The PPA's policy objectives renew RCRA's declaration that waste minimization is an integral part of the national hazardous waste policy.[82] The PPA establishes a national policy for promoting source reduction of pollution. The PPA creates a hierarchy of prevention options:

1. Reduction of pollutants at their source whenever feasible.
2. When source reduction possibilities are exhausted, recycling of pollutants in an environmentally safe manner.
3. When recycling options are exhausted, treating the pollutants in an environmentally safe manner.
4. As a last resort, releasing or disposing of the pollutants in an environmentally safe manner.[83]

Clearly the intent is to shift the focus of environmental waste management toward source reduction and away from treatment and disposal. Source reduction may be achieved by a variety of methods, including cost-effective changes in production, operation, and raw materials use, as well as by preventive maintenance and closed-loop recycling.

The PPA directs EPA to initiate pollution prevention strategies. These include establishing methods to measure source reduction and goals to be attained, streamlining public access to prevention data, facilitating development of source reduction technology by businesses, setting up a training program for state and federal officials

---

[78] COMAR 26.13.04.02.
[79] COMAR 26.13.04.03.
[80] 40 C.F.R. §302.6(a).
[81] 42 U.S.C. §13101, *et seq.*
[82] 42 U.S.C. §6902(b).
[83] 42 U.S.C. §13101(b).

on source reduction opportunities, and identifying opportunities to use federal procurement to encourage source reduction.[84]

Hazardous Waste Minimization

Hazardous waste minimization consists of the two most desirable pollution prevention measures: source reduction and environmentally sound recycling.[85] The PPA requires that facilities making annual reports for the Toxic Release Inventory (TRI) pursuant to the Emergency Planning and Community Right to Know Act (EPCRA) include in their reports a toxic chemical source reduction and recycling report.[86] In addition, RCRA requires large quantity generators and owners and operators of TSDFs to certify that a waste minimization program is in place.[87]

ENFORCEMENT

MDE administers enforcement actions for violations of state hazardous waste requirements and regulatory provisions authorized by the EPA under RCRA. EPA retains authority to enforce HSWA. Enforcement actions may include administrative orders with penalties for noncompliance, civil actions initiated in court, and criminal prosecution.

Administrative Enforcement

EPA has authority to issue three types of administrative orders. The first is a compliance order that may require a permittee to come into compliance with provisions of its permit immediately or within a specified time. A fine of $25,000 per day may be assessed for noncompliance. EPA also has authority to revoke or suspend any permit for noncompliance or failure to comply with a compliance order.[88] Second, EPA may issue a corrective action order. Such an order may require corrective action for releases of hazardous waste from interim status facilities, with penalties of $27,500 per day for noncompliance.[89] Third, EPA may require monitoring, analysis, and testing to be conducted by current or prior owners or operators of a waste management site, if a site may present a substantial hazard to human health or the environment.[90]

MDE has authority to suspend or revoke any permit or certificate issued by the Department for a violation of any state or federal law relating to hazardous substances.[91] Like EPA, MDE also has authority to issue a corrective action order for any violation of the state statute, regulation, or any provision of a permit or certificate issued

---

[84] 42 U.S.C. §13103(b).
[85] 58 Fed. Reg. 31114, 31115 (May 28, 1993).
[86] 42 U.S.C. §13106(a).
[87] 42 U.S.C. §6922(b).
[88] 42 U.S.C. §6928(a), (c).
[89] 42 U.S.C. §6928(h).
[90] 42 U.S.C. §6934.
[91] MD. CODE, ENVIR. §7-257.

by the Department.[92] MDE may impose penalties of up to $25,000 per day for each violation, not to exceed $100,000 total.[93] The Department's enforcement weapons include broad administrative search warrant authority and inspection authority, allowing it to inspect records and conduct tests at a facility.[94]

Civil Enforcement

For violations of Subtitle C of RCRA, EPA may seek civil penalties of up to $25,000 per day and may obtain injunctive relief.[95] If EPA receives evidence that a site may present an imminent and substantial endangerment to health or the environment, the agency may initiate a civil action to require any action that may be necessary. This action may be initiated for all past activities at the site where there are current effects.[96]

MDE may initiate a civil action for injunctive relief to enjoin an ongoing violation of any provision or to prohibit a violation that is about to occur. If the violation presents imminent danger to health or the environment, MDE may seek an immediate injunction.[97] Penalties of up to $25,000 per day may be imposed.[98]

Criminal Prosecution

EPA may seek criminal prosecution of any person who knowingly transports, or causes to be transported, any hazardous waste identified or listed under the statute to a facility that does not have a permit. Any person who knowingly treats, stores, or disposes of any hazardous waste identified under the statute without a permit, or knowingly violates any material condition or requirement of the permit, is also subject to criminal prosecution. Upon conviction, a defendant may be fined $50,000 per day for each violation and imprisoned for up to five years.

EPA may also seek criminal sanctions for a knowing violation of the record-keeping requirements under the statute. The penalty for such a violation is $50,000 per day for each violation and the possibility of imprisonment for a period not to exceed two years. A double penalty may be imposed for a subsequent offense.[99] If the violation is such that the defendant knows at the time of the violation that he places another person in imminent danger of death or serious bodily injury, the statutory penalty is $1,000,000 for a corporation and $250,000 for an individual. Imprisonment may be for up to 15 years.[100]

MDE may initiate criminal prosecution for any violation of the Maryland rules, regulations, orders, or permits. Upon conviction, a defendant is subject to a $25,000 fine or imprisonment not exceeding one year (or both) for a first offense, and a $50,000 fine or imprisonment not exceeding two years (or both) for a subsequent violation. A

---

92 MD. CODE, ENVIR. §7-259.
93 MD. CODE, ENVIR. §7-266.
94 MD. CODE, ENVIR. §7-256.
95 42 U.S.C. §6928(a), (g).
96 42 U.S.C. §6973(a).
97 MD. CODE, ENVIR. §7-263.
98 MD. CODE, ENVIR. §7-266.
99 42 U.S.C. §6928(d).
100 42 U.S.C. §6928(e).

penalty of a $25,000 fine or imprisonment not exceeding two years is available upon conviction of making false statements in any required records.[101] In addition, specific felony offenses are subject to a fine of $100,000 and imprisonment for five years. Knowing felony offenses are subject to fines of up to $250,000 and imprisonment for 15 years. Misdemeanor offenses are subject to a fine of $50,000 and imprisonment for not more than three years.[102]

---

[101] MD. CODE ANN., ENVIR. §7-267.
[102] MD. CODE ANN., ENVIR. §7-265.

Chapter 6

Remediation of Past Hazardous Substance Contamination

Superfund

Waste handling and disposal practices that were common prior to today's level of environmental awareness resulted in hazardous and toxic substances contaminating soil and groundwater. To combat this problem, Congress enacted the Comprehensive Environmental Response, Compensation and Liability Act (CERCLA or Superfund) in December 1980.[1] CERCLA has been amended a number of times, including substantial legislative revisions in 1986[2] and important liability protections signed into law in January 2002.[3]

In contrast to the Resource Conservation and Recovery Act, which generally regulates current hazardous waste handling and disposal, Superfund focuses on remediation of past contamination. The federal government has authority to use the Superfund to clean up a property, such as a waste disposal site, where there has been a release or threatened release of a "hazardous substance," and then to sue responsible parties for reimbursement of cleanup costs. Alternatively, the government may order responsible parties to clean up the site. Under CERCLA, responsible parties that pay for cleanup may sue other responsible parties for recovery of costs. CERCLA also imposes reporting requirements.

The Maryland Legislature has created a parallel state Superfund, the Hazardous Substance Control Fund (HSCF), which may finance identification and monitoring, as well as cleanup, of any Maryland site where there is a release or threatened release of "hazardous substances."[4] In addition, MDE possesses specific statutory authority to enter a site, compel cleanup, or seek injunctive relief if a site presents an imminent and substantial endangerment to public health and welfare or the environment.[5]

---

[1] 42 U.S.C. §9601, *et seq.*
[2] Superfund Amendments and Reauthorization Act of 1986 (Pub. L. 99-499) (SARA).
[3] Small Business Liability Relief and Brownfields Revitalization Act of 2001 (Pub.L. 107-118).
[4] MD. CODE, ENVIR. §7-220(s).
[5] MD. CODE, ENVIR. §7-222.

SUPERFUND HAZARDOUS WASTE SITE CLEANUPS

Hazardous Substances

The hazardous substances that may trigger CERCLA cleanup liability include all substances regulated under the Clean Water Act, the Clean Air Act, the Toxic Substances Control Act, and the Resource Conservation and Recovery Act, except certain petroleum and natural gas substances.[6] In addition, CERCLA authorizes EPA to designate additional substances as hazardous.

The Maryland Superfund statute regulates "hazardous substances," which include CERCLA hazardous substances and "controlled hazardous substances" identified by MDE.[7] "Controlled hazardous substances" are essentially synonymous with hazardous wastes regulated by the state under the RCRA program.[8]

Cleanup Site Selection

In 1981, there was a one-time federal reporting obligation imposed on certain transporters and on owners and operators of hazardous waste treatment, storage, and disposal facilities. From this list EPA compiled the original list of sites where hazardous substances may be located.[9] Since that time, EPA has frequently added sites to the list as a result of spill reports, citizen discoveries, state enforcement proceedings, etc. EPA evaluates the degree of hazard presented by each site and places the most hazardous ones on the National Priorities List (NPL) for cleanup.

Scope of Cleanup

Any federal government cleanup action and private remedial action must be consistent with the National Contingency Plan (NCP), EPA's regulatory blueprint for remediating Superfund sites.[10] Costs incurred by the remedying party consequent to actions not consistent with the NCP are *not* recoverable from liable parties.[11] Maryland has developed a state Hazardous Substance Response Plan, which generally follows the federal NCP.[12] Each plan describes governmental roles and procedures for evaluating remedial options. Evaluation of a site for cleanup is generally done through a remedial investigation and feasibility study (RI/FS).

The RI/FS is an intensive investigative study that collects data, evaluates alternative actions, and recommends selection of one of those remedial alternatives based on NCP criteria. A prime objective of the RI/FS is to determine the nature and extent of remediation required. Consideration is given to the benefits and detriments of containing the contamination on-site versus disposing of the waste off-site. The choices made

---

[6] 42 U.S.C. §9601(14).
[7] MD. CODE, ENVIR. §7-201(m).
[8] COMAR 26.13.01.03B(31).
[9] 42 U.S.C. §9603(c).
[10] 42 U.S.C. §9605.
[11] *Id.* §9607(a); see also *Weyerhaeuser Corp. v. Koppers Co.*, 771 F. Supp. 1406 (D. Md. 1991).
[12] COMAR 26.14.01, *et seq.*

affect the total cost of the cleanup and consequently the potential financial liability of the parties.

The NCP sets out nine criteria by which to judge alternative remedial plans. These criteria include: (1) overall protection of human health and the environment; (2) compliance with applicable or relevant and appropriate regulations; (3) long-term effectiveness and permanence; (4) reduction of toxicity, mobility, or volume through treatment; (5) short-term effectiveness; (6) implement-ability; (7) cost; (8) state acceptance; and (9) community acceptance.[13]

Remedy selection is a two-step process. The first step involves the presentation of a preferred remedy to the public for comment, followed by a review of those comments. Parties involved in an early cleanup decision will be able to request modifications of the remedial response plan to reflect new scientific information or technological advances.[14]

Review of EPA's Choice of Remedy

There are severe limitations on a party's ability to secure pre-enforcement judicial review of governmental remedial decisions on Superfund sites.[15] Therefore, a party should consider offering all pertinent information or opinions during the administrative decision-making process. The choice of cleanup method may be challenged later in court only when EPA seeks to collect from responsible parties the money it has spent or seeks to compel a cleanup by a responsible party. When such challenges are made, review is limited to the administrative record. A court will uphold the agency decision unless it is unlawful or arbitrary and capricious.[16]

LIABLE PARTIES

Responsible Parties

CERCLA places financial responsibility for on-site cleanup costs on the current owner or operator of a site and on the owner or operator of the site at the time of the disposal.[17] "Disposal" has been construed to include not only dumping and placing of hazardous substances, but also passive leakage and migration.

The "operator" may include a principal shareholder or a manager. Lessees may be liable as "operators" if they have the authority to control the facility at the time of the disposal; actual involvement is not necessary to impose liability. There have been federal lender liability protections enacted due to the Asset Conservation, Lender Liability, and Deposit Insurance Protection Act of 1996.[18] Under this Act, a lender will be considered "participating in the management of a facility," and liable only if

[13] 40 C.F.R. §300.430.
[14] 61 Fed. Reg. 19432 (May 1, 1996).
[15] 42 U.S.C. §9613(h).
[16] 42 U.S.C. §9613(j).
[17] 42 U.S.C. §9607(a).
[18] See 42 U.S.C. §9601(20)(A) (the "Lender Liability Amendments" to CERCLA).

the lender exercises daily control over the borrower's operation.[19] Also, if a lender promptly takes action to sell the property and complies with environmental laws, while still in possession of the property, the lender may foreclose on the property without becoming liable as an owner.[20]

As for off-site cleanups (e.g., landfills to which waste was transported), responsibility extends to all participants in the waste generation, handling, transportation, and disposal chain that resulted in the release or threatened release of a hazardous substance from a site requiring cleanup. Thus, the firm that generated a hazardous substance and/or made arrangements to have it transported to a disposal or recycling site may be considered a responsible party if the waste ends up at a site from which releases occur.

Corporate Successors

Corporate successors may incur the predecessor's Superfund liabilities if they acquire the predecessor's stock or if assets are acquired and there is substantial continuity of enterprise between the two.[21] Among the factors affecting continuity are: (1) retention of the same employees, supervisory personnel, facilities, production product, and name; (2) continuity of assets and business operations; and (3) whether the successor holds itself out to be the continuation of the same enterprise.[22]

Corporate Parent Liability

A parent corporation can be found liable under CERCLA for a subsidiary's contamination in two ways: (1) a parent corporation can be *directly liable* as an operator under CERCLA for contamination if it actively manages, directs, or otherwise conducts operations specifically related to the subsidiary-related pollution; and (2) a parent corporation can be *derivatively liable* as an operator under circumstances that warrant piercing the corporate veil under applicable state law.[23] To be held *directly liable* as an operator of a subsidiary's facility under CERCLA, the facts and circumstances of a particular case must demonstrate that the parent corporation manages, directs, or otherwise conducts subsidiary operations specifically related to the leakage or disposal of hazardous substances, or makes decisions about environmental compliance at the facility in question.[24] A parent corporation can also be found *derivatively* liable as an "operator" of a subsidiary's facility under CERCLA when, under principles of state law, the corporate veil of the parent may be pieced.[25] This typically occurs when, among other things, the parent misuses the corporate form for wrongful purposes (i.e., fraud).[26]

---

19 42 U.S.C. §9601(20)(F).
20 42 U.S.C. §9601(20)(E).
21 See *HRW Systems, Inc. v. Washington Gas Light Co.*, 823 F. Supp. 318 (D. Md. 1993), *United States v. Carolina Transformer Co.*, 978 F.2d 832 (4th Cir. 1992).
22 See *Carolina Transformer,* 978 F.2d at 838.
23 See *United States v. Bestfoods,* 524 U.S. 51 (1998).
24 *Id.* at 66–67.
25 *Id.* at 61–64.
26 *Id.*

Local Governments

Generators of municipal solid wastes (usually towns or counties) who provide for refuse collection or contract with a private party to do so may be liable for Superfund costs if the refuse collected and deposited at a contaminated landfill site contains hazardous substances like those found at the site.[27] Even trace amounts of hazardous substances found in municipal refuse may be sufficient to impose CERCLA liability upon a municipality.[28] A town may be liable as a transporter under CERCLA if the municipal refuse hauled to the contaminated landfill contains hazardous substances. In addition, a local government generally will be liable if it owned or operated the contaminated site, now or at the time of disposal.

Notice of Potentially Responsible Parties (PRPs)

EPA investigators identify potentially responsible parties (PRPs) with respect to a particular site and send them letters requesting further information. The "Dear PRP" letter may arrive at any stage during site identification, investigation, evaluation, and eventual cleanup as various parties' relationships to the site become clear. The decisions made in the early stages may have dramatic impacts on the potential liability of PRPs. Recipients of a "Dear PRP" letter should consult with counsel and consider becoming involved in EPA's decision-making process as early as possible.

Innocent PRPs

Congress intended CERCLA to make companies and individuals financially responsible for contamination resulting from past waste management practices, whether or not they acted in good faith, in accordance with the law, or used state-of-the-art waste management practices in disposing of materials. CERCLA imposes liability at all levels on a strict basis, without regard for whether the original disposal was appropriate and legal.[29]

The fact that a transporter was licensed by appropriate authorities or that a permitted disposal site was selected will not preclude liability for either the transporter or the generator. Both the owner and operator of a facility at the time it was used for disposal will be held liable without regard for causation or the appropriateness or legality of such use.

The current owner or operator of a site at which a hazardous substance release is discovered may be held liable under CERCLA despite having no knowledge of or involvement in the past contamination of the site.[30] The current owner provision encompasses municipalities that condemn properties, but not state or local governments that acquire property "involuntarily" (e.g., property that is abandoned or taken

---

[27] See *B. F. Goodrich Co. v. Murtha*, 754 F. Supp. 960 (D. Conn. 1991), *aff'd* 958 F.2d 1192 (2d Cir. 1992). However, in *B. F. Goodrich Co. v. Murtha*, 840 F. Supp. 180 (D. Conn. 1993), a related case, the court held that evidence of actual hazardous substance or hazardous waste disposal was required in a cost recovery action.

[28] *Id.*, 958 F.2d at 1200.

[29] See *Dent v. Beazer Materials and Services. Inc. et al.*, 156 F.3d 523, 529 (4th Cir. 1998).

[30] *Sherwin-Williams v. ARTRA Group, Inc.*, 125 F. Supp. 2d 739, 745 (D. Md. 2001).

to satisfy a tax delinquency), so long as the government entity did not contribute to the contamination and exercised due care.[31]

FEDERAL STATUTORY DEFENSES AND EXEMPTIONS TO LIABILITY

Act of God, Act of War, and Third-Party/Innocent Purchaser Defenses

Persons otherwise liable under CERCLA will not be held liable if the hazardous release was caused by an act of God, an act of war, or a third party contractually unrelated to the purchaser provided the purchaser exercised due care and took precautions against foreseeable acts and omissions of a third party.[32] The first two defenses are largely theoretical, and the third defense has been narrowly construed. The third-party defense is unavailable to a lessor or lessee because of the contractual relationship that existed when one or the other created the contamination. Moreover, it is unavailable to a buyer with respect to acts of a predecessor in title because "deeds" are contractual relationships *unless* a buyer qualifies as an "innocent purchaser." If the buyer is an "innocent purchaser," the contractual limitation on the third-party defense is removed.[33]

A buyer of property can assert "innocence" and thus avoid cleanup liability by showing that its predecessors in interest created the contamination and that the buyer did not know and had no reason to know that the hazardous substance was present. To establish "no reason to know" the buyer must have undertaken at the time of acquisition "all appropriate inquiry" into the previous ownership and uses of the property consistent with good commercial or customary practice. While it is clear that a buyer must perform an environmental site assessment at the time of acquisition in order to assert a meaningful defense to any subsequent "current owner" liability for cleanup of contamination, until recent amendments to CERCLA the statute was silent on the particular standard of inquiry necessary for a party to avail itself of the innocent purchaser defense.

The 2000 Brownfields Revitalization and Environmental Restoration Act[34] helps clarify the requirements for purchasers to meet the "appropriate inquiry" standard needed to satisfy the innocent purchaser defense.[35] The Brownfields Act provides that EPA must, within two years after its enactment, promulgate regulations establishing standards and practices for satisfying the requirements of performing "all appropriate inquiry" and satisfying other applicable requirements.[36]

The future EPA regulations must provide that the inquiry be conducted by an environmental professional and that the inquiry include or give effect to (1) interviews

---

[31] 42 U.S.C. §§9601(20)(A), (D).

[32] *Id.* §9607(b); see also *Dent* 156 F.3d at 529, citing *United States v. Monsanto Co.*, 858 F.2d 160 (4th Cir. 1988), *cert. denied*, 490 U.S. 1106 (1989) (subject only to "innocent party" exceptions in §9607(b), CERCLA liability is strict).

[33] 42 U.S.C. §9601(35)(A).

[34] Small Business Liability Relief and Brownfields Revitalization Act of 2001, Pub. L. 107–118.

[35] 42 U.S.C. §9601(35)(B).

[36] 42 U.S.C. §9601(35)(B)(ii).

with past and present owners, operators, and occupants of the facility; (2) reviews of historical sources to determine previous uses and occupancies of the real property; (3) searches for recorded environmental cleanup liens; (4) reviews of federal, state, and local government records concerning contamination at or near the facility; (5) visual inspections of the facility and adjoining properties; (6) any specialized knowledge of the defendant; (7) the relationship of the purchase price to the value of the property if the property were not contaminated; (8) commonly known or reasonably ascertainable information about the property; and (9) the degree of obviousness of the presence or likely presence of contamination at the property and the ability to detect the contamination by appropriate investigation.[37]

With respect to property purchased after May 31, 1997, and until EPA promulgates regulations concerning "all appropriate inquiry," the standards promulgated by the American Society for Testing and Materials (ASTM) in 1997 for the conduct of a phase I environmental site assessment apply to determine whether the purchaser has conducted "all appropriate inquiry."[38] However, the Brownfields Act provides that, in the case of property for residential or other similar use purchased by a nongovernmental or noncommercial entity, a facility inspection and title search that reveal no basis for further investigation constitute "all appropriate inquiry."[39]

Additionally, the Brownfields Act amends the "innocent landowner" provisions of CERCLA by requiring a buyer, as a prerequisite for liability protection, to provide full cooperation, assistance, and access to persons conducting a CERCLA response action on its property to be in compliance with any land use restrictions related to the response actions, and to not impede the effectiveness or integrity of any institutional control used at the facility.

Small Business Liability Protection

Title I of the Brownfields Act creates a *de micromis* exemption from CERCLA liability for small-quantity generators of hazardous substances that have been disposed of at sites on the NPL.[40] This *de micromis* exemption is available to parties who disposed of less than 110 gallons of liquid or less than 200 pounds of solid hazardous material before April 1, 2001.[41] However, the *de micromis* exemption is not available in any case in which EPA determines that the materials disposed of by such party have contributed significantly or could contribute significantly, either individually or in the aggregate, to the costs of cleanup or restoration of natural resources or in which the person has failed to comply with information requests or subpoenas issued by EPA under CERCLA.[42] The *de micromis* exemption also is not available to any person convicted of a criminal violation for the conduct to which the exemption would otherwise apply.[43] If any party (other than a federal, state, or local government) brings any

---

[37] 42 U.S.C. §9601(35)(B)(iii).
[38] 42 U.S.C. §9601(35)(B)(iv)(II); see also 68 Fed. Reg. 3430 (Jan. 24, 2003).
[39] 42 U.S.C. §9601 (35)(B)(v).
[40] 42 U.S.C. §9607(o).
[41] *Id.*
[42] 42 U.S.C. §9607(o)(2)(A).
[43] 42 U.S.C. §9607(o)(2)(B).

contribution action, that party bears the burden of proving that the conditions for the *de micromis* exemption have not been met by the generator defendant.[44]

Title I of the Brownfields Act also creates a new exemption from CERCLA liability for the following categories of generators of municipal solid waste ("MSW") disposed of at NPL sites:

1. owners, operators, and lessees of residential property from which the MSW was generated;
2. a business entity that, during its three taxable years preceding the date of EPA notification of potential liability under CERCLA, employed on average not more than 100 full-time individuals (or equivalent thereof) and that is a small business concern within the meaning of the Small Business Act; and
3. an organization described in Section 501(c)(3) of the Internal Revenue Code that, during the taxable year preceding the date of EPA notification of potential liability under CERCLA, employed not more than 100 paid individuals at the location from which was generated the MSW disposed of at the NPL site.[45]

However, the MSW exemption is not available in any case in which EPA determines

1. the MSW has contributed significantly, either individually or in the aggregate, to the cost of the cleanup or restoration of natural resources; or
2. the person has failed to comply with information requests or subpoenas issued by EPA under CERCLA; or
3. the person has impeded or is impeding, through action or inaction, the performance of response action or natural resource restoration at the NPL site.[46]

The Brownfields Act provides that, in some circumstances, a plaintiff in a CERCLA action has the burden of proving that the defendant is not entitled to the MSW exemption.[47] Further, nongovernmental parties are prohibited from bringing CERCLA contribution actions against parties entitled to the MSW exemption.[48] The Brownfields Act provides that, if a nongovernmental entity commences a CERCLA action after the date of enactment against a party entitled to the MSW exemption, the plaintiff is liable to the defendant for reasonable costs (including attorneys' fees and expert witness fees) of defending the action.[49]

The Brownfields Act defines MSW to include waste materials that are generated by a household (including a single or multifamily residence) or generated by a commercial, industrial, or institutional entity to the extent that the waste material is essentially the same as waste normally generated by a household, is collected and disposed of with other MSW as part of normal MSW collection services, and contains quantities of hazardous substances similar to those in MSW generated by a typical single-family

[44] 42 U.S.C. §9607(0)(4).
[45] 42 U.S.C. §9607(p)(l).
[46] 42 U.S.C. §9607(p)(2).
[47] 42 U.S.C. §9607(p)(5).
[48] 42 U.S.C. §9607(p)(6).
[49] 42 U.S.C. §9607(p)(7).

household.[50] MSW does not include combustion ash from resource recovery facilities or municipal incinerators, or wastes from manufacturing or processing operations.[51]

The Brownfields Act makes some technical amendments to CERCLA Section 122(g), which provides for expedited settlements of CERCLA liabilities for *de minimis*–responsible parties (i.e., those responsible parties under CERCLA whose shares of response costs are minor).[52] The amendments to Section 122(g) include (1) statutory authorization for the United States to reduce the amount of settlement payments from parties who have the inability or limited ability to pay their full shares, (2) requirement that any parties settling their liability under CERCLA Section 122(g) waive claims against other responsible parties (so as to reduce the volume of litigation), and (3) a bar on judicial review of any settlements by the United States with any *de minimis*–responsible party under CERCLA Section 122(g).[53]

"Brownfields" are generally defined as abandoned or under-used properties where redevelopment or expansion is complicated by real or perceived environmental contamination. Amendments to CERCLA under Title II, Subtitle B of the Brownfields Act were designed to encourage redevelopment of brownfields sites. These amendments include the clarifications of the innocent landowner defense discussed above, and the following additional liability protections: (1) limitations on CERCLA liability for certain owners of properties contiguous to contaminated sites; (2) limitations on CERCLA liability for prospective purchasers of certain contaminated sites; and (3) creation of liens in favor of the United States for unrecovered response costs incurred by the United States for sites acquired by prospective purchasers entitled to the limitations on liability.[54]

The Brownfields Act provides that an owner of real property ("contiguous owner") that has been contaminated by hazardous substances released on a contiguous site not owned by such contiguous owner is not considered an owner or operator of a contaminated site for purposes of CERCLA liability, provided that certain conditions are satisfied, including the following:

1. The contiguous owner did not cause, contribute, or consent to the hazardous substance release.
2. The contiguous owner is not (a) potentially liable under CERCLA on any other grounds; (b) affiliated with any other person that is liable under CERCLA through any direct or indirect familial, contractual, corporate or financial relationship; or (c) the result of a reorganization of a business entity that was potentially liable.
3. The contiguous owner takes reasonable steps to stop any continuing release; prevent any future release; and prevent or limit human, environmental, or natural resource exposure to any hazardous substance released on or from property owned by that contiguous owner. However, the contiguous owner is not required to conduct groundwater investigation or remediation except in accordance with EPA's existing policy dated May 24, 1995, concerning owners of property containing contaminated aquifers.

---

[50] 42 U.S.C. §9607(p)(4)(A).
[51] 42 U.S.C. §9607(p)(4)(c).
[52] 42 U.S.C. §9622(g).
[53] *Id.*
[54] 42 U.S.C. §9607(r).

4. The contiguous owner provides full cooperation, assistance, and access to persons who are authorized to conduct response actions or natural resource restoration at the facility from which there has been a hazardous substance release.
5. The contiguous owner (a) is in compliance with any land-use restrictions established or relied on in connection with the response action, and (b) does not impede the effectiveness or integrity of any institutional control employed in connection with a response action.
6. The contiguous owner is in compliance with any request for information or administrative subpoena issued by EPA under CERCLA.
7. The contiguous owner provides all legally required notices with respect to the discovery or release of any hazardous substances at the facility.
8. When the contiguous owner acquired its real property, the contiguous owner conducted all appropriate inquiry with respect to its real property and did not know or have reason to know that the property was or could be contaminated by hazardous substances released from other sites not owned by such contiguous owner.[55]

The Brownfields Act provides that a bona fide prospective purchaser whose potential liability for a hazardous substance release is based solely on the purchaser's being considered an owner or operator will not have owner or operator liability under CERCLA so long as the bona fide prospective purchaser does not impede the performance of a response action or natural resource restoration.[56] The Brownfields Act defines a "*bona fide* prospective purchaser" as a person (or a tenant of such person) that acquires ownership of a facility after the enactment of the Brownfields Act and that establishes each of the following by a preponderance of the evidence:

1. All disposal of hazardous substances at the facility occurred before the person acquired the facility.
2. The person made all appropriate inquiries into the previous ownership and uses of the facility in accordance with generally accepted good commercial and customary standards and practices. The criteria to be the basis for these standards are described below in the section relating to innocent landowners.
3. The person provides all legally required notices with respect to the discovery or release of any hazardous substances.
4. The person takes reasonable steps to stop any continuing release; prevent any future release; and prevent or limit human, environmental, or natural resource exposure to any hazardous substance found at the facility.
5. The person provides full cooperation, assistance, and access to persons who are authorized to conduct response actions or natural resource restoration at the facility from which there has been a hazardous substance release.
6. The person (a) is in compliance with any land use restrictions established or relied on in connection with the response action, and (b) does not impede the effectiveness or integrity of any institutional control employed in connection with a response action.

---

[55] 42 U.S.C. §9607(q).
[56] 42 U.S.C. §9607(1).

7. The person is in compliance with any request for information or administrative subpoena issued by EPA under CERCLA.
8. The person is not (a) potentially liable under CERCLA on any other grounds; (b) affiliated with any other person who is liable under CERCLA through any direct or indirect familial, contractual, corporate, or financial relationship; or (c) the result of a reorganization of a business entity that was potentially liable.[57]

However, if the United States does not recover any response costs with respect to a property owned by a person qualifying as a bona fide prospective purchaser, and if the response action increases the fair market value of the property over the fair market value that existed before the response action was initiated, then the United States may have a lien on the property (or, with the agreement of the owner, on any other property or other assurance of payment satisfactory to EPA) for the amount of the United States' unrecovered response costs.[58] The amount of such lien cannot exceed the increase in the fair market value of the property attributable to the response action at the time of a sale or other disposition of the property.[59]

Maryland's Brownfields Program: The Voluntary Cleanup Program

The state's Voluntary Cleanup Program (VCP) is the core of Maryland's brownfields program.[60] The VCP is a voluntary program that requires appropriate cleanup of properties while providing eligible participants limited liability protection from government action related to past contamination. Applicants eligible for the VCP include "Responsible Persons," who have not knowingly or willfully violated controlled hazardous substance laws, and "Inculpable Persons." A Responsible Person under the VCP is defined in Md. Code, Envir. §7-201(t), to include: a current owner or operator, an owner or operator at time of disposal, arrangers, and transporters.[61] An Inculpable Person under the VCP is defined as a person who has no current or prior ownership interest in the property at the time of application and who did not cause or contribute to contamination.[62] An inculpable person includes a successor-in-interest to an eligible property acquired from an inculpable person.

Not all properties are eligible for the VCP. Under the VCP statute, a property is "eligible" if it is contaminated or perceived to be contaminated, unless the property is listed on the CERCLA National Priorities List; the property is under "active enforcement" (property that has received a notice of violation, order, consent order, or other enforcement action from MDE until completion of activities required by the action); or the property is subject to a controlled hazardous substance permit.[63]

57 42 U.S.C. §9601(40).
58 42 U.S.C. §9607(r)(l)–(3).
59 42 U.S.C. §9607(r)(4).
60 MD. CODE, ENVIR. §§7-501 to 7-516.
61 MD. CODE, ENVIR. §7-501(n).
62 MD. CODE, ENVIR. §7-501(j).
63 MD. CODE, ENVIR. §7-501(g).

Application and Processing

In submitting a VCP application to MDE, an applicant must demonstrate that it is an "eligible applicant" and that the property in question is an "eligible property" (as discussed above).[64] The VCP application must also include a report of specified information on the property, including environmental site assessments complying with ASTM assessment principles. The application must also include a summary of the proposed cleanup, proposed cleanup criteria, a description of the proposed future use of property, and a $6,000 application fee.[65]

The statute provides MDE 45 days to review the VCP application.[66] At the end of the 45-day period, MDE can either approve the application, deny the application, or issue a "No Further Requirements" (NFR) determination.[67] MDE issues an NFR determination if it determines that the applicant is an eligible party and that no additional remedial action is required at the property. An NFR determination allows an applicant to participate in and receive the benefits of the VCP program without performing cleanup activity, but subject to the terms and conditions of the NFR determination letter. Such terms and conditions frequently include construction and deed restrictions designed to protect public health and the environment from any potential future hazards related to contamination or potential contamination on the site (e.g., no excavation or residential use).

MDE must deny a VCP application if it determines that an applicant or the property is not "eligible," or if it determines the property was contaminated after October 1, 1997 (unless it was caused by an act of god or the property was acquired by an inculpable person).[68]

If MDE approves an application, an applicant has 30 days to decide whether to proceed or withdraw from the program.[69] If an applicant decides to proceed, it must submit a Response Action Plan (RAP) to MDE. A RAP must include: a description of all planned response actions, including long-term monitoring; a demonstration to MDE's satisfaction that the plan will protect public health and the environment and achieve approved cleanup criteria; a certification of zoning compliance; an outline of responsibilities of the participant and MDE; an agreement to implement the RAP subject to VCP withdrawal provisions; a proposal for financial assurances; and protective cleanup criteria based on uniform risk-based standards, measurable standards on site-specific risk assessment, background levels, and other federal or state standards.[70]

A VCP participant must meet public notice and comment requirements.[71] MDE reviews the RAP and public comments (if any), applying a standard of protection of health and the environment. Within 120 days of receiving the RAP, MDE must either approve the RAP or reject it.[72] If the department rejects the RAP, it must state

---

[64] MD. CODE, ENVIR. §7-506(a).
[65] *Id.*
[66] MD. CODE, ENVIR. §7-506(e).
[67] *Id.*
[68] MD. CODE, ENVIR. §7-506(f).
[69] MD. CODE, ENVIR. §7-506(g).
[70] MD. CODE, ENVIR. §7-508.
[71] MD. CODE, ENVIR. §7-509.
[72] MD. CODE, ENVIR. §7-511.

the modifications necessary to obtain approval. A party has 120 days to resubmit a rejected RAP.[73]

If the RAP is approved, the participant receives a RAP approval letter that specifies: (1) any necessary limitations on use of the property; (2) that no further action will be required other than that specified in the RAP (subject to certain limitations discussed below); and (3) that the participant will receive a Certification of Completion ("COC") upon MDE's determination that the RAP has been fully implemented and the plan has achieved the stated cleanup criteria.[74]

The VCP statute allows a participant to voluntarily withdraw while a VCP application or proposed RAP is still pending, or after a COC is received.[75] A party must give MDE 10 days' notice of the withdrawal, stabilize the site to MDE's satisfaction, and forfeit any expended application/oversight fees. A party may be involuntarily withdrawn if it fails to notify MDE of an intent to proceed within 30 days of an approved application.

Once MDE is notified by the participant that the RAP has been successfully implemented, the department has 30 days to issue a COC. The COC serves to affirm the RAP is complete; establish permissible uses/restrictions on the property; affirm the achievement of cleanup criteria; affirm that MDE may not bring an enforcement action against a participant at the eligible property (subject to reopeners); affirm a participant is released from liability to the state for contamination identified in environmental site assessment; and affirm that a participant is not subject to contribution action by a responsible person.[76]

Benefits of the VCP Program

The VCP program offers a number of significant benefits to developers, lenders, property owners, and other parties to projects involving brownfields. First, the VCP process greatly reduces the risk of future cleanup cost by providing predictability and finality of cleanup requirements. The VCP program also offers protections from state action for past contamination and protection from a contribution suit by a responsible party for past contamination.[77]

The program also offers limited protection from federal Superfund liability. Under a Memorandum of Agreement (MOA) with MDE, EPA agrees to consider VCP approved sites in Maryland as having "no federal interest" for the purpose of federal CERCLA enforcement action. The MOA provides assurance to a VCP participant (and related parties, such as lenders) that federal enforcement action by EPA will not likely occur with respect to a VCP approved property in the state. The MOA does not apply to several categories of sites, including those already subject to federal orders or enforcement action and sites subject to RCRA corrective action orders.

---

[73] *Id.*
[74] *Id.*
[75] MD. CODE, ENVIR. §7-512.
[76] MD. CODE, ENVIR. §7-513.
[77] MD. CODE, ENVIR. §7-513(b)(3).

Limitation on VCP Protections

The liability protection afforded to a VCP participant is not absolute. The VCP statute expressly reserves MDE's right before, during, or after the VCP process to take action against any person in connection with imminent and substantial endangerment; take action concerning new contamination or exacerbated contamination; take action to enforce use restrictions in RAP approval; take action against persons responsible for long-term monitoring and maintenance; require additional actions to meet applicable cleanup criteria (subject to withdrawal provision); void RAP approvals or certification of completion if based on fraud or misrepresentation.[78]

It is important to note that after a VCP Certification of Completion is issued, a responsible person remains liable for undiscovered contamination, zoning is not affected, and tort liability of any party is not affected.[79]

Maryland Statutory Defenses

The Maryland Superfund statute largely parallels, with some notable exceptions, the liability scheme set forth in CERCLA. The Maryland statute contains an innocent purchaser defense virtually identical to that provided by CERCLA. It also excludes from liability persons who hold a security interest in property unless they participate in the day-to-day management of the site or directly cause the discharge of a hazardous substance on or from the site.[80] Fiduciaries who have legal title to a site or property for purposes of administering an estate or trust and lenders who acquire title through foreclosure or deed in lieu of foreclosure are also excluded from liability if they do not participate in day-to-day management or directly cause a discharge.[81] Governmental owners and operators are excluded from liability except in the case of gross negligence or willful misconduct.[82]

The day-to-day management that will void the exclusion under state law includes "directing or controlling operations, production or treatment of a hazardous substance, storage or disposal of a hazardous substance, or remediation of a hazardous substance release." It does *not* include "rendering advice on financial matters, rendering financial assistance, or actions taken to protect or secure the site or property located on the site if the advice, assistance or actions do not involve the treatment, storage or disposal of a hazardous substance or remediation of a hazardous substance release."[83]

The Maryland Estates and Trusts Article authorizes certain environmental actions by personal representatives, trustees, and fiduciaries.[84] When these actions are taken prudently and in good faith, the fiduciary is protected from liability for a decrease in the value of the assets of the estate, trust, or fiduciary estate.[85]

---

78 MD. CODE, ENVIR. §7-514.
79 *Id.*
80 MD. CODE, ENVIR. §7-201(t)(2)(vi).
81 MD. CODE, ENVIR. §7-201(t)(2)(v).
82 MD. CODE, ENVIR. §7-201(t)(2)(vii).
83 MD. CODE, ENVIR. §7-201(t)(6).
84 MD. CODE, EST. & TRUSTS §15-102(z)(1).
85 MD. CODE, EST. & TRUSTS §15-102(z)(2).

COST RECOVERY

Share of Liability for PRPs

Under CERCLA, potentially responsible parties are liable for all cleanup response costs incurred at the site and for damages (up to $50 million) to natural resources owned, managed, or controlled by a federal, state, or local governmental authority. Cleanup costs include the costs of investigation, monitoring, testing, and evaluating the site. The statute also makes it clear that government enforcement costs, including legal fees, are recoverable, as is interest from the date of the request for payment. The statute does not expressly address the recoverability of legal costs by private parties. The Supreme Court, however, has decided that the statute does *not* provide for the award of litigants' attorney's fees associated with bringing a private cost recovery action, although certain costs expended in identifying other PRPs may be recoverable.[86] Finally, parties seeking recovery for cleanup costs or damages stemming from federally permitted releases must look to other provisions of state, federal, or common law in lieu of the CERCLA statute.[87]

"Joint and several liability" means that any one party may be liable for the costs of the entire cleanup, although that party may seek contribution from other parties. The courts have consistently supported EPA's position that CERCLA imposes joint and several liability on responsible parties whenever the contamination is "indivisible." Only where there is a clear basis to apportion liability will the damages be assessed according to an individual defendant's contribution to the problem.[88]

The Maryland statute reverses the federal scheme by ordinarily requiring the state to seek recovery from responsible persons on an apportioned, rather than joint and several, basis in accordance with a person's contribution to the situation or problem. Only when there is no reasonable basis for apportionment is liability joint and several.[89]

Contribution

CERCLA, as amended, expressly authorizes any person who is liable or potentially liable to seek contribution against other liable or potentially liable parties for an equitable portion of remedial and natural resource damage costs.[90] The party seeking contribution has the burden of proving the opposing party's equitable share of response costs.[91] Importantly, CERCLA further provides that responsible parties that enter into a judicially or administratively approved settlement are not liable for claims

---

[86] See *Key Tronic Com. v. United States of America*, 511 U.S. 809 (1994).

[87] 42 U.S.C. §9607(j).

[88] See *Dent*, 156 F.3d at 529-530, *citing Monsanto Co.*, 858 F.2d 160; *United States v. Alcan Aluminum Co.*, 990 F.2d 711 (2d Cir. 1993); *United States v. Alcan Aluminum Co.*, 964 F.2d 252 (3rd Cir. 1992); *United States v. Ottati & Goss*, 630 F. Supp. 1361 (D. N.H. 1985).

[89] MD. CODE, ENVIR. §7-221(b).

[90] 42 U.S.C. §9613(f).

[91] See *Minyard Enterprises v. Southeastern Chemical and Solvent Co.*, 184 F.3d 373, 385 (4th Cir. 1999).

for contribution regarding matters addressed in the settlement.[92] Settling parties may, however, seek contribution from any non-settling responsible party.[93] The Maryland Uniform Contribution among Tortfeasors Act is expressly applicable to liability for releases under the Maryland statute.

Cost Reimbursement

CERCLA also provides that private parties who are not responsible parties and who incur response costs as a result of a release or threatened release of hazardous substances may bring an action to recover those costs from the responsible parties.[94] Parties seeking recovery must demonstrate: (1) the site in question is a "facility" within the CERCLA statute, (2) a release or threatened release of a hazardous substance occurred, and (3) the response costs incurred are consistent with the National Contingency Plan.[95] "Facility" may include a building, structure, container, or simply a general area where a hazardous substance has been deposited.[96] In order to be consistent with the NCP, costs must be "necessary"—unnecessary costs are not recoverable.[97] However, to prove a *prima facie* case of liability, the plaintiff need only prove that at least some of the response costs it incurred were in compliance with the NCP.[98]

Insurance

Parties liable for the costs of cleanup at a contaminated site may be able to recover those costs through pollution insurance. Currently, most standard comprehensive general liability (CGL) policies contain "pollution exclusion" clauses that severely limit the insured's coverage for costs associated with the cleanup of a contaminated site. However, most CGL policies issued in Maryland before the mid-1980s did not contain such clauses, and decisions by the Maryland Court of Appeals may allow insureds to recover costs associated with environmental cleanup, depending upon the specific policy terms and the underlying facts.[99]

The language of most CGL policies is identical—the insurer will pay all sums the insured becomes "legally obligated to pay" as "damages" because of "property damages" resulting from an occurrence during the course of the policy. Usually, a "legal obligation to pay" stems from the insured's liability, established in a lawsuit,

---

[92] 42 U.S.C. §9613(f). A plaintiff may bring an action for contribution under §9613(f) even though it has not been the subject of an action under §§9606 or 9607. *1325 "G" Street Assoc., L.P. v. Rockwood Pigments NA, Inc.*, 235 F. Supp. 2d 458 (D.Md. 2002).

[93] *Id.*

[94] 42 U.S.C. §9607(a). See also *Axel Johnson, Inc. v. Carroll Carolina Oil Co.*, 191 F.3d 409, 415 (4th Cir. 1999) and *Minyard*, 184 F.3d at 385 *citing Pneumo Abex Corp. v. High Point, Thomasville and Denton R.R.*, 142 F.3d 769 (4th Cir. 1998) (PRP may only bring an action for contribution under §113 and not for cost recovery under §107).

[95] *Weyerhaeuser*, 771 F. Supp. at 1410 *citing Retirement Community Developers, Inc. v. Merine*, 713 F. Supp. 153, 155 (D. Md. 1989).

[96] *Nurad*, 966 F.2d at 842.

[97] *Washington Gas*, 823 F. Supp. 318 (D. Md. 1993).

[98] *Weyerhauser*, 771 F. Supp. at 1414.

[99] See *Bausch & Lomb, Inc. v. Utica Mutual Insurance Co.*, 330 Md. 758, 625 A.2d 1021 (1993); *Harford County v. Harford Mutual Insurance Co.*, 327 Md. 418, 610 A.2d 286 (1992).

to reimburse contaminated site cleanup costs. However, when an insured party acts in cooperation with state or federal agencies to comply with remedial action laws or regulations, that party may be acting under a tacit threat of EPA or MDE action even though the cooperative actions are ostensibly voluntary. In Maryland, the insured in such cases assumes a legal obligation to remediate the contamination, and insurance may cover the remediation costs.[100] In other words, an insured need not actually be sued by MDE or EPA in order to collect defense and indemnification costs from the insurance carrier.[101]

Maryland courts have interpreted "damages" broadly and in accordance with its ordinary and accepted meaning, absent any clear intention to the contrary manifested in the policy.[102] Using this interpretation, compensatory outlays of various kinds, including expenditures made to comply with administrative orders, are considered recoverable "damages."[103]

CGL policies typically categorize "property damages" as damages to third parties; without proof of injury to another's property, the insured cannot recover.[104] Thus, recovery can also turn on whether a third party has a sufficient property interest in the contaminated property to satisfy the CGL definition of "property damage."[105]

CGL coverage is triggered when environmental damage occurs, not when it is first discovered.[106] Therefore, insureds that can demonstrate that contamination occurred under prior CGL policies may be able to recover policy limits under multiple expired policies.

CERCLA Section 122 explicitly authorizes EPA to negotiate settlements with potentially responsible parties. There are expedited "cash-out" settlement procedures for *de minimis* contributors to a site's contamination.[107] Low-volume or low-toxicity contributors to a waste site are candidates for *de minimis* consideration. In these situations, EPA is authorized to accept a cash payment in return for which the PRP is released from further liability.[108]

Also, the EPA may enter into "mixed-funding" agreements with potentially responsible parties.[109] Under a "mixed-funding" agreement, the party may agree to perform cleanup actions and be reimbursed from the fund for a portion of the cleanup for which the party was not responsible.[110] In order to bring about prompt cleanup of a site, EPA may be willing to relax its position on joint and several liability. In such

---

[100] *Bausch & Lomb*, 330 Md. at 781–82.

[101] The mere threat of legal action by a private party, however, will not create a "legal obligation to pay." See *Bausch & Lomb,* 330 Md. at 780.

[102] *Bausch & Lomb*, 330 Md. at 781–82.

[103] *Id.* These outlays may include site investigation, testing, planning, and cleanup, but cannot include penalties, fines, or assessments.

[104] *Id.* at 783.

[105] In cases of contaminated subterranean percolating waters, for instance, while the state has a regulatory interest in groundwater, it is not a "property interest" within the meaning of a CGL policy, and thus contamination thereof does not constitute "property damages." *Bausch & Lomb*, 330 Md. at 788.

[106] See *Harford County*, 327 Md. 418, 610 A.2d 286.

[107] 42 U.S.C. §9622(g).

[108] *Id.*

[109] 42 U.S.C. §9622(b).

[110] *Id.*

cases, EPA pays the "orphan share" of the response costs (i.e., the portion attributable to unidentified or insolvent parties).

Remedial Investigations

Private parties will have notice and the opportunity to conduct their own remedial investigation and feasibility study subject to EPA oversight.[111] EPA must provide, to the extent available, the names and addresses of all other responsible parties at the particular site, as well as information concerning the volume, nature of the substances, and a hazard and volume ranking of wastes contributed by each.[112] EPA will allow the parties 60 days to make a good faith proposal for undertaking or financing the operation.

CERCLA also attempts to facilitate cleanup settlements by authorizing, but not requiring, EPA to prepare a "non-binding preliminary allocation of responsibility" (NBAR) among potentially responsible parties when it believes this will promote settlement.[113] The NBAR does not establish legal grounds for allocating liability, is not admissible as evidence in a subsequent proceeding, and cannot be reviewed by the courts. However, it does provide an allocation opinion that the parties can look to as an aid in negotiation.

RELEASE REPORTING

Definition of Release

CERCLA imposes a continuing reporting obligation upon every person in charge of a vessel or facility when and if a hazardous substance is spilled, or "released," and enters the environment.[114] A "release" for which notification is required is a release into the environment of any hazardous substance in an amount greater than its statutory or final regulatory reportable quantity within a 24-hour period.[115] A release includes virtually any contact with the environment: spilling, leaking, pumping, discharging, leaching, dumping, etc.[116] The environment is broadly defined and includes surface water, groundwater, ambient air, land surface, and subsurface.[117]

Substance Reporting Requirements

The reporting obligation applies to releases of reportable quantities of any CERCLA hazardous substance that includes waste characterized as toxic, ignitable, corrosive, or reactive within the meaning of RCRA.[118]

---

[111] 42 U.S.C. §9622(e).
[112] *Id.*
[113] *Id.*
[114] 42 U.S.C. §9603.
[115] 42 U.S.C. §9603(a); 40 C.F.R. §302.6.
[116] 42 U.S.C. §9601(22).
[117] 42 U.S.C. §9601(8).
[118] 42 U.S.C. §9601(14).

Reportable Quantities

EPA has assigned five reportable quantity levels of 1, 10, 100, 1,000, or 5,000 pounds depending on the potential for harm from the release of any given hazardous substance.[119] Reporting requirements do not depend on the medium into which the substance is released. The notification requirement is triggered by the release of an amount equal to or greater than the reportable quantity within a 24-hour period.[120]

Release of a hazardous substance in excess of its reportable quantity but in compliance with a federal permit (e.g., a Clean Water Act permit) need not be reported.[121] Continuous releases that have already been reported to the federal government require only annual reports unless the quantity being released increases significantly.[122]

Notification of a Release

Any person in charge of a facility must notify the National Response Center as soon as there is knowledge of any release of a hazardous substance in a reportable quantity.[123] The owner and operator of a facility at which a release occurs must also notify potentially injured parties by publication in local newspapers serving the affected area.

ENFORCEMENT

Federal Enforcement Tools

When EPA determines that an actual or threatened release of a hazardous substance from a facility represents an imminent and substantial endangerment to the public health, welfare, or the environment, it may take such steps as are necessary to abate the danger.[124] This could include administrative orders or resort to the federal district courts for injunctive relief. However, a party in compliance with an administrative order may petition for recovery of the costs of compliance.[125] Reimbursement will follow if the party demonstrates that (1) it is not a liable party within the meaning of the statute, or (2) EPA's orders were arbitrary and capricious.[126] If a party willfully violates, or fails to comply with, an EPA order, however, the statute provides for a fine of $27,500 for each day in which the violation occurs, and treble damages if EPA must conduct the cleanup after the order is violated.[127]

---

[119] 40 C.F.R. §302.4.
[120] 42 U.S.C. §9603(a); 40 C.F.R. §302.6.
[121] *Id.* §9603(a); 40 C.F.R. §302.6(a).
[122] 40 C.F.R. §302.8.
[123] 42 U.S.C. §9603(a); 40 C.F.R. §302.6(a).
[124] 42 U.S.C. §9606(a).
[125] 42 U.S.C. §9606(b).
[126] *Id.*
[127] 42 U.S.C. §§9606(b), 9607(c)(3), 40 C.F.R. §19.4.

Penalties for Noncompliance

The civil and criminal penalties for noncompliance with CERCLA reporting requirements are significant. Criminal penalties of up to three years' imprisonment, or five years for subsequent violations, exist for violations of reporting requirements, submission of false or misleading information, or destruction of records.[128] EPA is also authorized to assess civil penalties administratively of up to $25,000 per violation.[129]

---

[128] 42 U.S.C. §9603(b), 40 C.F.R. §19.4.
[129] 42 U.S.C. §9609(a), 40 C.F.R. §19.4.

Chapter 7

Regulation of Solid Waste

The oversight of nonhazardous solid waste management is largely a matter of state and local government responsibility.[1] Since 1988, Maryland's regulation of nonhazardous solid waste has extended to any "solid waste acceptance facility" installed, altered, or extended after July 1, 1988[2] (i.e., a sanitary landfill, incinerator, transfer station, or plant with the primary purpose of solid waste disposal, treatment or processing).[3]

Each county in Maryland must adopt and maintain a comprehensive 10-year waste management plan, subject to MDE approval.[4] State statutory and regulatory provisions provide broad policy guidelines that dictate the substance of the plans. The state, however, has delegated implementation of these plans largely to local authorities. Despite general deference to state responsibility for nonhazardous solid waste management, the Resource Conservation and Recovery Act ("RCRA") provides the basic framework for state solid waste management planning and regulation. Accordingly, states that administer their own solid waste programs must develop five-year waste management plans that are at least as stringent as federal requirements.[5] Only states with approved plans are eligible to receive federal funds.[6]

Subtitle D of RCRA generally prohibits "open dumping" of solid waste and requires EPA to establish criteria for distinguishing approvable "sanitary landfills" from "open dumps."[7] Implementation of those criteria is left to the states. Furthermore, the regulations are enforceable only by the states or through citizen suits under RCRA §7002.[8] These federal standards were expanded considerably in October 1991 when EPA

---

1 An express objective of the Resource Conservation and Recovery Act (RCRA) is to "provide for the promulgation of guidelines for solid waste collection, transport, separation, recovery, and disposal practices and systems." Consequently, "the collection and disposal of solid wastes should continue to be primarily the function of State, regional, and local agencies." 42 U.S.C. §6901(a)(4).

2 MD. CODE, ENVIR. §9-204(a).

3 MD. CODE, ENVIR. §9-501(n); COMAR 26.04.07.02B(29).

4 MD. CODE, ENVIR. §9-503; COMAR 26.03.03.02.–.05.

5 40 C.F.R. §256.02(d).

6 42 U.S.C. §6948.

7 42 U.S.C. §§6944–45.

8 42 U.S.C. §6945(a).

supplemented its general standards for classification of solid waste disposal facilities[9] with extensive criteria for municipal solid waste landfills (MSWLFs).[10] These Subtitle D regulations encompass location restrictions, design and operating criteria, groundwater monitoring and corrective action protocol, closure and post-closure care, and financial assurance requirements. Generally speaking, the new regulations took effect in 1993, and MDE received a final partial approval of its MSWLF program in 1995.[11]

APPLICABILITY OF REGULATIONS

Definition of Solid Waste

Under the Maryland statute, "solid waste" is defined as "any garbage, refuse, sludge, or liquid from industrial, commercial, mining, or agricultural operations, or from community activities."[12] The Maryland statute specifically includes in this definition "scrap tires" that are defined as tires no longer suitable for their original intended purpose—as opposed to "used tires."[13] Scrap tires accumulated in excess of 15,000 cubic feet must be returned to the marketplace, used as fuel in an approved resource recovery incinerator, or otherwise disposed of properly within 90 days of the time of storage.[14] Organic material capable of being composted is also a solid waste.[15]

MDE regulations define "solid waste" to include:

1. materials that are abandoned by burning, incineration, disposal, or that are stored or treated prior to the foregoing events;
2. "inherently waste-like" materials; and
3. recycled secondary materials if used in a manner constituting disposal, burned for energy recovery, used to produce a fuel or contained in a fuel, being reclaimed, or accumulated speculatively.[16]

Any substance that is disposed, regardless of its physical state, generally falls within the solid waste definition.

The statutory and regulatory definitions of solid waste exclude solid and dissolved materials in domestic sewage or in irrigation return flow, compost, industrial wastewater discharged under a Clean Water Act permit, and certain commercial wastes (i.e., pulping liquors, spent sulfuric acid, and materials subjected to *in-situ* mining techniques). Furthermore, certain materials that ordinarily would be solid waste are not deemed so when they are recycled. These are:

---

9 40 C.F.R. Part 257.
10 40 C.F.R. Parts 257 and 258.
11 60 Fed. Reg. 39385 (August 2, 1995). To obtain full and final approval of the program, EPA will require MDE to modify its regulations regarding closure and post-closure care requirements and financial assurance criteria.
12 MD. CODE, ENVIR. §9-101(j)(1).
13 MD. CODE, ENVIR. §§9-101(j)(2), 9-201(f); COMAR 26.04.08.02B(32).
14 MD. CODE, ENVIR. §9-228; COMAR 26.04.08.02B(29).
15 MD. CODE, ENVIR. §9-101(j)(2)(ii).
16 COMAR 26.04.07.02(28), adopting COMAR 26.13.02.02. COMAR 26.13.02.02E(1).

1. recycled materials used or reused as ingredients in an industrial process to make a product;
2. materials used or reused as effective substitutes for commercial products; and
3. materials returned to the original process from which they are generated without first being reclaimed as a substitute for raw material feedstock.[17]

Regulated Solid Waste Systems

Maryland law governs any *publicly* used "refuse disposal system" (i.e., incinerator, transfer station, landfill, landfill system, solid waste processing facility, and any other disposal system).[18] The law also applies to *any* "solid waste acceptance facility" (i.e., incinerator, transfer station, sanitary landfill or solid waste disposal unit, treatment or processing plant) that was installed, altered, or extended after July 1988.[19] The state's regulation and permitting of such facilities preempts local legislation prohibiting them by moratorium.[20]

MARYLAND PERMIT REQUIREMENTS

Permitted Activities

Permits are required for all *publicly* used refuse disposal systems, such as sanitary landfills, incinerators, and transfer stations; and for *all* solid waste acceptance facilities installed, altered, or extended after July 1988.[21] Sewage sludge management systems will not be treated in this chapter, though there are regulatory permitting requirements for such systems.[22]

Maryland regulations establish detailed permit, performance, and reporting criteria for managing solid waste. The requirements for permitting a sanitary landfill may vary depending upon the type of waste accepted and the type of facility (i.e., municipal, rubble, land-clearing debris, or industrial waste landfill).[23] No solid waste acceptance facility may accept infectious or liquid wastes or controlled hazardous substances without specific authorization from MDE.[24]

Exemptions

No permit is required for the following:

---

[17] MD. CODE, ENVIR. §9-101(j)(3); COMAR 26.13.02.04A.
[18] MD. CODE, ENVIR. §§9-204(a), 9-201(e).
[19] MD. CODE, ENVIR. §9-204(a), 9-501(n); COMAR 26.04.07.02B(29).
[20] *Mayor of Baltimore v. New Pulaski Co. Ltd. P'ship,* 112 Md. App. 218 (1996), *cert. denied*, 344 Md. 717 (1997).
[21] MD. CODE ANN., ENVIR. §9-204(a), (d).
[22] See generally COMAR 26.04.06.
[23] COMAR 26.04.07.05–.22.
[24] COMAR 26.04.07.03B(5), (6), (8).

- land disposal of solid waste generated from a single-family residence and disposed of within the property limits of the residence;[25]
- land disposal of agricultural waste on agricultural land; land disposal of mining operations overburden; and certain filling operations consisting solely of clean earthen fill;[26]
- land disposal areas that are not part of a system of refuse disposal for public use;[27] and
- facilities that are otherwise regulated under Maryland environmental statutes and regulations.[28]

Permit Application Procedures

Parties seeking permits may submit a preliminary statement on the proposed system to MDE. Upon request, MDE shall outline the general requirements that must be satisfied to achieve final approval.[29]

The actual application process for a refuse disposal system permit commences with submittal to MDE of a Phase I report. The Phase I report must describe the type of facility, the waste streams to be accepted, the actual site, and zoning and land use surrounding the proposed facility. Furthermore, the applicant or MDE must publish public notice of the application in the geographical area where the landfill will be located.[30] Interested citizens may request a public information meeting within 10 working days after public notice.[31] MDE must forward copies of the Phase I reports to various local, state, and federal agencies for comment.[32] MDE will review the submission for completeness and may deny the application at this stage if it determines that the site is not suitable for the intended use.[33]

For a land-clearing debris landfill, or incineration, transfer, or processing facility, there are fewer stages to the process.[34] However, MDE requires submittal of more information at the initial phase with the application—detailed operations manuals, drawings of the proposed facilities, and detailed engineering plans.

If, after reviewing the Phase I material, MDE determines that the site is suitable for the proposed landfill, the applicant must submit a Phase II report describing the soils, geology, meterology, and hydrology of the site.[35] On the basis of these surveys, the applicant must include a preliminary conceptual design satisfying minimum standards. The landfill design must consider leachate control, permeability of the liner,[36] and buffer zones above the expected groundwater elevation. Like the Phase I report,

---

25 COMAR 26.04.07.04C.
26 *Id.*
27 COMAR 26.04.07.04C(2).
28 COMAR 26.04.07.04C(6).
29 MD. CODE, ENVIR. §9-204(c).
30 MD. CODE, ENVIR. §§1-602(b), 1-603(a).
31 MD. CODE, ENVIR. §1-603(c)(l).
32 COMAR 26.04.07.06C.
33 See COMAR 26.04.07.06C(4).
34 COMAR 26.04.07.11.
35 COMAR 26.04.07.07A.
36 COMAR 26.04.07.07C(12).

the Phase II report is subject to comment by various federal, state, and local agencies, and approval by MDE.

If MDE allows the application to proceed, the applicant must submit a Phase III report that provides detailed operating information and facility plans, including emergency procedures, a construction schedule, and a five-year post-closure plan.[37]

Before issuance of a permit to install, materially alter, or extend a landfill, incinerator, or rubble landfill, the public may request a public hearing.[38] Upon a final decision to issue the permit, an aggrieved party may request a contested case hearing.[39] The contested case hearing, which is adjudicatory or trial-like in nature, is judicially reviewable. This can substantially increase the time required to obtain a permit.

After construction is completed, the applicant must submit a certified copy of the plans showing the work as built.[40]

County Solid Waste Management Plans

The county solid waste management plan is a 10-year waste management plan that must be approved by MDE. It must address systems for water supply, sewage, and solid waste disposal, as well as solid waste acceptance facilities, collection, and disposal.[41] One component of the management plan is a comprehensive county recycling plan.[42] The regulations prescribe the detailed the contents of the county plan.[43] Special plan provisions exist for Montgomery and Prince George's Counties.[44]

Each county plan is subject to local review on a triennial or more frequent basis.[45] Public hearings are mandated before a county may adopt an amendment to or revision of an existing plan.[46]

MDE is precluded by statute from issuing a permit for a refuse disposal system until the system is determined to be in conformity with the county solid waste management plan and local zoning and land use requirements.[47] The county has the opportunity to determine whether the proposed facility is consistent with the county solid waste plan.[48] However, once a solid waste acceptance facility has been included in the county plan, the county cannot revise one plan to remove the facility in reaction to public concern of permitting.[49] MDE may not issue an incinerator permit for "disposal of a solid waste stream" unless the county where the incinerator is located has an approved county recycling[50] and solid waste management plan.[51] Local determination

---

37 COMAR 26.04.07.08.
38 MD. CODE, ENVIR. §l-604(a).
39 MD. CODE, ENVIR. §§1-601(b), 1-605(a).
40 MD. CODE, ENVIR. §9-204(i).
41 MD. CODE ANN., ENVIR. §9-503(a).
42 MD. CODE ANN., ENVIR. §9-505.
43 COMAR 26.03.03.03.
44 MD. CODE, ENVIR. §9-515.
45 MD. CODE, ENVIR. §§9-503(b), 9-515.
46 MD. CODE, ENVIR. §9-503(d).
47 MD. CODE, ENVIR. §§9-210(a), 9-511; COMAR 26.04.07.09D(l).
48 COMAR 26.04.07.09D.
49 *County Comm'ers v. Days Cove Reclamation Co.*, 122 Md. App. 505 (1998).
50 MD. CODE ANN., ENVIR. §9-204.1; COMAR 26.04.07.25G.
51 MD. CODE ANN., ENVIR. §9-210(a); §9-511.

that a proposed system is inconsistent with the county plan can bar further processing of the application.[52]

Financial Requirements

Prior to receiving a permit, private party landfill permit applicants must file a bond in the amount of $10,000 for each acre of a landfill, but not less than $250,000. Land-clearing debris landfills must file bonds in the amount of $2,000 per acre, but not less than $25,000. MDE has the authority to set security requirements for incinerators and transfer stations and does so through the permit terms. The bond moneys are to be applied to the proper closure of a facility in the event that the facility is not properly closed.[53] Federal financial assurance requirements for MSWLFs are discussed below.

Permit Issuance and Renewal

MDE may not issue a refuse disposal system permit until the applicant provides a written statement from the county that the disposal system meets all zoning and land use requirements.[54] Where the permit application is for a rubble fill, no permit may be issued until the county in which the proposed facility will be located has specified the types of waste that may be disposed of in a rubble fill.[55] Disposal of asbestos and white goods in rubble landfills is permissible if the county expressly approves such disposal in its county solid waste management plan.[56] MDE may deny landfill permits to nongovernmental persons if the owner of the land, the operator, or the applicant has violated any state sanitary landfill law or regulation, or upon a finding that the landfill would harm public health or the environment.[57]

Duration

Landfill permits are valid for up to five years from the date of issue unless suspended or revoked. Permit renewal requires: (1) an application to MDE, (2) a notice of the renewal application to each member of the General Assembly in whose district the landfill system is located, and (3) an approval from MDE.[58] MDE may revoke or refuse to renew a landfill permit on a finding that the permit holder is violating any regulation or the terms of the permit. MDE may also refuse to renew a permit on the finding of injury to the public health, the environment, or for "any other good cause."[59]

---

[52] MD. CODE ANN., ENVIR. §9-511.
[53] MD. CODE, ENVIR. §9-211.
[54] MD. CODE, ENVIR. §9-210(a)(3); COMAR 26.04.07.09D(1).
[55] MD. CODE, ENVIR. §9-210(c).
[56] MD. CODE, ENVIR. §9-210(c)(3).
[57] MD. CODE, ENVIR. §9-212. l.
[58] MD. CODE, ENVIR. §9-213.
[59] MD. CODE, ENVIR. §9-214.

OPERATIONAL REQUIREMENTS

General Restrictions

No person may engage in solid waste handling in a manner that will create a nuisance, be conducive to insect or rodent infestations, harbor wild dogs or other animals, pollute the air, cause discharges to waters of the state not otherwise permitted under Maryland Environment Code §7-232 or §9-323, impair the quality of the environment, or create other hazards to the public health, safety, or comfort as determined by MDE.[60]

Definition of Open Dumping

Among the specific prohibitions relating to refuse disposal is the absolute ban on "open dumping."[61] Open dumps must be upgraded or closed. Any disposal facility that does not meet MDE's and EPA's sanitary landfill criteria is considered an open dump.[62] MDE has closed or upgraded open dumps primarily through the permit issuance or renewal process.

Restrictions on Solid Waste Disposal Facility Locations

Federal criteria require siting restrictions addressing the location of solid waste disposal facilities in floodplains and wetlands[63] and additional restrictions for municipal solid waste landfills located near airports, unstable areas, Seismic Impact Zones, and Fault Areas.[64] Maryland addresses these location restrictions during Phase II of the permitting process, which involves hydrogeologic and topographic siting to evaluate appropriateness of a site.

Definition of Sanitary Landfills

Every landfill must be "designed and operated in accordance" with the pertinent regulations to be considered a "sanitary landfill."[65] In other words, landfills are either "sanitary landfills" or "open dumps" regardless of the nature of the waste disposed of therein. Maryland recognizes four distinct types of sanitary landfills: (1) municipal landfills, (2) land-clearing debris landfills, (3) rubble landfills, and (4) industrial waste landfills.

Sanitary Landfills Generally

Burning is prohibited without MDE approval.[66] Controlled hazardous substances must be excluded unless specifically authorized by a valid permit issued under COMAR

---

[60] COMAR 26.04.07.03A.
[61] COMAR 26.04.07.03B(4).
[62] COMAR 26.04.07.02B(19).
[63] 40 C.F.R. §§257.8–.9.
[64] 40 C.F.R. §§258.10–.15.
[65] COMAR 26.04.07.02B(27).
[66] COMAR 26.04.07.03B(3).

26.13.07.[67] Infectious waste must also be excluded, unless specifically authorized by the Approving Authority.[68] Differing requirements govern the operation of rubble landfills,[69] land-clearing debris landfills,[70] and industrial waste landfills.[71] Every landfill must also comply with the general restrictions applicable to all solid waste handlers.

Municipal Landfills

Maryland requires daily or more frequent covering with at least six inches of clean earth, along with intermediate cover of at least one foot of earth over each portion of a lift.[72] Other requirements address public access, run-on and run-off control, litter and noise control, fire protection, and periodic reporting.[73] Federal criteria require that careful attention be given to explosive gas control. Quarterly monitoring of methane levels must be performed to ensure that the maximum level—25 percent of the lower explosive limit (LEL) in structures, LEL at the property boundary—has not been exceeded. If the maximum level has been exceeded, the MSWLF must take immediate steps to protect human health, record the incident, notify the proper authorities, and implement a remediation plan within 60 days.[74]

Random inspections of incoming loads and training of all relevant personnel are now required.[75] Federal regulations impose an extensive record-keeping protocol. Records are to be made of location restriction demonstrations, inspections, training and notification procedures, gas monitoring and remediation plans, leachate design, groundwater monitoring or demonstration, closure and post-closure plans, cost estimates, and financial assurance documentation.[76]

Air Quality Requirements for MSWLFs

In accordance with Section 111(d) of the Clean Air Act, MDE submitted a municipal solid waste landfill plan to EPA in 1999 establishing emission limits for existing MSWLFs. The plan was codified at COMAR 26.11.19.20. The Maryland regulations require compliance plans, closure reports and equipment removal, and regular testing, reporting, and record keeping.

New Source Performance Standards (NSPS)

Under EPA's NSPS for MSWLFs, owners or operators of new, reconstructed, or modified MSWLFs having a design capacity less than 2.5 million megagrams or 2.5 million

---

67 COMAR 26.04.07.03B(5).
68 COMAR 26.04.07.03B(6).
69 COMAR 26.04.07.18.
70 COMAR 26.04.07.11C.
71 COMAR 26.04.07.19E.
72 COMAR 26.04.07.10D, E.
73 COMAR 26.04.07.10.
74 40 C.F.R. §258.23.
75 40 C.F.R. §258.20.
76 40 C.F.R. §258.29.

cubic meters are required to submit an initial design capacity report to EPA.[77] Larger facilities (with capacities greater than 2.5 million megagrams or 2.5 million cubic meters) and a nonmethane emission rate equal to or greater than 50 megagrams per year (Mg/yr) must, among other things,

1. submit a design plan for a gas collection and control system;
2. install a system that meets regulatory standards within 18 months; and
3. operate the system in accordance with regulatory standards.[78]

If the facility meets the capacity threshold but the emission rate is less than 50 Mg/yr, the owner or operator must submit annual emission reports to EPA and comply with the aforementioned requirements if the Non-methane Organic Compound (NMOC) rates exceed the threshold emission rate. Provisions for operation of a gas collection and control system, determining compliance of the system, testing, monitoring, reporting, record keeping, and collection system specifications are included in the NSPS.[79]

The federal Subtitle D landfill regulations require that methane gas be monitored during landfill operations and a remediation plan be implemented when gas levels exceed regulatory limits. Monitoring must continue after landfill closure.[80]

NSPS for MW Combustors

In 1995, EPA issued NSPS and emission guidelines for municipal waste combustors (MWCs).[81] The regulations define MWCs to include any non-exempt "setting or equipment" that combusts municipal waste.[82] The NSPS applies to MWCs for which construction began after September 20, 1994, or for which modification or reconstruction began after June 19, 1996. This NSPS applies to MWC units located with a combustion capacity of more than 250 tons per day of municipal waste.[83] Separate emission standards apply to MWCs for which construction began on or before September 20, 1994.[84]

The NSPS establishes emission limits for opacity, dioxin/furan, sulfur dioxide, hydrogen chloride, NOx, carbon monoxide, cadmium, lead, mercury, and fugitive ash.[85] It also sets forth operating practices and requirements for training and certification and requires siting analysis.[86]

Land-Clearing Debris Landfills

A land-clearing debris landfill is one that is restricted to accepting only earthen materials, topsoil, tree stumps, root mats, brush and limbs, logs, vegetation, and rock.[87]

---

[77] 40 C.F.R. §60.752(a).
[78] *Id.* §60.752(b).
[79] *Id.* §60.752.
[80] 40 C.F.R. §§258.23; 258.61(a)(4); see also COMAR 26.04.07.21E(5).
[81] 40 C.F.R §§60.50b *et seq.*) Maryland adopted the regulations in COMAR 26.11.08.
[82] 60 Fed. Reg. at 65387, 65421.
[83] 40 C.F.R. §60.50(b).
[84] *Id.* §60.50(a).
[85] *Id.* §60.52(b).
[86] *Id.* §§60.53b, .54b, .57b.
[87] COMAR 26.04.07.11.

These facilities are required to follow the design and operational requirements found in COMAR 26.04.07.11–.12, including placing six inches of soil on top of waste every third operating day, one foot of soil on top of each lift, and two feet of cover material at the completion of each lift.[88] Permit applications for Land Clearing Debris Landfills must include submission of a topographical map of the area and proposed operational procedures.[89] After the plan passes initial review, it must be shown that the proposed facility is consistent with all local solid waste management plans.[90]

Rubble Landfills

Rubble landfills are those that can accept land-clearing debris, demolition debris, construction debris, scrap tires, asbestos waste, household appliances, white goods, processed debris, and any other material if approved by the appropriate authority.[91] Rubble landfills are required to follow a three-step process when obtaining a permit. Phase I is a preliminary site inspection,[92] Phase II requires the submission of a detailed report of the geography of the site,[93] and Phase III requires the submission of engineering plans and project specifications.[94] The Maryland Court of Special Appeals held that a County zoning board of appeals could not deny a conditional use permit for a rubble landfill permit in the absence of evidence of unsuitability based on factors unique to the site in question.[95]

Industrial Waste Landfills

Industrial waste landfills may only accept nonhazardous industrial waste. The location and design of the facility must take into account the prevention of surface and groundwater contamination.[96] Permit applications must include proposed operational procedures as well as background water quality data.[97]

LANDFILL CLOSURE AND MONITORING

Under current MDE regulations, upon exhaustion of the site capacity, expiration or refusal by MDE to renew the permit, or on order by MDE to cease accepting waste, closure shall begin no later than 24 months from the date of completion of the final landfill lift and shall be completed not later than 36 months from the date of the final lift.[98] The closure cap shall minimize infiltration into the landfill and shall comply

[88] *Id.*
[89] COMAR 26.04.07.12.
[90] *Id.*
[91] COMAR 26.04.07.13.
[92] COMAR 26.04.07.14.
[93] COMAR 26.04.07.15.
[94] COMAR 26.04.07.16.
[95] *Days Cove Reclamation Company v. Queen Anne's County*, 146 Md. App. 469 (2002).
[96] COMAR 26.04.07.19.
[97] COMAR 26.04.07.20.
[98] COMAR 26.04.07.21.

with minimum design features specific to the waste buried at the site. The cap shall be seeded with perennial species appropriate to the area. Sanitary landfill permittees must also monitor the site for a period of not less than five years after the completed closure. The permittee must inspect the post-closure site at least twice yearly.[99]

The federal criteria are significantly more stringent than Maryland's current requirements. Closure under the federal criteria must begin within 30 days of the last deposit and be complete within 180 days.[100] Post-closure groundwater, gas, and leachate monitoring must be performed for 30 years, although states approved to implement the Subtitle D regulations may vary that time provided that no additional risk to human health or the environment arises.[101] Furthermore, the federal criteria require a more extensive routine groundwater monitoring system than Maryland currently prescribes.

The federal Subtitle D regulations also impose substantial financial assurance requirements to assure an MSWLF's ability to pay a third person to perform closure, post-closure care, and corrective action.[102] The owner or operator of the MSWLF must supply a written estimate in current dollars but adjusted for inflation and including a worst-case scenario. Allowable mechanisms include:

1. trust fund with a "pay-in period," whereby annual payments are made over the term of the initial permit or the remaining life of the MSWLF, whichever is shorter;[103]
2. surety bond, letter of credit, or insurance;[104]
3. financial test through which a corporate or local government owner or operator may demonstrate ability to pay;[105]
4. corporate guarantee by a parent corporation of an owner or operator;[106]
5. state or local guarantee, whereby the state or local government assumes legal responsibility for the owner/operator's compliance, or assurance that funds will be made available from state or local sources; and[107]
6. any alternative mechanism acceptable to an approved state.[108]

Innovative alternatives such as subsidized loans, grants, certificates of deposit, escrow accounts, enterprise funds, local government planning, and a Financial Assurance Fund, are encouraged.[109] Use of multiple mechanisms is also expressly authorized.[110]

---

99 COMAR 26.04.07.22.
100 40 C.F.R. §258.60(f), (g).
101 40 C.F.R. §258.61.
102 40 C.F.R. §§258.70–.74.
103 40 C.F.R. §258.74(a).
104 40 C.F.R. §§258.74(b), (c), (d).
105 40 C.F.R. §§258.74(e), (f).
106 40 C.F.R. §258.74(g).
107 40 C.F.R. §§258.74(h), (j).
108 40 C.F.R. §258.74(i).
109 56 Fed. Reg. at 51118.
110 40 C.F.R. §258.74(k).

RECYCLING INITIATIVES

County Recycling Activities

Counties must develop and implement recycling plans as a component of the comprehensive ten-year solid waste management plan.[111] Counties are required to report to MDE on the total solid waste collected and disposed of at solid waste acceptance facilities, the amount of waste recycled, and the percentage reduction in the amount of solid waste needing disposal that has been achieved.[112]

Newsprint Requirements

Newsprint used by newspaper publishers must meet a recycled content percentage requirement, which was 40 percent for 2005 and all subsequent calendar years.[113] Publishers must submit to MDE quarterly and annual reports documenting recycled content.[114] Failure to comply with the schedule subjects the publisher to newsprint recycling incentive fees of $10 for each ton of the recycled content deficiency.[115] Publishers may seek an excuse from the requirements if they show that there was not an adequate supply of recycled newsprint comparable in quality to virgin newsprint.[116]

ENFORCEMENT AND PENALTIES

Federal Enforcement Powers

Under RCRA Subtitle D, "open dumping" is a federal offense.[117] The statute does not define open dumping, though case law indicates that EPA regulations may supply the necessary definitions.[118] EPA does not have the power to enforce the ban; rather, enforcement is solely by citizen suit.[119]

Citizen suits, which may only seek injunctions, must be filed in federal court in the district where the violation occurred. The person bringing suit must give 60 days' notice to EPA prior to filing suit. EPA takes the position that entering into a compliance order with the state provides an absolute shield to liability. The court may award the prevailing party with costs, including attorney's fees.[120]

---

[111] MD. CODE, ENVIR. §§9-505, 9-1703, 9-1704.
[112] MD. CODE, ENVIR. §9-1705.
[113] MD. CODE, ENVIR. §9-1707(c).
[114] MD. CODE, ENVIR. §9-1707(d).
[115] MD. CODE, ENVIR. §9-1707(e).
[116] MD. CODE, ENVIR. §9-1707(h).
[117] 42 U.S.C. §6945(a).
[118] *O'Leary v. Moyer's Landfill, Inc.*, 523 F. Supp. 642 (E.D. Pa. 1981) (applying open dump regulations found at 40 C.F.R. Part 257 and concluding open dump existed).
[119] 42 U.S.C. §6972.
[120] *Id.*

Maryland Enforcement Powers

MDE has broad injunctive powers.[121] MDE may require industrial establishments to alter waste disposal methods in any way MDE determines to be necessary to protect public health and comfort.[122]

MDE may conduct enforcement through suit, notice, or order. MDE may revoke or temporarily suspend a permit after notice and the opportunity for a hearing if the holder fails to comply with the requirements of the regulations, the permit, or a corrective order. If necessary to protect public health or the environment, MDE may immediately discontinue any permit, though the permittee has a right to a prompt hearing if requested in writing within 10 days of the discontinuance.[123]

MDE may collect civil penalties of up to $10,000 per violation through a civil action, with each day constituting a separate violation. MDE may impose administrative penalties of $1,000 per violation, up to $50,000 total.[124]

Upon presenting proper identification, MDE inspectors have the right to inspect and conduct tests to ascertain whether the facility is in compliance with all regulations, orders, and permits.[125] Right of entry is also gained by consent because it is a term of each permit issued by MDE.

SPECIAL MEDICAL WASTE REGULATIONS

MDE and the Department of Health and Mental Hygiene (DHMH) regulate special medical wastes.[126] The DHMH regulations enumerate the acceptable means of handling and rendering special medical waste non-infectious. The MDE regulations govern identification, packaging, manifesting, and transportation to a treatment or disposal facility. The term of art used by both agencies is "special medical waste." Until special medical waste receives proper treatment as described in the regulations, it is considered infectious waste. Maryland law prohibits the disposal of infectious waste in landfills, though landfill disposal of properly treated medical waste is permissible.[127]

Special Medical Waste Defined

Special medical waste is a solid waste as defined in COMAR 26.13.02.02. Special medical wastes are also Controlled Hazardous Substances as defined by COMAR.[128] Specifically, special medical waste includes:

1. anatomical material (both human and animal);
2. blood (both human and animal);

---

[121] MD. CODE, ENVIR. §9-339.
[122] *Id.* §9-224.
[123] COMAR 26.04.07.27A.
[124] MD. CODE, ENVIR. §9-342.
[125] COMAR 26.04.07.27D.
[126] COMAR 10.06.06, COMAR 26.13.11, .12, .13.
[127] MD CODE, ENVIR. §9-227; COMAR 10.06.06.03D.
[128] COMAR 26.13.11.01C and 26.13.11.02B(10).

3. blood-soiled articles;
4. contaminated material;
5. microbiological laboratory wastes; or
6. sharps.

The regulations broadly define "sharps" to include "a syringe, needle, surgical instrument, or other article that is capable of cutting or puncturing human skin."[129] "Contaminated material" includes microbiological laboratory waste, the feces of a person diagnosed as having a disease that may be transmitted to another through feces, articles soiled with such feces, and articles that have come into contact with a known infectious agent.[130]

Regulations exclude certain material from the definition of special medical waste. Excluded are:

1. household waste (which includes single and multiple residences, hotels, and motels) including garbage, trash, and sanitary wastes in septic tanks;
2. wastes generated in the handling of an animal (unless the generator knows or has reason to know that the animal has a disease that is capable of being transmitted to humans);
3. the ash or by-product from an incinerator authorized by a state to burn special medical waste; and
4. wastes not generated in the ordinary course of business.[131]

Generators

Generation of special medical wastes triggers the regulatory requirements for identification, record keeping, treatment, transport, and disposal. The generator is the key figure in overseeing compliance with these requirements. A generator is any person, business, government entity, or group of people whose act or process produces a special medical waste.[132]

Generator's Responsibilities

Responsibility for determining which wastes are special medical wastes as defined by regulation rests solely on the generator. Once identified, the generator has two options for managing special medical wastes: (1) to treat the wastes on-site according to regulations, or (2) off-site for treatment and disposal. In either instance, the generator must ensure the waste is properly managed. All generators of special medical waste must obtain an identification number from MDE.[133]

---

129 COMAR 26.13.1 l.02B(8).
130 COMAR 26.13.11.02B(4).
131 COMAR 26.13.11.03A.
132 COMAR 26.13.11.02B(5), (7).
133 COMAR 26.13.12.03.

A small-volume generator that produces less than 50 pounds of special medical waste in any given calendar month need not conform to the MDE manifest and transport requirements.[134] However, a generator that accumulates special medical wastes in quantities over 50 pounds must meet all regulatory requirements.[135] Those generators who are below the 50-pound limit must nonetheless determine whether generated solid wastes are special medical wastes, package them according to regulation, and meet all treatment provisions that the regulations may otherwise require.[136]

Generators may elect to treat special medical wastes on-site rather than transport the wastes to a separate treatment facility. Generators who treat on-site must follow the same methods prescribed by DHMH for other treatment facilities.[137] The regulations attempt to minimize the risk of infection or piercing of skin from special medical wastes should a generator choose to treat special medical wastes on-site.

A special medical waste generator must ensure appropriate packaging of wastes for transport. Sharps must be in a container impervious to puncture.[138] Blood and blood-soiled articles must be in containers that will prevent spills or other leaks.[139] Anatomical materials and other special medical wastes must be in a leakproof bag or bags with a combined thickness of at least three mils or equivalent strength. The bags must be inside a clearly labeled rigid container to protect the bags from puncture.[140] The used container must be thoroughly disinfected if it is intended to be used again.[141] Each package label must be clearly visible. The label must include the generator's identification number and the words "Special Medical Waste."[142]

Manifests No Longer Required

While MDE previously mandated that generators complete and maintain manifests for the transportation of special medical waste, the state has since repealed this requirement.[143] MDE now requires generators to prepare "shipping papers" in accordance with federal Department of Transportation (DOT) requirements.[144] The DOT regulations require generators to include on shipping papers detailed descriptions of hazardous materials to be transported, the name of the shipper, an emergency response telephone number, and a certification that shipping requirements have been met.[145] In addition, shippers may still have to provide hazardous waste manifests as required by the federal Environmental Protection Agency pursuant to 40 C.F.R. 262.20.[146]

[134] COMAR 26.13.11.03B.
[135] COMAR 26.13.11.03C.
[136] COMAR 26.13.11.03D.
[137] COMAR 10.06.06.
[138] COMAR 26.13.12.05A(3), 10.06.06.06A.
[139] COMAR 26.13.12.05A(l), 10.06.06.04A.
[140] COMAR 26.13.12.05A(2), (4); and COMAR 10.06.06.05A(1), .07B.
[141] COMAR 10.06.06.05A(2), .07B(3).
[142] COMAR 26.13.12.05B.
[143] COMAR 26.13.12.04A.
[144] *Id.*
[145] 49 C.F.R. Part 172.
[146] 49 C.F.R. Part 172.205.

Record Keeping

Generally speaking, a generator must keep all records, including annual reports and exception reports, relating to special medical wastes for a period of three years. The generator must also retain all test results, including waste analyses or determinations that the waste is or is not excluded or is a special medical waste, for three years from the date the generator last sent the waste to on-site or off-site treatment storage or disposal. All record retention periods are automatically extended during the course of any unresolved enforcement action or when requested by MDE.[147]

International Shipments

Those who export or import special medical waste internationally must still comply with the requirements of COMAR 26.13.12.07[148] along with certain additional modifications. When shipping special medical waste outside the United States, the generator must prepare shipping papers and notify MDE in writing four weeks before the initial shipment to each country in each calendar year. The generator must also identify the waste to be shipped, as well as the name and address of the foreign consignee, and require that the foreign consignee confirm delivery. Those who import special medical waste into the state from outside the United States also must conform to the requirements of the Maryland regulations, including preparing shipping papers.[149]

TRANSPORTERS

Maryland requires a person transporting special medical waste from a source within the state or to a facility within the state to obtain a state identification number and certificate. The certificate shall be prominently displayed on the outside of the left door of the vehicle's cab. Generators may not offer special medical waste to transporters who do not have a state identification number.[150]

General Transportation Requirements

Transporters must purchase a yearly hauling certificate for $50 per vehicle and submit a certificate of safety inspection for each vehicle. The transporter must secure a $10,000 bond to indemnify the state for abatement of pollution resulting from improper transport or spills. Requests for hauling certificates must be made in writing and include descriptions of the nature, quantity, source, and destination of the waste to be transported, and the method of transportation. Specific information must describe the vehicle, its age, and construction. Interstate certificates are available to carriers with more than 10 trucks operating in and out of the state and servicing more

---

[147] COMAR 26.13.12.06A.
[148] COMAR 26.13.12.07.
[149] COMAR 26.13.12.07C.
[150] COMAR 26.13.12.03C.

than three states. Furthermore, the transporter must have five vehicle certificates currently issued and meet the insurance requirements of 49 C.F.R. Part 387 in order to qualify for an interstate certificate. Interstate certificates are transferable among vehicles.[151] Because transferable certificates do not indicate vehicle-specific information, the transporter must notify MDE 24 hours before using a certificate and describe the vehicle to be used, including type, make, model, serial number, state of registration, license, destination, and material transported.[152]

Spill or Discharge Response

The transporter must notify MDE and any local authorities within one hour of a spill or, if not immediately discovered, within one hour of discovery.[153] The transporter should take any immediate steps, such as diking the area, that are necessary. All transporters, whether water, air, rail, or highway, who have discharged special medical waste must give notice to the National Response Center at (800) 424-8802 if required by 40 C.F.R. §171.15. A bulk shipment water transporter must give additional notice to the state. Any transporter who has discharged special medical waste shall submit a written report to MDE.[154] If any special medical waste is discharged during transport, the transporter shall clean up or take such actions that are required or approved by federal, state, or local authorities to ensure that the discharge no longer presents a hazard to human health or the environment.[155]

TREATMENT AND DISPOSAL

Treatment and disposal of special medical wastes are two separate activities. Special medical wastes must receive treatment before they may be finally disposed.

All special medical waste, except sharps, must be incinerated, autoclaved, chemically disinfected, cremated, disinfected, mechanically destroyed after decontamination, or incinerated.[156] If allowed by state and local law, treatment may be by mechanical destruction followed by discharge to a sanitary sewer.

Sharps must either be encapsulated, incinerated, or mechanically destroyed. Autoclaving, chemical disinfection, or microwave disinfection must precede mechanical destruction of the sharps.[157] Following treatment of contaminated materials or of sharps, the residue must be disposed of at a place approved of for disposing solid waste.[158]

---

[151] COMAR 26.13.13.01C.
[152] *Id.*
[153] COMAR 26.13.13.03A.
[154] *Id.*
[155] COMAR 26.13.13.03B.
[156] COMAR 10.06.06.04.
[157] COMAR 10.06.06.06.
[158] COMAR 10.06.06.07C.

ENFORCEMENT

Failure to comply with the DHMH treatment regulations is a criminal misdemeanor. A violator is subject to a $500 per violation fine upon conviction. Suspension or revocation of any license, permit, or certificate issued by DHMH is also authorized.[159] Because MDE's generator and transporter regulations are promulgated under the authority of Maryland Environment Code §7-201 *et seq.*, failure to comply with those regulations may result in the imposition of much stiffer penalties.[160] MDE may impose a civil penalty of $25,000 per day or prosecute criminally. A criminal conviction may result in a fine of $25,000 for each day of violation and imprisonment for a period of up to a year for a first offense. Subsequent violations can result in fines of $50,000 per day and two years' imprisonment.[161]

In addition, Section 113 of the Clean Air Act authorizes federal EPA to seek both civil and criminal penalties for alleged violations of regulations governing stationary sources, including new source performance standards.[162] Under these provisions, EPA can seek administrative penalties of up to $25,000 per day for ongoing violations of its medical waste incinerator standard.[163] The agency also can seek civil penalties of up to $25,000 per day[164] and bring criminal enforcement.

---

159 COMAR 10.06.06.08.

160 See *American Recovery Co. v. Department of Health and Mental Hygiene,* 306 Md. 12, 506 A.2d 1171 (1986) (civil penalties are not conditioned upon a finding of actual harm to the environment).

161 MD CODE, ENVIR. §§7-266 and 7-267.

162 42 U.S.C. §7413.

163 42 U.S.C. §7413(d).

164 42 U.S.C. §7413(b).

Chapter 8

Employee and Community "Right-to-Know"

The Maryland Access to Information about Hazardous and Toxic Substances law requires employers to conduct an inventory of their work areas to identify "hazardous chemicals" they use or store, create a list of covered chemicals, report the presence of chemicals to the Maryland Department of Environment (MDE), maintain safety reports on these chemicals, and develop employee training programs. Employees, past and present, who may be or might have been exposed to a "hazardous chemical" while in the workplace must be given access to the gathered information. In addition, the Emergency Planning and Community Right-to-Know Act (EPCRA),[1] enacted as Title III of the Superfund Amendments and Reauthorization Act of 1986 (SARA), includes other chemical record-keeping and reporting requirements designed to ensure that citizens have access to information about chemicals present in their communities. EPCRA, or SARA Title III as it is often called, also includes a chemical release reporting requirement, as well as major emergency planning provisions to address potential releases of hazardous substances.

INFORMATION LISTS AND SAFETY REPORTS

Since 1985, the U.S. Occupational Safety and Health Administration (OSHA) has approved Maryland's occupational safety and health plan and has relinquished authority to enforce the federal standards concerning any matters covered under the Maryland plan. The approved Maryland plan includes the employee right-to-know provisions of the Maryland Access to Information about Hazardous and Toxic Substances statute.[2]

The Maryland employee right-to-know law applies to all employers who use or store any "hazardous chemical." Such employers must comply with state reporting,

---

[1] 42 U.S.C. §§11001, *et seq.*

[2] MD. LAB. AND EMP. CODE, §§5-401, *et seq.*, Maryland's statutory framework adopts by reference the federal standards promulgated by OSHA and found at 29 C.F.R. §§1910.1200 and supplements those standards as appropriate.

labeling, and worker training and education requirements.[3] Maryland exempts railroads, landfills, commercial or residential refuse services, and certain laboratories from some of the state statutory requirements, but still requires that they adhere to the federal guidelines.[4]

Hazardous Chemical

"Hazardous chemical" is broadly defined for right-to-know purposes. The term includes substances that scientific evidence indicates may be a physical or health hazard.[5] The statute identifies a physical hazard as: a combustible liquid, a compressed gas, an explosive or flammable chemical, an organic peroxide, oxidizer, a pyrophoric chemical, or an unstable or water-reactive chemical. Determining whether a chemical falls under one of these categories requires a technical review of relevant scientific studies and reference to the standards. OSHA has not created a "master" list of hazardous chemicals but has enumerated certain source references for hazardous chemicals that persons evaluating chemical dangers must consult.[6]

Certain materials are exempt from the employee right-to-know law. For example, consumer products and foodstuffs, including tobacco products, intended for use by the general public or for personal consumption by employees are specifically excluded from coverage of the law when they are used in the workplace consistent with the manner of use expected of consumers.[7] If employee use of the product is more extensive than normal consumer use such that there is a substantial risk of hazard exposure to the employee, then the product is *not* exempt.

The law also exempts manufactured items that qualify as "articles." An "article" is any item manufactured to a specific shape or design, with an end use dependent on that shape or design, and which does not result in exposure to hazardous chemicals under normal conditions of use.[8] Examples of exempt articles include vinyl upholstery, tires, and office supplies such as pens and pencils.

Material Safety Data Sheets

A Material Safety Data Sheet (MSDS) is a document that provides key hazard information about a hazardous chemical. Both OSHA's Hazard Communication Standard and the Maryland statute require that an MSDS for each substance be compiled by the original manufacturer or importer of the chemical. The MSDS must be written in

---

[3] 29 C.F.R. §1910.1200(b)(l).

[4] See MD. LAB. AND EMP. CODE §§5-402, 5-403.

[5] 29 C.F.R. §1910.1200(c). "Health hazard" means a chemical for which there is statistically significant evidence based on at least one scientific study that acute or chronic health effects may occur in exposed employees. *Id.*

[6] 29 C.F.R. §1910 Subpart Z (Toxic and Hazardous Substances); "Threshold Limit Values for Chemical Substances and Physical Agents in the Work Environment" (American Conference of Government Industrial Hygienists, latest edition); "Annual Report of Carcinogens" (National Toxicology Program, latest edition); "Monographs" (International Agency for Research on Cancer, latest edition). See 29 C.F.R. §1910.1200(d)(3) and (4). In addition, the Maryland Department of the Environment's Toxic Information Center maintains a list of known hazards and toxic substances.

[7] 29 C.F.R. §1910.1200(b)(6).

[8] 29 C.F.R. §1910.1200(c).

English and must include the specific identity of the chemical;[9] its common name; the physical and chemical characteristics of the "hazardous chemical"; any physical or health hazards; primary route(s) of entry; applicable exposure limits; whether the substance is a carcinogen; precautions for safe handling and use; control measures; emergency and first aid procedures; the date of preparation or last update of the MSDS; and the name, address, and telephone number of the party preparing or distributing the MSDS who can provide additional information on the "hazardous chemical" or emergency procedures. MSDSs must be updated within three months of discovery of any new information on the chemical.

Obtaining MSDS Reports

Manufacturers and distributors are required to provide employers with the MSDS for each hazardous chemical.[10] An employer must keep an MSDS for each hazardous chemical that is used or stored in the workplace.[11]

A purchaser of hazardous chemicals must request an MSDS as soon as possible if one is not on hand or provided with the shipment.[12] It is advisable to keep a record of efforts made to obtain an MSDS since the law holds the purchaser ultimately responsible for obtaining an MSDS for each hazardous chemical in the workplace.

In rare cases an employer may be unable to obtain an MSDS for a product from the manufacturer or distributor. In these cases, the employer should review the information on the product label, and any other available sources, to assess the hazards of the product. If the employer concludes that the product qualifies as a "hazardous chemical," the employer should either create an MSDS or remove the product promptly from the workplace. In either event, the employer is advised to seek the assistance of a qualified industrial hygienist.

Chemical Information Lists

All Maryland employers using or storing a hazardous chemical are also required to compile and maintain a Chemical Information List covering all hazardous chemicals used or stored in the workplace.[13] The list must specify the chemical and common name of each hazardous substance and identify the location where each substance is found. The information on the MSDS may be used to find the chemical name and to identify the substance. In determining whether a given chemical is "hazardous" and therefore should be placed on the list, employers may rely on the evaluation performed by the chemical's manufacturer or importer as reflected in the MSDS. Although the employer need not second-guess information provided on the chemical's MSDS, MSDS information known by the employer to be wrong must not be used.

---

[9] In limited circumstances, the chemical's specific identity, if a trade secret, may be protected. See 29 C.F.R. §1910.1200(i).

[10] 29 C.F.R. §1910.1200(g)(7).

[11] 29 C.F.R. §1910.1200(g)(8).

[12] 29 C.F.R. §1910.1200(g)(6).

[13] MD. CODE ANN., LAB. AND EMP. §5-405(b), 29 C.F.R. §1910.1200(e)(l).

The first page of the list must note the complete name and telephone number of a company contact person, and the date of preparation or revision. The Chemical Information List must be arranged alphabetically every two years. The employer must maintain the list for 40 years. A "hazardous chemical" not already on the list must be added within 30 days of its introduction into the workplace and the date of introduction recorded.[14]

Recipients of Chemical Information Lists

Upon request, the employer must provide access to the Chemical Information List and applicable MSDSs to any employee who is exposed to a hazardous chemical.[15] Access to the information must be provided within one working day of the request. In addition, within five working days after the request, the employer must provide one copy of the requested information or the means to produce a copy free of charge.[16] A reasonable charge may be assessed for any additional copies.[17]

The employer must also provide the Chemical Information List and applicable MSDSs to other employers or independent contractors who will be working at the employer's workplace. When possible, the information should be given before the work commences.[18]

Upon request, the employer is also required to provide information to the local fire department administration. An MSDS must be provided for each substance on the Chemical Information List. The fire department official may request that the Chemical Information List be broken down by work areas into smaller lists and that the work areas be identified by location.[19]

Employees' Work Obligations

If the employer refuses to grant access or fails to provide the Chemical Information List and applicable MSDSs as required, an employee requesting the information about a hazardous chemical may refuse to work with that particular hazardous chemical.[20] An employer may not request that an employee "waive" rights granted under the right-to-know law. Any waiver of rights is void.[21] Employers also may not discharge, discipline, or otherwise discriminate against an employee because the employee has exercised a statutory right, such as requesting the hazardous chemical information or

---

[14] MD. CODE ANN., LAB. AND EMP. §§5-405(b)(2), 5-405(c).

[15] Exposed employees include those actually exposed and those who might potentially be exposed in the normal conduct of business or during foreseeable emergencies. See, generally, MD. CODE ANN., LAB. AND EMP. §§5-401(b)(l), 5-407(a). In addition, former employees have the right to review MSDS information. MD. CODE ANN., LAB. AND EMP. §§5401(b)(l), 5-407(a).

[16] MD. CODE ANN., LAB. AND EMP. §5-407(a)(2).

[17] MD. CODE ANN., LAB. AND EMP. §5-407(a)(3).

[18] MD. CODE ANN., LAB. AND EMP. §§5-408(a)–(b).

[19] MD. LAB. AND EMP. CODE ANN. §5-409(b).

[20] MD. CODE ANN., LAB. AND EMP. §5-407(a)(5).

[21] *See* MD. CODE ANN., LAB. AND EMP. §5-404.

refusing to work with a hazardous chemical for which the employer has not provided requested information.[22]

LABELING REQUIREMENTS

The Maryland Employee Right-to-Know law requires chemical manufacturers, importers, and distributors to label hazardous chemical containers with the substance's chemical identity, appropriate hazard warning, and the name and address of the manufacturer, importer, or distributor before the chemical is shipped. Employers must ensure that each container of hazardous chemicals in the workplace is labeled with the chemical's identity and hazard warnings.[23] The label must be in English, legible, and prominently displayed.

In most cases, containers of hazardous chemicals entering the workplace will have already been labeled by the chemical manufacturer, importer, or distributor; an employer need not affix a new label to a container that already is properly labeled.

Portable containers, filled from a labeled container and intended for immediate use by the transferring employee, are exempt from the requirement.[24] While pipe systems are not considered "containers" *per se*, in practice, pipes are covered by the law's information requirements, especially in situations where chemicals contained in the pipes present a potential hazard to the employee.[25]

In lieu of affixing a label to an individual stationary process container, an employer may use a sign, placard, or other written material if it conveys the chemical identity and the appropriate hazard warnings and is readily accessible to employees in the work area throughout each work shift.[26]

The labeling requirements of the right-to-know law do not apply to chemicals whose labeling is regulated under other federal laws. For example, pesticides are subject to the labeling requirements of the Federal Insecticide, Fungicide, and Rodenticide Act and therefore are exempt from the labeling provisions of the Maryland (and federal) worker right-to-know requirements.[27]

EMPLOYEE TRAINING AND EDUCATION

Every employer who uses hazardous chemicals in Maryland must provide a training and education program to all employees who may be exposed under normal operating conditions or in foreseeable emergencies.[28]

The regulations require all new employees to undergo a training program *prior* to initial assignment. Current employees must receive training as new information

[22] MD. CODE ANN., LAB. AND EMP. §5-604(b)(4).
[23] 29 C.F.R. §1910.1200(f)(4).
[24] 29 C.F.R. §1910.1200(f)(7).
[25] *Cf.* 29 C.F.R. §1910.1200(e)(l)(ii).
[26] 29 C.F.R. §1910.1200(f)(6).
[27] 29 C.F.R. §1910.1200(b)(5).
[28] 29 C.F.R. §1910.1200(h).

becomes available. Additional instruction must be provided to an employee whenever that employee may be subjected to increased or different exposures due to changes in work practices, including changes in equipment, work assignment, or the introduction of new hazardous chemicals into the workplace.[29]

The training and education programs must include instruction on employee rights under the right-to-know law, the employer's hazard communication program, and the dangers associated with the substances to which an employee is or may be exposed.[30]

The employer must make the employee aware of the existence of hazard information, such as Chemical Information Lists, MSDSs, and identifiers or placards within the workplace. The employer should also instruct the employee in the proper procedure for obtaining that information. The employee should also be informed that there is a right to additional training as the work environment changes or new "hazardous chemicals" are introduced.

The training program should make the employee aware of the nature of the hazards of the various substances in the workplace. Instruction about appropriate work practices, control programs, and protective measures must be included, as well as procedures to be followed in the event of an emergency.[31]

PENALTIES FOR NONCOMPLIANCE

OSHA requires states like Maryland enforce their own employee right-to-know law to implement penalty provisions equal in force to OSHA's. During an inspection, an employer who fails to comply with requirement of Maryland's right-to-know law will be issued a citation for each violation by the Division of Labor and Industry. An employer may be assessed a base civil penalty up to $7,000 for each "serious" violation.[32] Penalties are assessed at the Commissioner's discretion for lesser violations, if a risk of harm exists. If the employer fails to correct a cited violation within the time permitted for its correction, the Division may assess a penalty of up to $7,000 for each day that the violation continues. Willful or repeated violations will subject the employer to a possible penalty of $70,000 for each violation.[33] Under appropriate circumstances, criminal sanctions also may be imposed.[34]

EPCRA/SARA TITLE III

The federal Emergency Planning and Community Right-to-Know Act (EPCRA), also known as SARA Title III, is a separate and free-standing law included as Title III of

---

[29] *Id.*

[30] 29 C.F.R. §1910.1200(h)(2).

[31] *Id.*

[32] MD. CODE ANN., LAB. AND EMP. §§5-809, 5-810. A serious violation exists if there is a substantial probability of death or significant physical harm from a condition that exists, or a practice, means, method, operation, or process that is adopted or in use, unless the employer did not and with the exercise of due diligence could not know of the condition or violation. *Id.*

[33] MD. CODE ANN., LAB. AND EMP. §5-810.

[34] MD. CODE ANN., LAB. AND EMP. §§5-804, 5-806.

the Superfund Amendments and Reauthorization Act of 1986 (SARA).[35] EPCRA has two basic purposes: first, to promote local emergency planning to respond to releases of dangerous chemicals; and second, to ensure that information regarding hazardous and toxic substances present in the community is reported and made available to the public. These two purposes are implemented in two subtitles to the law, discussed below under the headings "Emergency Planning Requirements" and "Community Right-to-Know Reporting Requirements."

In order to implement the provisions of EPCRA, the law mandates the establishment of State Emergency Response Commissions (SERCs) and Local Emergency Planning Committees (LEPCs) in every state of the nation. The SERCs and LEPCs are charged with the responsibility of developing comprehensive emergency plans to be followed in the event of a chemical release. In addition, these agencies (together with local fire departments) are the entities that receive, maintain, and make available to the public most of the information submitted under the "community right-to-know" reporting requirements imposed by EPCRA.

EMERGENCY PLANNING REQUIREMENTS

Facility Notification

The first reporting requirement that went into effect under EPCRA was the "emergency planning notification" requirement of EPCRA §302.[36] This requirement applied to any facility owner or operator having any listed "extremely hazardous substance" present in greater than the substance's "threshold planning quantity" (TPQ).[37] Facilities have stringent reporting requirements to MDE.[38]

Extremely Hazardous Substances

An "extremely hazardous substance" is any substance listed by the Environmental Protection Agency (EPA) under EPCRA §302. EPA's regulations currently list approximately 360 extremely hazardous substances.[39] EPA's regulations also specify a "threshold planning quantity" for each listed chemical.

Consequences of Facility Notification

Facilities that notify under EPCRA §302 are subject to the emergency planning provisions of EPCRA. Those provisions require each LEPC to develop a comprehensive emergency response plan to address potential releases of "extremely hazardous substances" from facilities within the LEPC's jurisdiction that have notified under

[35] 42 U.S.C. §§11001, *et seq.*

[36] 42 U.S.C. §11002.

[37] "Facility" is defined broadly to include all buildings, equipment, and other stationary items that are located on a single, adjacent, or contiguous site and that are under common ownership. 42 U.S.C. §11049(4).

[38] https://perma.cc/R6N8-383Y.

[39] 40 C.F.R. §355, App. A, B.

EPCRA §302.[40] The plans must be updated by the LEPC annually. The plans also must be reviewed annually or more frequently as changed circumstances in the community or at the facility may require by the SERC.[41]

In order to promote the emergency planning process, each facility that notifies must thereafter identify an individual who will serve as a "facility emergency coordinator."[42] This person is expected to provide information and assistance to the LEPC in its planning efforts. The law requires that, upon request by the LEPC, each facility notifying under EPCRA §302 must provide any information to the committee "necessary" for the development and implementation of the local comprehensive emergency response plan.[43] Notifying facilities must also promptly inform the LEPC of any "relevant changes" at the facility.[44]

Chemical Release Reporting

In addition to facility notification and local emergency response planning, EPCRA also imposes an expanded duty on businesses to provide immediate notification of releases of certain chemicals. This requirement appears in EPCRA §304.[45] Notification is required for any release of a "reportable quantity" (RQ) within a 24-hour period of either an "extremely hazardous substance" identified under EPCRA or a "hazardous substance" identified under CERCLA. As noted above, there are currently approximately 360 "extremely hazardous substances" and over 800 CERCLA "hazardous substances."[46] EPA has established RQs for each of these substances in its regulations. The RQs range from 1 pound to 5,000 pounds.

Notification Procedures

Upon discovery of the release, one must *immediately* notify by telephone or other oral communication the SERC and the LEPC for any planning district likely to be affected. A written follow-up emergency notice is also required and must be sent to the SERC and LEPC as soon as practicable thereafter.[47]

The oral notification must convey the following information, if known: the chemical name; quantity; time and duration of the release; medium or media into which the release occurred; any known or anticipated health risks; proper precautions to take; and name and number of the facility's contact person. The follow-up report should reiterate and update information provided in the oral notice and must include a statement of the actions taken to respond to the release.

---

[40] 42 U.S.C. §11003.
[41] 42 U.S.C. §11003(a).
[42] 42 U.S.C. §11003(c)(3).
[43] 42 U.S.C. §11003(d)(3); 40 C.F.R §355.30(d)(2).
[44] 42 U.S.C. §11003(d)(2); 40 C.F.R. §355.30(d)(l).
[45] 42 U.S.C. §11004.
[46] See 40 C.F.R. §302.4.
[47] 42 U.S.C. §11004(b), (c); 40 C.F.R. §355.40. Transportation vehicles are specifically covered under EPCRA §304. However, compliance in the event of a release can be satisfied by calling 911 or the local emergency personnel and reporting the release.

Penalties for Noncompliance

EPCRA provides for civil penalties of up to $25,000 per day for the first violation and up to $75,000 per day for any subsequent violation of the emergency notification requirements. However, on December 31, 1996, the EPA issued a "Civil Monetary Penalty Inflation Adjustment Rule,"[48] as mandated by the Debt Collection Improvement Act of 1996.[49] As a result, maximum civil penalties were increased by 10 percent to $27,500 and $82,500, respectively. Willful failure to notify invites criminal penalties of up to a $25,000 fine and two years' imprisonment for the first offense and up to a $50,000 fine and five years' imprisonment for subsequent offenses.[50] These penalties are in addition to any penalties that may be imposed under the release reporting requirement of CERCLA §103.

Exemptions

Both CERCLA §103 and EPCRA §304, and EPA's regulations implementing these provisions,[51] exempt certain categories of releases from emergency release notification requirements. Most important, "federally permitted releases" need not be reported under either section. The term "federally permitted release" is defined in CERCLA §101(10) and generally includes releases in compliance with an environmental permit or regulation.

In addition to "federally permitted releases," both CERCLA and EPCRA also exempt so-called "continuous releases" from emergency reporting; however, such releases must still be reported under an alternative (less burdensome) reporting scheme.[52] EPA's regulations define "continuous release" broadly to include any release that is "routine, anticipated, and intermittent and incidental to normal operations."[53] A facility that has a release that qualifies as a continuous release must provide initial telephone and written reports describing the release. A written follow-up report one year later, verifying and updating the information in the initial reports, is also required. Any "statistically significant increases" in the release must be reported immediately as a new emergency release under CERCLA §103 and EPCRA §304.[54]

COMMUNITY RIGHT-TO-KNOW REPORTING REQUIREMENTS

EPCRA imposes three other reporting requirements, designed to ensure that the public has access to information about chemicals in their communities. These "community

[48] 40 C.F.R. parts 19 and 27.
[49] 31 C.F.R. part 285.
[50] EPCRA §325(b); 40 C.F.R. §355.50.
[51] 40 C.F.R. §302.6 (CERCLA §103); 40 C.F.R. §355.40 (EPCRA §304).
[52] CERCLA §103(f)(2); 42 U.S.C. §11004(a)(2)(C).
[53] 40 C.F.R. §302.8(b).
[54] *Id.* §302.8(d)–(h).

right-to-know" requirements are found in Section 311 (MSDS reporting),[55] Section 312 (inventory reporting),[56] and Section 313 (toxic chemical release reporting).[57]

MSDS Reporting Requirements of EPCRA §311

Every facility that is required to prepare or maintain an MSDS under the federal OSHA Hazard Communication Standard must submit a copy of their MSDSs to the SERC, LEPC, and local fire department.[58] Alternatively, the facility may submit a list of the "hazardous chemicals" present at the facility.[59] If a request for the MSDS of any chemical on the list is made, then one must be submitted. The initial filing was due October 17, 1987, for facilities in the manufacturing sector (SIC codes 20–39). For non-manufacturing facilities, the initial submission deadline was September 24, 1988.[60]

EPA has established certain minimum quantity thresholds for reporting under EPCRA §311 (and §312).[61] Specifically, the reporting threshold for "extremely hazardous substances" is the substance's "threshold planning quantity" or 500 pounds, whichever is less. For all other "hazardous chemicals," the threshold is 10,000 pounds.[62]

Inventory Reporting Requirements of EPCRA §312

A facility that must comply with EPCRA §311 (MSDS reporting) must also submit annual Emergency and Hazardous Chemical Inventory Forms to the SERC, LEPC, and local fire department pursuant to EPCRA §312. These reports cover the same "hazardous chemicals" covered by EPCRA §311, and the same minimum reporting thresholds discussed above apply. The initial deadline for the annual inventory report was March 1, 1988, for manufacturing facilities and March 1, 1989, for non-manufacturing facilities.[63]

There are two separate annual inventory report forms.[64] The "Tier I" form is a more general report that allows the facility to aggregate information on chemicals that pose similar hazards.[65] The "Tier II" form requires more detailed information for each "hazardous chemical." The facility has the option of submitting Tier I forms, but the facility must submit the more detailed Tier II forms if requested by the SERC, LEPC, or fire department. For this reason, many facilities file Tier II forms in the normal course.

---

[55] 42 U.S.C. §11021.

[56] 42 U.S.C. §11022.

[57] 42 U.S.C. §11023.

[58] 42 U.S.C. §11021(a), (d).

[59] If a list is submitted, the chemicals must be grouped under the five hazard categories established by EPA: acute health hazard, chronic health hazard, fire hazard, release of pressure hazard, and reactivity hazard. 40 C.F.R. §§370.2; 370.21.

[60] Pursuant to Executive Order 12856, the initial filing deadline for federal facilities was March 3, 1994.

[61] 40 C.F.R. §370.20(b).

[62] "Hazardous chemicals" do not include: (1) food, food additives, or drugs regulated by the Food and Drug Administration; (2) any solid substance in a manufactured item to the extent exposure to the substance does not occur under normal use; (3) any substance to the extent it is used for personal, family, or household purposes; (4) any substance to the extent it is used in a research laboratory or hospital or other medical facility; and (5) any substance to the extent it is used in routine agricultural operations or is a fertilizer held for sale by a retailer to the ultimate consumer. EPCRA §311(e).

[63] Pursuant to Executive Order 12856, the initial filing deadline for federal facilities was March 1, 1995.

[64] For copies of the forms and an explanation of how they should be filled out, *see* 40 C.F.R. §§370.40, 370.41.

[65] The information must be aggregated under EPA's five hazard categories for "hazardous chemicals."

Any Tier I or Tier II report must be made available to the public by the LEPC or the SERC. A facility may request, by noting on the report, that the specific location of the chemical be withheld. A limited exception also applies, as it does for Maryland's Chemical Information List, for the specific chemical identity if it is a protected trade secret.

Penalties for Noncompliance

Civil penalties of up to $10,000 per day may be imposed for violating the §311 MSDS requirements and up to $25,000 for each day in violation of the §312 Inventory Form requirements.[66]

TOXIC CHEMICAL RELEASE INVENTORY (TRI) REPORTING

EPCRA §313 requires the submission of Toxic Chemical Release reports (known as "Form R" reports).[67] This reporting program is also referred to as the Toxic Release Inventory or TRI. TRI reports must be filed with the EPA and with Maryland Emergency Response Commission. The reports must be submitted each July 1, covering the previous calendar year.

Facilities Subject to TRI

Under EPCRA §313, facilities are required to report releases and other waste management activities of specifically listed chemicals. Facilities meeting the following three criteria are subject to TRI reporting requirements:

1. the facility has a primary Standard Industrial Classification (SIC) code listed by EPA under EPCRA §313;
2. the facility has ten or more full-time employees; and
3. the facility manufactured, processed, or otherwise used in the course of the calendar year any listed "toxic chemical" in quantities greater than the applicable threshold.

The threshold quantity for the manufacture[68] or processing[69] of a toxic chemical is 25,000 pounds per year.[70] The threshold quantity for "use" of a toxic chemical is 10,000 pounds per year.[71]

---

[66] 42 U.S.C. §11045(c)(1).

[67] 40 C.F.R. §372.

[68] "Manufacture" is defined as producing, preparing, importing, or compounding a toxic chemical. 40 C.F.R. §372.3.

[69] "Processing" is defined as the preparation of a toxic chemical, after its manufacture, for distribution in commerce—(1) in the same form or physical state as, or in a different form or physical state from, that in which it was received by the person so preparing such chemical, or (2) a part of an article containing the toxic chemical. *Id.*

[70] See 40 C.F.R. §372.25(a).

[71] Several types of "uses" are exempt from reporting, including: (1) use as a structural component of the facility; (2) use of products for routine facility, grounds, or motor vehicle maintenance; and (3) use of toxic chemicals present in process water, non-contact cooling water, or air used either for compression or combustion. *See* 40 C.F.R. §372.38(c).

Definition of Toxic Chemical

The list of toxic chemicals subject to reporting consists of approximately 600 chemicals and categories of chemicals.[72]

Completing a Toxic Chemical Release Form

Completion of "Form R" reports (EPA's toxic chemical release reporting form) is a difficult and time-consuming task. Although the law only requires the preparer to rely on available data, in cases where data are not available, EPA requires the preparer to develop estimates, using engineering judgments, of the amounts of each toxic chemical that have been released into the environment. Form R requires the following information for each chemical:

1. A general description of how the chemical is used in the facility;
2. An estimate of the maximum amount (in ranges) present at any one time during the preceding year;
3. A description for each waste stream of the disposal or treatment method used, and an estimate of the treatment efficiency achieved;
4. The annual quantity of the toxic chemical entering the environment, broken down by each medium of entry (e.g., stack releases, fugitive air releases, NPDES discharges, run-off, etc.); and
5. A description of source reduction and recycling activities, including a list of quantities released, recovered, recycled, and treated both on- and off-site.

Identifying Listed Toxic Chemicals

Manufacturers and distributors of trade name products and mixtures containing "toxic chemicals" listed by EPA are required to notify downstream purchasers of the name and concentration of each "toxic chemical" contained in their products. This notification must accompany the first shipment in each calendar year.[73]

Penalties for Noncompliance

Civil penalties of up to $25,000 per day of violation of the §313 reporting requirements may be assessed for failure to submit the required information.[74] However, as noted previously, EPA increased the maximum civil penalty for EPCRA violations by 10 percent to $27,500 per day, pursuant to the Debt Collection Improvement Act of 1996.[75]

---

[72] 40 C.F.R. §372.65.
[73] 40 C.F.R. §372.45.
[74] EPCRA §325(c)(l). Furthermore, submission of §§311, 312, and 313 information is required notwithstanding passage of a due date.
[75] 40 CFR parts 19 and 27.

TRADE SECRET INFORMATION—STATE AND FEDERAL

EPCRA provides for the limited protection of trade secret information.[76] The protection is available for emergency planning, community right-to-know, and toxic chemical release reporting. Specific chemical identity information may not be withheld by a facility giving emergency notice of a release of an "extremely hazardous substance" or a "hazardous substance." Trade secret protection is also provided to industry through OSHA regulations.[77] These regulations limit the disclosure of trade secret information associated with the MSDS requirements.

Procedures for Obtaining Trade Secret Protection

As provided in EPCRA, any person may withhold the specific chemical identity of a hazardous chemical if that information is claimed to be a trade secret.[78] In order to establish a trade secret claim, the claimant must separately submit the trade secret information to the EPA administrator, together with an explanation of the reasons why such information is entitled to trade secret protection.

To qualify, the claimant must demonstrate that: (1) the information has not been disclosed to any other person, except under a confidentiality agreement; (2) the information is not required to be disclosed under any other law; (3) disclosure would likely cause substantial competitive harm; and (4) the chemical's identity is not readily discoverable through reverse engineering.[79] A process of appeal for negative determinations and for challenge by individuals or the state is also provided in the statute.

Even if chemical identity information can legally be withheld, provisions in EPCRA allow access to the information by health professionals.[80] Where no medical emergency exists, a statement of need for the information is required, and the person requesting the information must first enter into a confidentiality agreement. In cases where a treating physician or nurse determines that a medical emergency exists, the chemical identity information must be disclosed immediately. The physician or nurse can then be required to sign a confidentiality agreement as soon as circumstances permit thereafter.

---

[76] 42 U.S.C. §11042.

[77] 29 C.F.R. §1910.1200(i).

[78] Even if the chemical identity is withheld, the generic class or category of the chemical must be provided.

[79] 42 U.S.C. §11042(b).

[80] 42 U.S.C. §11043.

Chapter 9

Regulation of Indoor Air Pollutants

ASBESTOS

Asbestos is a generic term and usually refers to any one of many mineral compounds that share desirable fibrous qualities. It normally includes anthophyllite, chrysotile, crocidolite, amosite, tremolite, and actinolite.[1] Regulated asbestos-containing material (RACM) includes both friable and non-friable asbestos-containing materials (ACM).[2]

"Friable" ACM refers to any asbestos-containing material applied on ceilings, walls, structural members, piping, ductwork, or any other part of a building that, when dry, can be crumbled, pulverized, or reduced to powder by hand pressure and contains more than 1 percent asbestos by weight.[3] "Non-friable" ACM is any material that contains more than 1 percent by weight asbestos, but that when dry, cannot be crumbled, pulverized, or reduced to powder by hand pressure.[4]

Federal and State Role in Asbestos Control

Several federal agencies regulate asbestos, including EPA, OSHA, and DOT. This chapter discusses the regulation of owners and operators of buildings that may contain asbestos. These federal regulations are enforced primarily by EPA and OSHA. OSHA's role in asbestos control focuses on protection for employees in the workplace.[5]

EPA's role in asbestos control in buildings is five-fold. First, EPA oversees the training and accrediting of asbestos control professionals. Second, EPA implements building inspection requirements for both public and non-public buildings. Third, EPA regulates the repair, renovation, and demolition activities involving ACM. Fourth, it also regulates the disposal of ACM. Fifth, and finally, EPA implements requirements

---

1 29 C.F.R. §1910.1001(b).
2 40 C.F.R. §61.141; see also COMAR 26.11.21.01E.
3 *Id.*
4 *Id.*
5 29 C.F.R. §§1910.1001 and 1926.1101.

that protect state and local government employees from the health risks of exposure to asbestos to the same extent that OSHA protects private sector workers through its adoption of OSHA's Asbestos Standards.[6] The State of Maryland has implemented additional regulations governing the control of asbestos[7] and the accreditation of asbestos control professionals.[8]

Licensing and Accreditation of Asbestos Control Professionals

EPA does not license or accredit individuals involved in asbestos control in Maryland. This activity is carried out by the State of Maryland Department of the Environment (MDE). EPA's involvement consists only of its approval of licensing and accreditation courses offered by the states.[9]

Any business entity or public unit must be licensed or have its contractor licensed by the State of Maryland prior to engaging in any "asbestos project."[10] Asbestos projects include any activities involving the "demolition," "renovation," or "encapsulation" of friable asbestos material.[11] Demolition includes the wrecking or taking out of any load-supporting structural member and any related removal or stripping of friable asbestos material.[12] Renovation includes the removal or stripping of friable asbestos materials used on any pipe, duct, boiler, tank, reactor, turbine, furnace, or structural member.[13] "Encapsulation" means activities that coat, bind, or resurface walls, ceilings, pipes, or other structures to prevent friable asbestos from becoming airborne.[14] The term "structural member" includes load-bearing beams and walls, as well as non-supporting members such as ceilings and non-load-supporting walls.[15]

Maryland also requires accreditation for each person engaged in an "asbestos occupation" involving any school project or public or commercial building.[16] An asbestos occupation is any job such as asbestos abatement worker, asbestos abatement contractor/supervisor, inspector, management planner, or abatement project designer.[17] Any individual, while engaged in an asbestos occupation, must carry the photo identification card issued by either the training provider or by the State of Maryland or other state with an EPA-approved Model Accreditation Plan.[18]

Licensing

Anyone, including public and private entities, must be licensed before conducting any asbestos project.[19] Once it is known that asbestos is present in a building or structure,

---

[6] 40 C.F.R. §§763.91 and 763.120.
[7] COMAR 26.11.21.
[8] COMAR 26.11.23.03.
[9] See, e.g., 15 U.S.C. §53.2646(a).
[10] MD. CODE, ENVIR. §6-419; COMAR 26.11.21.04.
[11] COMAR 26.11.21.01C, D, and L.
[12] COMAR 26.11.21.01C.
[13] COMAR 26.11.21.01L.
[14] COMAR 26.11.21.0ID.
[15] COMAR 26.11.21.0IM.
[16] COMAR 26.11.23.03A.
[17] COMAR 26.11.23.01B(6).
[18] COMAR 26.11.23.03C.
[19] COMAR 26.11.21.04.

the owner or operator must decide whether to seek a license to work with asbestos-containing materials or to avoid these materials and have licensed contractors do any required work involving asbestos. Under the Maryland regulations, even routine maintenance work requires a state license if asbestos will be disturbed, and there is no exception for an "emergency."[20]

An application and license fee ($625 for three or more employees; no fee for fewer than three employees) must be submitted to MDE,[21] which should act on a completed application within 60 days.[22] Approval will be based on the applicant's demonstration of ability to comply with the requirements of COMAR 26.11.21 and applicable EPA and OSHA standards. If a license is denied, all but $25 of the fee will be returned to the applicant.[23]

Generally the applicant must demonstrate the following in order to obtain a license: workers will be initially, and annually thereafter, medically examined for their physical capacity for work while wearing respirators; each employee who will come in contact with asbestos will complete approved initial and annual health and safety training; protective clothing and equipment, including respirators, will be provided to and used by employees whenever working on an asbestos project; accurate records will be maintained of all training and asbestos projects performed; appropriate control measures will be used on all asbestos projects to limit the emission of asbestos fibers into the environment; and asbestos waste will be properly labeled and disposed of at an authorized facility.[24]

The license remains in effect for one year from the date of issuance unless revoked or suspended for failure to comply with appropriate requirements.[25] It may be renewed annually by MDE if a renewal application and the appropriate fee are submitted 30 days prior to expiration and the applicant complies fully with all applicable requirements.[26]

Accreditation

Maryland requires accreditation only for those persons engaged in an asbestos occupation involving any school project or any public and commercial building.[27] MDE will accredit an individual for an asbestos occupation upon submission of proof that the individual has successfully completed either a state- or EPA-approved initial training or review course or an EPA-approved course as provided in the Maryland regulation.[28] MDE will also accredit an individual who maintains a current accreditation from an EPA-approved accreditation plan of another state.[29] MDE issues a photo identification

---

20 *Id.*
21 COMAR 26.11.21.10.
22 COMAR 26.11.21.11.A.
23 COMAR 26.11.21.11B(2).
24 COMAR 26.11.21.01–26.11.21.13.
25 COMAR 26.11.21.12A.
26 COMAR 26.11.21.12B.
27 COMAR 26.11.23.03A.
28 COMAR 26.11.23.03B.
29 *Id.*

card as proof that an individual is properly accredited.[30] The identification card must be carried at all times an individual is engaged in an asbestos occupation.[31]

The accreditation is valid only for the asbestos occupations for which the candidate qualifies.[32] For example, if a person has obtained accreditation to conduct only building inspections, he or she is not authorized to design abatement projects.

Building Inspection

EPA has promulgated a comprehensive federal inspection requirement for school buildings, commonly known as the Asbestos-in-Schools Rule.[33] The rule requires local education agencies to implement and carry out a management plan for the identification and proper management of any asbestos-containing building material (ACBM) in each building leased, owned, or otherwise used as a school building.[34] The management plan must provide for, among other items: training of all custodial and maintenance employees; informing all workers and building occupants, at least annually, about inspections and response actions; notifying all temporary workers who may come into contact with ACBM of the locations of any ACBM or suspected ACBM; and posting appropriate warning labels in routine maintenance areas that may contain any friable or non-friable ACBM.[35] At least once every three years after the management plan is in effect, local education agencies must reinspect each school building.[36] As discussed in the previous sections, those individuals responsible for the management plan required in the Asbestos-in-Schools Rule must be accredited by the state.[37]

In addition, OSHA has promulgated regulations that require building and facility owners to identify the presence, location, and quantity of known asbestos-containing materials (ACM) and presumed asbestos-containing materials (PACM) in their buildings.[38] Building or facility owners must inform employers and employees who work within their buildings about the presence and location of ACM and PACM.[39] Employers are responsible for informing all affected employees.[40] Records regarding the identification of asbestos must be kept for the duration of ownership of the building and must be transferred to successive owners.[41] OSHA regulations also specify signage and labeling requirements for regulated areas.[42]

OSHA also requires monitoring for airborne concentrations of asbestos fiber in all areas where persons "are, or may reasonably be expected to be exposed" to airborne asbestos at or above either: (1) "permissible exposure limit" of 0.1 fibers per cubic

---

[30] COMAR 26.11.23.03C.
[31] *Id.*
[32] COMAR 26.11.23.03D.
[33] 40 C.F.R. §763.80.
[34] 40 C.F.R. §§763.84 *et seq.*
[35] *Id.*
[36] 40 C.F.R. §763.85(b).
[37] See COMAR 26.11.23.02.
[38] 29 C.F.R. §1910.1001(j)(2).
[39] 29 C.F.R. §1910.1001(j)(2)(i).
[40] *Id.*
[41] 29 C.F.R. §1910.1001(j)(2)(ii).
[42] 29 C.F.R. §1910.1001(j)(3)-(4).

centimeter of air on an eight-hour time-weighted average; and/or (2) the "excursion limit" of 1.0 fibers per cubic centimeter as averaged over a sampling period of 30 minutes.[43] This requirement applies to all industries, except for construction work and shipbuilding activity.[44] Those individuals conducting inspection and monitoring in compliance with the OSHA requirements must be accredited by the state as discussed in the previous section.[45]

While no definite legal standard exists for determining where a "reasonable" expectation of exposure may exist, building owners and managers should monitor wherever there is visible deterioration of friable asbestos. Particularly with regard to the "excursion levels," owners and managers should monitor where any work involving ACM is taking place, unless those activities have been demonstrated to produce no exceedances. An owner or manager should consider conducting voluntary air monitoring in any building that was constructed prior to 1975 because of the prevalent use of asbestos-containing construction materials prior to this date. Inspection and monitoring may confirm a suspicion of a potential asbestos problem and provide the impetus for the adoption of appropriate operation and maintenance programs that will ensure compliance with the law. Inspection and monitoring, however, may prove that the suspect material does not contain asbestos and that the programs need not be put into place.

Renovation and Demolition

Buildings must be inspected for asbestos before demolition or renovation in order to comply with EPA's Asbestos National Emission Standard for Hazardous Air Pollutants.[46] Renovation, which may include maintenance and repair, and demolition of buildings containing asbestos is strictly regulated.[47] The regulations include not only requirements for notification of the activity and management of materials containing or potentially containing asbestos, but also include requirements for monitoring and controlling employee exposure.[48]

Most renovation and demolition activities involving asbestos are governed by the National Emission Standard for Hazardous Air Pollutants for Asbestos (Asbestos NESHAP). The state has supplemented the federal standards with additional requirements. For those activities not governed by the Asbestos NESHAP, the state has promulgated its own requirements to regulate the renovation, demolition, and encapsulation of asbestos.

---

[43] 29 C.F.R. §1910.1001(d)(2).

[44] 29 C.F.R. §1910.1001(a).

[45] COMAR 26.11.23.02.

[46] *See* 40 C.F.R. §61.145.

[47] 29 C.F.R. §1926.1101 (OSHA regulations for construction activities); 40 C.F.R. §61.140 (EPA regulations regarding renovation and demolition); 40 C.F.R. §763.91 (EPA regulations regarding response action in management of asbestos-containing materials in schools); 40 C.F.R. §763.120 (EPA regulations regarding asbestos abatement projects by employers of state and local government not covered by OSHA); MD. CODE, ENVIR. §6-401, *et seq.*; COMAR 26.11.21 (Maryland regulations for control of asbestos from an asbestos project).

[48] *Id.*

Notifications

The owner or operator of a facility[49] undergoing demolition that is subject to the Asbestos NESHAP is responsible for giving notification of the activity to EPA, regardless of the amount of regulated asbestos-containing materials (RACM) involved.[50] Even if a facility inspection reveals no RACM present, the facility must still notify EPA 10 days prior to demolition.[51] If a facility that is subject to the Asbestos NESHAP is undergoing renovation, the owner or operator must notify BEA if the activity involves the disturbance of at least 260 linear feet of RACM on pipes, 160 square feet of RACM on other facility components, or at least 1 cubic meter of RACM on facility components where the length or area could not be measured.[52] Renovation includes activities that alter a facility or a facility's components "in any way," and may include activities such as repair and maintenance.[53]

Owners or operators subject to the Asbestos NESHAP, through demolition or renovation activity, must also notify the Maryland Air and Radiation Management Administration if the renovation or demolition of the facility involves friable asbestos material.[54] Notification to the state is not required, however, if the activity involves the removal, encapsulation, or disturbance of less than 10 square feet or 20 linear feet of friable ACM and the activity is associated with small repairs or maintenance.[55]

Sources not subject to the Asbestos NESHAP (e.g., residential units with four or fewer dwelling units) must notify the Maryland Air and Radiation Management Administration of any activity involving the demolition, removal, stripping,[56] or encapsulation of friable asbestos materials.[57] If the activity involves encapsulation only, notification to the state is required only if the activity will encapsulate more than 160 square feet or 260 linear feet of asbestos.[58]

Notice should be sent to EPA and the Maryland Air and Radiation Management Administration as early as possible (and generally at least 10 days pursuant to EPA requirements) before a renovation or demolition begins.[59] The notice must describe the type of operation (i.e., renovation or demolition); describe the size, age, location, and present and prior use of the facility; and identify both the owner or operator of the facility and the contractor, including name, address, and telephone number.[60] The notification also must estimate the amount of RACM present at the site and describe the work methods and compliance procedures to be used, as well as provide the scheduled

---

[49] "Facility" does not include residential buildings with four or fewer dwelling units. 40 C.F.R. §61.141.

[50] 40 C.F.R. §61.145(b); COMAR 26.11.21.03. Limited notification is required when the combined amount of RACM involved is less than 260 linear feet on pipes, less than 160 square feet on other facility components, and less than 35 cubic feet of facility components where the length or areas could not be measured previously or there is no asbestos. See 40 C.F.R. §61.145(a)(2).

[51] See 40 C.F.R. §61.145(b)(3)(i).

[52] 40 C.F.R. §61.145(a)(4).

[53] 40 C.F.R. §61.141.

[54] COMAR 26.11.21.03A.

[55] COMAR 26.11.21.03D and 26.11.21.01I.

[56] COMAR 26.11.21.01L.

[57] COMAR 26.11.21.03C and 26.11.21.03D.

[58] COMAR 26.11.21.03B.

[59] 40 C.F.R. §61.145(b)(3); MD. CODE, ENVIR. §6-414.1(a); COMAR 26.11.21.03.

[60] 40 C.F.R. §61.145(b)(4).

start and completion date of the removal project.[61] The notification also must provide the name and location of the waste disposal site to be used.[62] In addition, various other data elements must be included in the notification depending on the circumstances surrounding the activity. One should check the regulations prior to making a notification on a specific activity to ensure that all the requirements are met.

Management of Asbestos Emissions from a Facility Subject to Asbestos NESHAP

EPA has promulgated regulations governing the removal of RACM from facilities subject to the Asbestos NESHAP.[63] The requirements include, among other things: removing all RACM from a facility before beginning any activity that may break up, dislodge, or similarly disturb the material, if possible; adequately wetting any RACM during cutting, separation, or stripping; and carefully handling any RACM so as not to drop, throw, slide, or otherwise disturb or damage the material. Exceptions to these procedures may be used if other requirements are met.[64] In addition, there are additional requirements for special situations such as removal of large facility components (e.g., large tanks and steam generators);[65] periods when temperatures are below freezing;[66] demolition of buildings or structures by order of the state because they are structurally unsound;[67] and demolition by intentional burning.[68] In addition, there must be a person trained in the requirements of the regulations on-site at all times activities are occurring.[69]

Maryland regulations supplement the federal standards with additional requirements for asbestos projects (i.e., removal of friable asbestos).[70] Facilities subject to the Asbestos NESHAP must also post "Danger Signs" and "Project Notification Signs."[71]

Small Projects (Less Than 260 Linear Feet or 160 Square Feet of ACM)

On any project involving the stripping or removal of less than 260 linear or 160 square feet of friable asbestos material, the licensee is required to take reasonable precautions to prevent asbestos from becoming airborne.[72] Examples of reasonable precautions include wetting the asbestos with a surfactant, isolating and containing the asbestos to be removed, and using appropriate work practices to minimize the dispersal of particulate asbestos. When the project is complete, there should be no visible residue

---

[61] *Id.*; COMAR 26.11.21.03B and .03C.
[62] 40 C.F.R. §61.145; COMAR 26.11.21.03. The NESHAP regulations also require notice of the procedures used for detecting the presence of ACMs, the procedures to be used to comply with the NESHAP, the procedures to be followed if unexpected ACMs are encountered, and the estimated volume of ACM to be generated.
[63] 40 C.F.R §61.145(c).
[64] See, e.g., 40 C.F.R. §61.145(c)(5).
[65] 40 C.F.R. §61.145(c)(5).
[66] 40 C.F.R. §61.145(c)(7).
[67] 40 C.F.R. §61.145(c)(9).
[68] 40 C.F.R. §61.145(c)(10).
[69] 40 C.F.R. §61.145(c)(8).
[70] COMAR 26.11.21.06.
[71] COMAR 26.11.21.06.
[72] COMAR 26.11.21.07A.

of asbestos. Following the OSHA guidelines for employee safety will ordinarily keep the licensee in compliance with the emission control requirements for small projects.[73]

Asbestos Waste Disposal

The following disposal procedures should be followed: all waste from the asbestos project must be deposited in plastic bags, of specified thickness and the bags sealed. All insulation, wallboard, tiles, used protective clothing, filters, tape, plastic sheeting, etc. should be included. Objects that cannot be bagged must be wrapped in plastic sheeting. The waste should be labeled with the contractor license number and the date of sealing.[74] Additionally, a caution label identifying the waste as asbestos and warning against opening the container or breathing asbestos particles must be attached.[75] Waste from small project sites must be removed within 24 hours of the project's conclusion. Waste from large projects must be removed within seven days after completion. All waste must be transported to a state-approved disposal facility, if disposed of in Maryland, and a copy of the disposal manifest must be submitted to the Department within 10 days.[76]

At the time of application for licensing, the applicant may request authorization to store asbestos in rigid containers on an interim basis. If granted, authorization is limited to no more than 20 cubic yards of waste. Such authorization is at the sole discretion of MDE.[77]

Cleanup of Asbestos Material

All asbestos material must be removed and properly disposed of following project completion. Before removing any plastic barriers, all surfaces in the work area must be cleaned with a wetting solution and, once dry, vacuumed with a high-efficiency particulate air (HEPA) filter–equipped vacuum to remove any visible residue.[78]

After cleanup, air monitoring must be performed to ensure that the airborne concentration of asbestos fibers longer than 5 microns is less than .01 fibers per cubic centimeter, using the specified procedures. Barriers may not be removed if monitoring indicates a higher concentration of fibers. Final monitoring results must be submitted in writing to the Maryland Air and Radiation Management Administration.[79]

Penalties

Any person who willfully violates any of the Maryland provisions for the licensing of contractors or control and disposal of asbestos may be subject to a $25,000 civil

[73] 29 C.F.R. §§1926.1101, *et seq.*
[74] COMAR 26.11.21.08.
[75] 40 C.F.R. §61.150(a)(l)(iv).
[76] COMAR 26.11.21.08B and D. The federal NESHAP regulations require all ACM waste generators to keep detailed records for at least two years of the quantity of waste generated, place and date of disposal, and the name of the transporter. 40 C.F.R. §61.150.
[77] COMAR 26.11.21.08C.
[78] COMAR 2611.21.06B(3).
[79] *Id.*

penalty per violation. Each day a project is in violation constitutes a separate violation. Subsequent willful violations constitute a misdemeanor subject to a fine of up to $25,000 and/or two years' imprisonment.[80]

Under federal law, civil penalties can be issued at levels not to exceed $27,500 per violation, with each day constituting a separate violation.[81] Criminal penalties can be imposed for knowing or willful violations, for which similar fines can be imposed, and a potential additional penalty of imprisonment for up to one year.[82]

Employee Protection

The federal Occupational Safety and Health Administration (OSHA) promulgated comprehensive asbestos worker protection standards codified at 29 C.F.R. §1910.1001 for general industry employees, at 29 C.F.R. §1926.1101 for construction employees, and at §1915.1001 for shipyard employees.

In 2000, OSHA promulgated revisions to the Asbestos Worker Protection Rule (WPR),[83] which provides the same level of protection to state and local government employees as non-governmental employees protected by OSHA's comprehensive Asbestos Worker Protection Standards.[84] The revisions to the WPR incorporate by reference OSHA Asbestos Standards for Construction and for General Industry set out at 29 C.F.R. §1926.1101 and 29 C.F.R. §1910.1001, respectively.

The Maryland Occupational Safety and Health Administration (MOSH) adopted by reference the revised federal OSHA standards for occupational exposure to asbestos.[85] As a result, any Maryland employer engaged in any activity likely to involve asbestos exposure, demolition, asbestos abatement, building renovation, and even routine maintenance and repair operations, must comply with relevant portions of the standards. Many of the requirements of the Maryland emission control regulations can be met by compliance with the standards for employee exposure.

Presumed ACM or PACM

The revised OSHA standards establish a rebuttable presumption that certain materials contain asbestos and are, therefore, subject to OSHA's management standards. PACM or "presumed ACM" means thermal system insulation (TSI), sprayed or troweled-on surfacing material (such as fireproofing material on steel beams or acoustical ceiling plaster), resilient flooring, and debris from asbestos removal/repair work activities and from areas where ACM/PACM is not intact.[86] The presumption applies in buildings and vessels constructed before 1980.

---

[80] MD. CODE, ENVIR. §6-422.

[81] 40 C.F.R. §19.4.

[82] 15 U.S.C. §2615.

[83] OSHA promulgated the first WPR in 1987, which only provided limited protection to state and local employees not covered by an OSHA-approved state plan. See Fed. Reg. 69,210 (November 15, 2000).

[84] 40 C.F.R., Part 763; see also 65 Fed. Reg. 69,210 (November 15, 2000).

[85] COMAR 09.12.20.

[86] 29 C.F.R. §1926.1101(b).

Establishing a Regulated Area

The employer must establish a regulated area designated by sign and enclosure for each area where airborne concentrations of asbestos exceed or can reasonably be expected to exceed either the short-term "excursion limit" or the long-term "time weighted average" limit (TWA).[87] The TWA is 0.1 fibers per cubic centimeter of air as an eight-hour time weighted average. The excursion limit is 1.0 fiber per cubic centimeter, averaged over a 30-minute sampling period.[88] Collectively the excursion limit and TWA are called the permissible exposure limits (PEL).

The regulated area must be demarcated in a manner that minimizes the number of persons in the area and protects persons outside the area from exposure to airborne concentrations of asbestos.[89] Other employees who share the same facility must be made aware of the nature of the asbestos work being performed at the project site and informed that access to the regulated area is limited to authorized persons.[90]

Warning signs must demarcate the regulated area so that an employee reading a sign can take any necessary protective steps prior to entering the area.[91] Waste containers and all asbestos-containing material, where feasible, must carry a warning label.[92]

Enclosing a Regulated Area

Wherever feasible, the employer shall establish a negative-pressure enclosure before commencing removal, demolition, and renovation operations. A "competent person" fully trained in asbestos abatement procedures must perform or supervise the setting up of the enclosure, ensure the integrity of the enclosure, control access to the area, and ensure that the employees are using appropriate protective clothing and respirators.[93] All employee exposure must be monitored, and employees must be trained in the use of engineering controls, work practices, and personal protective equipment.[94] The "competent person" must be trained in asbestos management and safety practices through an EPA-approved course.[95]

MOSH standards require hygiene facilities for persons working within the enclosure. There must be a decontamination area containing a clean (change) room, an equipment room for the storage of contaminated equipment and for the removal and disposal of contaminated equipment and protective clothing, and a shower facility connecting the two rooms.[96]

---

[87] 29 C.F.R. §§1926.1101(c)(1) and (2).
[88] *Id.*
[89] 29 C.F.R. §1926.1101.
[90] 29 C.F.R. §1926.1101(d) and (e)(3).
[91] 29 C.F.R. §1926.1101(k)(7).
[92] 29 C.F.R. §1926.1101(k)(7).
[93] 29 C.F.R. §1926.1101(o). The federal NESHAP regulations require all demolitions and NESHAP-source renovations have at least one trained individual on-site during any ACM work. 40 C.F.R. §61.145. This requirement supplements, but does not replace, the OSHA "competent person" rule. The federal OSHA rules also require the continual presence of a "competent" person for the most hazardous work.
[94] 29 C.F.R. §1926.1101(k)(9).
[95] 29 C.F.R. §§1926.1101(b) and 1926.1101(0).
[96] 29 C.F.R. §19261101l(j).

Classes of Asbestos Work

OSHA established four classes of asbestos work based on their relative hazards. *Class I* work means the removal of thermal system insulation (TSI), sprayed or troweled-on surfacing asbestos-containing material, and "presumed ACM."[97] Activities in this high-risk category include, for example, the removal of decorative ceiling plaster, fireproofing on structural steel, and asbestos-laden insulated pipes, tanks, and boilers, as well as demolition operations involving these materials.

Class II work means the removal of asbestos-containing material that is *not* TSI or surfacing ACM.[98] Activities in this category include the removal of resilient flooring, ceiling tiles, siding, shingles, roofing felts, transite panels, and cement pastes.

Class III work means maintenance and repair activities involving the potential or intentional disturbance or disruption of ACM/PACM, including TSI and surfacing material. Activities in this category are limited to the incidental cutting or disturbance (less than a standard glove or waste bag) of ACM/PACM during the course of routine repair or maintenance efforts.

Class IV work means maintenance and custodial activities during which employees come into contact with ACM/PACM or asbestos-contaminated waste in an incidental fashion.[99] Activities in this category include dusting or vacuuming surfaces, mopping or buffing resilient flooring, cleaning up ACM/PACM debris from TSI or surfacing ACM, or cleaning up ACM/PACM after an asbestos removal job.

Required Work Practices

Several specific fiber control methods are specified for Class I work (i.e., the removal of TSI and surfacing ACM). These control methods are:

- Negative pressure enclosure systems of any configuration, in which air movement is directed away from the work source and toward a HEPA filtration collection device.
- Glove bag systems used to remove ACM/PACM from piping. Glove bags are made from six mil plastic and must be smoke-tested before use. Each glove bag may be used only once and must be collapsed prior to disposal by means of a HEPA vacuum.
- Negative pressure glove bag systems also used to remove ACM/PACM from piping. This control method uses the same work practices as regular glove bag systems.
- Negative pressure glove box systems built from rigid material capable of withstanding the cumulative weight of ACM/PACM and removal water. The box is outfitted with glove apertures, a HEPA filtration system, and a bagging outlet.

---

[97] 29 C.F.R. §1926.1101(b).
[98] *Id.*
[99] *Id.*

- Water spray process systems, in which 360° high-pressure water spray forms a liquid aerosol barrier between the worker and the ACM/PACM. Removal and bagging activities are to be performed inside the water barrier by at least two highly trained individuals, while a third person checks the continued proper operation of the system.
- Mini-enclosure systems. If the ACM/PACM disturbance or removal can be contained by a portable, isolated enclosure that accommodates no more than two persons, then this control method may be used. The enclosure must be built of 6 mil plastic or its equivalent, placed under negative pressure by a HEPA-fitted vacuum or similar venting unit, inspected for leaks before use, and, after use, completely washed and HEPA vacuumed.

- If another dust isolation or containment control method is used, or a listed method is modified, a certified industrial hygienist or licensed professional engineer/project designer must certify to the enforcement agency the safety of the alternate method, using the criteria set forth in §1926.1101(g).[100]

Class II work—the removal of ACM/PACM that is *not* TSI or surfacing ACM (i.e., asbestos-containing wallboard or transite panels, floor tile, siding, shingles, and roofing felts)—poses fewer asbestos exposure risks than Class I work. Accordingly, the control methods are somewhat less rigorous.

- HEPA-equipped vacuums, wet methods (continual misting of the points of operation), and prompt ACM/PACM waste containment and disposal are universal precautions to be observed, as is the use of barriers across regulated area openings and impermeable drop cloths. Certain operations, such as the removal of ACM/PACM flooring, paneling, and roofing, involve additional work precautions. Sanding, dry sweeping, and dry scraping are prohibited, as is the cutting, ripping, breaking, or abrasion of resilient materials, siding, shingles, or wallboard.[101]

Class III work—the repair and maintenance of building or equipment components containing previously installed ACM/PACM—includes work performed on boilers, air handling units, heat exchangers, and gasket or valve replacements; activities performed above suspended ceilings or on insulated pipes or conduits; and the replacement of light fixtures or ceiling tiles. As a general matter, work operations must minimize employee and bystander exposures and feature the use of wet methods, local exhaust ventilation, respirators, impermeable drop cloths, and mini-enclosure or glove bag systems.[102]

---

100 29 C.F.R. §1926.1101(g).
101 29 C.F.R. §§1926.110l(g)(7) and (8).
102 29 C.F.R. §1926.1101(g)(9).

Class IV work includes any maintenance or custodial activity during which employees may contact ACM/PACM in the form of debris or waste from friable or disturbed asbestos-containing materials. Asbestos awareness training must be provided to all Class IV workers; wet methods of housekeeping, HEPA vacuums, and prompt clean-up practices are required. When a custodial worker is assigned to a Class I, II, or III location where respirators are used, the custodian also must be provided with and wear a respirator, selected, used, and fit-tested in accordance with the requirements of the standard.[103]

The regulations permit alternate work practices and controls so long as the employer can demonstrate with data that the employee exposure during the use of alternate methods will not exceed the PELs.[104]

Employee Exposure Monitoring

Prior to commencing an activity likely to involve asbestos exposure, an initial assessment must be performed by a "competent person" to ascertain expected asbestos exposures. A "competent person" means an individual capable of identifying existing asbestos hazards in the workplace, selecting the control strategies, and exercising authority to take prompt corrective measures to eliminate exposures.[105] The initial assessment must be completed in time to comply with requirements, which are triggered by exposure data or the lack of a "negative exposure assessment."[106]

The initial assessment must include, if feasible, exposure monitoring of employees, as well as consideration of all observations, information, or calculations that indicate employee asbestos exposure, including previous monitoring results. For Class I asbestos work, the employer must presume exposures exceed the PEL, until exposure monitoring is conducted or a negative assessment is completed demonstrating otherwise.[107] The employer may demonstrate exposures are below PEL's by performing a "negative exposure assessment" by compiling data conforming to and satisfying one of three sets of criteria.[108]

In Class I and Class II asbestos work, the employer must continue exposure monitoring daily, unless the employer can satisfactorily make a negative exposure assessment. For all asbestos work other than Class I or II, the employer must conduct periodic monitoring at intervals sufficient to document the validity of the exposure prediction.[109] This ongoing monitoring may be discontinued if employees are provided with positive pressure–supplied air respirators, or if statistically reliable measurements indicate employee exposures are below the PEL.[110]

---

[103] 29 C.F.R. §§1926.1101(g)(10) and (h).
[104] See, e.g., 29 C.F.R. §1926.1101(g)(8)(vi).
[105] 29 C.F.R. §1926.1101(b).
[106] 29 C.F.R. §1926.1101(f)(2)(i).
[107] 29 C.F.R. §1926.1101(f)(2)(ii).
[108] 29 C.F.R. §1926.1101(f)(2)(iii).
[109] 29 C.F.R. §1929.1101(f)(3).
[110] 29 C.F.R. §§1929.1101(f)(3)(iii) and 1101(f)(4)(i).

Respirators and Protective Clothing[111]

The regulations require the employer to provide and ensure the use of respirators by employees in the following circumstances:

1. During all Class I asbestos jobs.
2. During Class II asbestos jobs where ACM is not removed substantially intact.
3. During Class II and III work not utilizing wet methods.
4. During Class II and III work where there has been no negative exposure assessment.
5. During Class III work where TSI or surfacing ACM or PACM is disturbed.
6. During Class IV work in regulated areas where other employees are required to use respirators.
7. During all work covered by the standard whenever exposure levels exceed a PEL.
8. During emergencies.[112]

Respirators and associated equipment must be supplied at no cost to the employee.[113] Appropriate respirators must be selected by the employer.[114] Employees must wear protective clothing, such as head and foot coverings and coveralls, whenever exposed to asbestos levels in excess of the PEL.[115] While federal standards direct the employer to inform launderers that the protective clothing is contaminated,[116] Maryland regulations circumvent this issue by requiring the use of disposable protective clothing at asbestos projects[117] (i.e., those projects involving friable asbestos). In addition, Maryland regulations require that the business entity or public unit provide protective clothing to workers and supervisors.[118]

Excessive Exposure

Employers must incorporate all feasible engineering controls and work practices that serve to reduce the amount of asbestos fiber in the air to a level below the PEL.[119] Such practices and controls include: using local exhaust ventilation with a HEPA filter for all power tools used in the projects; the prompt disposal of waste in leak-tight containers; and the use of wet methods and good general housecleaning practices whenever asbestos-containing materials are handled, cut, removed, or cleaned up.[120] These methods must be utilized regardless of the levels of exposure.

Medical surveillance is mandatory for any construction employee who is exposed to asbestos at or above the TWA and/or the excursion limit for more than 30 days per

---

[111] See 29 C.F.R. §1926.1101; 40 C.F.R. §763.120; 40 C.F.R. §763.91(b) (application of OSHA regulations in 29 C.F.R. §1926.1101 or EPA regulations in 40 C.F.R. §763.120, whichever is applicable, to local school agencies.

[112] 29 C.F.R. §1926.1101(h)(l).

[113] *See* 29 C.F.R. §1910.134(c)(4).

[114] 29 C.F.R. §1926.1101(h)(3).

[115] 29 C.F.R. §1926.1101(i).

[116] 29 C.F.R. §1926.1101(i)(2).

[117] COMAR 26.11.21.05D(l).

[118] COMAR 26.11.21.05D.

[119] 29 C.F.R. §1926.1101(g).

[120] *Id.*

year, and who is required to wear a negative pressure respirator or who engages in Class I, II, or III asbestos work.[121] Prior to assignment to an area where negative pressure respirators must be worn or within 10 days following the 30th day of exposure above the PEL, a licensed physician must perform, at no cost to the employee, an initial medical examination, which must be repeated at least annually thereafter.[122] The exams must include a complete physical, with emphasis on the digestive tract, cardiovascular system, and respiratory system.[123] The employer must obtain, and make available to the employee, a written opinion assessing the employee's health risks and any medical conditions resulting from exposure to asbestos, any recommended limitations on the employee's use of protective equipment, a statement that the employee was informed of the results and of the increased risk of lung cancer attributable to the combined effects of smoking and asbestos exposure.[124]

If it is likely that an employee will be exposed to asbestos in excess of the TWA and/or the excursion limit, the employer must provide initial and annual training requirements by MOSH.[125] This training requirement is similar to that required by MDE regulations governing control of asbestos emissions during asbestos projects.[126] A training course approved by MDE will likely encompass the MOSH requirements; nonetheless, care should be taken to ensure compliance with both programs.

Generally, MOSH requires training in the following areas: identification of asbestos-containing material; health effects associated with asbestos exposure; appropriate engineering controls and work practices, including proper disposal procedures; operation of respirators and use of protective clothing; employer responsibilities as to medical surveillance; and the content of regulations governing work with asbestos.[127] Training materials must be made accessible to all employees at no cost.[128]

Record-Keeping Requirements

Employers must maintain records of employee exposure monitoring for a period of 30 years.[129] Medical surveillance records must be maintained for the duration of an employee's employment plus an additional thirty years.[130] Employee training records must be maintained for the duration of an employee's employment plus one year.[131] Upon written request, the employer must make the medical training and exposure monitoring records available to the employee, or anyone having the employee's written consent, for examination and copying.[132] If the employer goes out of business before a prescribed period elapses and has no successor, the employer must notify

121 29 C.F.R. §1926.1101(m)(l)(i).
122 29 C.F.R. §1926.1101(m)(2)(i).
123 29 C.F.R. §1926.1101(m)(2)(ii).
124 29 C.F.R. §1926.110l(m)(4)(i).
125 29 C.F.R. §1926.1101(k)(9).
126 See COMAR 26.11.21.05C.
127 29 C.F.R. §1926.110l(k)(9).
128 29 C.F.R. §1926.110l(k)(9)(i).
129 29 C.F.R. §1926.1101(n)(2)(iii).
130 29 C.F.R. §1926.110l(n)(3)(iii).
131 29 C.F.R. §1926.1101(n)(4).
132 29 C.F.R. §1926.1101(n)(7).

the Maryland Commissioner of Labor and Industry 90 days prior to disposal of the records and, if so requested, transfer them to the Maryland Division of Labor and Industry.[133] Building owners must maintain written records of information received concerning the identification, location, and quantity of ACM or PACM for the duration of ownership and transfer these records to the successive owner.[134]

RADON

Radon is an odorless naturally occurring gas that is a by-product of the deterioration of underground uranium. High levels of exposure may result in an increased risk of lung cancer.

Suggested Standards

At the present time there are neither federal nor state established "safe" levels for radon. EPA, on an advisory basis, recommends that remedial steps to decrease radon levels should be taken where the exposure level exceeds 4.0 picocuries per liter of air.

Responding to Excessive Radon

If the initial screening results for a building exceed the EPA suggested standard of 4.0 picocuries, then more detailed follow-up testing should begin immediately. If both the initial and follow-up testing indicate that radon levels in a building exceed the EPA standard, then an abatement plan, usually consisting of either creating an airtight barrier between the ground and the building or improving the building's outdoor/indoor air exchange and circulation, should be implemented. While there currently are no federal or Maryland certification programs for radon abatement training, there are a number of reputable environmental consulting firms and contractors that can design and execute an adequate plan.

Governmental Action

The Maryland General Assembly has considered, but not passed, bills that would require all radon testing facilities to be certified by MDE. Maryland Environment Code §8-305 requires that all non-self-analyzing radon test devices be analyzed by a facility listed in the latest round of the EPA Radon/Radon Progeny Measurement Proficiency Program. Maryland provides financial assistance to low-income parties for radon abatement through a loan program.[135]

At the federal level, EPA has established a radon information clearinghouse; created a model program for controlling radon exposure in new construction and

---

133 29 C.F.R. §1926.110l(n)(8)(ii).

134 29 C.F.R. §1926.1101(n)(6). The OSHA standards require the identification of certain materials presumed to contain asbestos. 29 C.F.R. §1926.1101(k)(l).

135 MD. CODE, Art. 83B, §62.

remediating radon levels in existing buildings; and established a certification program for radon measurement devices and a proficiency program for their use. EPA has also commissioned a study of the health effects of radon in schools and federal buildings.

OTHER INDOOR AIR POLLUTANTS

A variety of other indoor air pollutants (IAPs) beyond asbestos and radon have attracted national attention. They include: formaldehyde and other volatile organic compounds (VOCs), ozone, pesticides, solvents, fiberglass particles, dust, molds and fungi, carbon monoxide, and all other hazardous substances that may be found in a building (including cigarette smoke).

Indicia of IAPs

The most common way for IAPs to manifest themselves is through what is known as Sick Building Syndrome (SBS) or Building Related Illness (BRI). Persons having SBS claim symptoms such as headaches; fatigue; eye, nose, throat, and/or skin irritation; shortness of breath; coughing; sneezing; and nausea. According to the generally accepted definition of the American Society of Heating, Refrigeration and Air Conditioning Engineers (ASHRAE), SBS is suspected when, for at least two weeks, 20 percent or more of a building's occupants complain of any of the same symptoms and the cause is unknown.

Newly Constructed Buildings

New construction may suffer from acute IAP problems.[136] These problems will manifest themselves in building occupants through the same types of symptoms as SBS. The reason for this is the presence of VOCs in petrochemically based construction and furnishing materials. These materials can emit VOCs at levels up to 100 times higher than those found in the ambient outdoor air and up to 30 to 50 times higher than those found in older buildings. While VOC levels were found to decrease over time, up to a ten-fold reduction in the first two months after installation, it took anywhere from 3 to 12 months for VOC levels to reach the levels found in "old" buildings.

The types of materials primarily responsible for the emission of VOCs are molding and carpet adhesives; latex caulks and paints; vinyl and rubber moldings; prefabricated partitions; and cleaning solutions. Secondary emitters may include telephone cable, linoleum, carpet, and particle board.

State or Federal Laws

Since the IAPs that contribute to SBS often are present at relatively low levels, currently no state or federal laws or regulations, such as OSHA's various permissible

---

[136] EPA, Indoor Air Quality in Public Buildings (1988).

exposure limits or the American Conference of Governmental Industrial Hygienists' threshold limit values for many industrial VOCs and toxics, are applicable.

MOLD

Although there are currently no federal or Maryland standards specifically regulating exposure to mold, the trend in Maryland, as with a number of other states, is increased governmental effort to regulate mold, increased effort by insurers to exclude mold-related claims from coverage, and increased numbers of plaintiff suits alleging both property damage and illness caused by mold.

There are over 100,000 species of mold, approximately 50 of which are toxic to human health. Molds and other fungi are ubiquitous in the environment, with outdoor concentrations typically higher than indoor concentrations, unless an indoor source of mold exists.[137] Because conditions favorable for the growth of indoor mold are quite common (moisture, oxygen, light, and a suitable substrate),[138] it is not very surprising that indoor mold is also fairly common.

LEAD PAINT

Maryland has adopted comprehensive legislation relating to the maintenance and inspection of lead paint in rental housing.[139] Under that legislation, landlords of properties constructed before 1950 must take certain steps to protect tenants from exposure to lead paint.[140] These steps include registration with MDE, inspection and certification of the house as lead-free or lead-safe,[141] and annual renewals of registration.[142]

In addition, the MDE regulates the process of abating lead-based paint from residential properties and day care centers.[143] The regulations set standards for abatement methods and procedures for determining compliance.[144]

Federal Requirements

EPA has developed various guidance materials related to lead-based paint hazards. These guidance materials include a lead hazard information pamphlet. This pamphlet, or an equivalent EPA-approved pamphlet, must be provided to purchasers and tenants of all housing constructed before 1978. In addition, a lead warning statement must

---

137 Maryland State Task Force on Indoor Air Quality, Final Report, July 1, 2002, pp. 10–11.
138 *Id.*
139 MD CODE, ENVIR. §§6-801 *et seq.*
140 COMAR 26.16.02.
141 The inspection must be conducted by a state-accredited lead paint inspector or risk assessor (COMAR 26.16.01). Lead-free housing contains no lead paint, except factory-applied coatings on metal components (COMAR 26.16.02.05). "Lead-safe" refers to housing built after 1978 or housing with lead-free windows and a satisfactory inspection for lead-contaminated dust (COMAR 26.16.02.0). Lead-safe certification is effective for two years.
142 MD. CODE, ENVIR. §6-812.
143 COMAR 26.02.07.
144 COMAR 26.02.07.12.

be included in every contract for the purchase and sale of any pre-1978 housing, and purchasers must sign a statement that they have read and understood the warning statement, received the lead hazard pamphlet, and had 10 days to inspect the house. If a seller is represented by a real estate agent, the Act expressly places the burden of compliance on the agent.[145]

In 1992 Congress also adopted amendments to the Toxic Substances Control Act—the "Lead-Based Paint Exposure Act."[146] As directed in the act, EPA adopted regulations governing lead-based paint and the certification of contractors.[147] In addition, EPA developed renovation and remodeling guidelines applicable to all residential and commercial buildings constructed before 1978.[148] These guidelines are distributed through paint and hardware stores, employee organizations and trade groups, state and local governments, and other appropriate means. In addition, beginning in April 1996, the lead hazard information pamphlet also was required to be provided to persons having renovations performed on pre-1978 housing by paid contractors.

Enforcement Powers

The Residential Lead-Based Paint Hazard Reduction Act provides three enforcement mechanisms for "knowingly" violating the disclosure requirements: (1) civil monetary penalties; (2) injunctive relief by HUD; and (3) civil money damages up to treble damages. The Act also provides for recovery of court costs, attorney fees, and expert witness fees.[149]

Contractors who fail to provide information on lead hazards to homeowners pursuant to federal requirements could face penalties of up to $11,000 for failing to comply with the disclosure requirements.[150] In addition, violators may be subject to civil and criminal sanctions pursuant to the Toxic Substances Control Act for each violation. These provisions provide for additional penalties of up to $11,000.[151]

State Requirements for Rental Housing

The Lead Poisoning Prevention[152] bill required MDE to establish a lead poisoning prevention program under which owners of "affected properties" (principally rental housing constructed before 1950) are required to register those properties with MDE.[153] Under these requirements, affected property owners must register each affected property with MDE, using appropriate state forms. The registration requires information to be provided to the owner; address of the affected property; property

---

145 42 U.S.C. §4852d(a)(4).
146 15 U.S.C. §§2681–2688.
147 40 C.F.R. part 745.
148 EPA, Reducing Lead Hazards When Remodeling Your Home (April 1994).
149 42 U.S.C. §§4852d(b)(3), (b)(4).
150 40 C.F.R. §745.118.
151 *Id.*, 40 C.F.R. §745.118(f).
152 MD. CODE, ENVIR. §§6-801 through 6-852, and 6-1001 through 6-1005.
153 MD. CODE, ENVIR. §6-811. "Affected property" means a property constructed before 1950 that contains at least one rental dwelling unit and any other residential rental property that the owner elects to bring into compliance with the law.

managers, if applicable; insurance coverage; age of the property; date of latest change in occupancy; lead reduction treatments performed to attain or maintain the state risk reduction standard; and the date of last certification of compliance with the risk reduction standard. This registration must be renewed annually.

Risk Reduction Requirements

Owners of affected rental property must verify compliance with the risk reduction standards by either conducting an inspection for lead-contaminated dust or by conducting a visual inspection using methods specified in COMAR 26.16.02. The inspection for lead-contaminated dust must be conducted by an accredited lead paint inspector[154] and involves a laboratory analysis of dust samples, collected and tested according to specified methods.[155] MDE must be notified 24 hours in advance of lead dust testing. The visual inspection must be conducted by an accredited lead paint visual inspector or lead paint risk assessor, using the specified methods. Property owners must obtain, record, and maintain specified information regarding contractors, supervisors, or workers involved in any lead hazard reduction treatment.[156] Contractors must submit a copy of the certificate of compliance to MDE within 10 days following an inspection.

Housing can be certified as lead-free after an inspection verifies that: (1) the interior is certified lead-free; (2) all exterior painted surfaces of the affected property that were chipping, peeling, and flaking have been restored; and (3) no exterior painted surfaces are chipping, peeling, or flaking. Every two years, the property must be re-certified.[157] An inspection for lead content in paint must be conducted by an accredited lead paint inspector technician or lead paint risk assessor.

The law provides that if owners are in compliance with the risk reduction program, they can achieve significant protection from lawsuits. A person may not bring a suit against a property owner for injury caused by lead unless: (1) elevated blood lead levels exceed 25 micrograms per deciliter (lowered to 20 ug/dl by February 24, 2001), and (2) written notice has been given to the landlord giving him an opportunity to make a "qualified offer."[158] The qualified offer must include an offer to reimburse medical expenses, relocation expenses, and similar expenses, but the maximum that the landlord or its insurer is required to pay is $17,000.[159]

The law also provides for the creation of a lead poisoning prevention fund, to be funded by an annual fee for an affected property of $30 and an annual fee of $5 for certain properties that are "not affected" until such time as the owner certifies that the property is lead-free.[160] At least part of the annual fees collected is dedicated to community outreach and education.[161]

---

154 COMAR 26.16.01.
155 COMAR 26.16.01 .03B.
156 COMAR 26.16.02.03C(5).
157 COMAR 26.16.02.01–.07.
158 MD. CODE, ENVIR. §6-828.
159 MD. CODE, ENVIR. §§6-839 and 6-840.
160 MD. CODE, ENVIR §§6-843 and 6-844.
161 MD. CODE, ENVIR. §6-848.

Chapter 10

Criminal Liability under Environmental Statutes

STATUTORY PROVISIONS

Illegal Acts

CERCLA provides criminal sanctions for owners and operators of a facility at which hazardous substances are stored, treated, or disposed of who fail to provide proper notice of the existence of such a facility and who fail to maintain adequate records. It also imposes liability for failure to provide the required notice of a hazardous substance spill, or for providing false or misleading information in the notice.[1]

RCRA provides severe criminal sanctions for storing, treating, or disposing of any hazardous waste without a permit or in violation of a condition or requirement of the permit. It also imposes liability upon transporters for transporting any hazardous waste without a permit, or to a facility that does not have a permit, or in violation of any condition in the permit. Generators of hazardous waste are subject to criminal liability for arranging for the transport of hazardous waste by an unpermitted transporter or to a facility without a permit, or in violation of any condition in the permit.[2] The Maryland Controlled Hazardous Substances statute prohibits the same conduct.[3] In addition to permit violations, both the federal and state statutes make criminal the violation of any regulations promulgated under the statute.[4]

The Clean Air Act establishes criminal liability for violation of an applicable implementation plan after notice, and for violation of permit conditions and certain orders.[5] The Clean Air Act is especially tough on violators because no leniency is provided for facilities that investigate and report their own emissions violations.

The Clean Water Act provides criminal sanctions for discharging without a permit, for violation of any permit condition for a direct discharger, and for introducing into a publicly owned treatment works (POTW) any pollutant that causes the POTW to

1 42 U.S.C. §9603(b), (c), (d)(2).
2 42 U.S.C. §6928(d), (e).
3 MD CODE, ENVIR. §7-265.
4 42 U.S.C. §6928(d), (e); MD CODE ANN., ENVIR. §7-267(a).
5 42 U.S.C. §7413(c).

exceed effluent limitations or conditions in its permit.[6] The Maryland water pollution statute imposes criminal sanctions for violating any rule, statute, regulation, order, or permit and for failing to perform duties imposed by law.[7]

Record-Keeping Requirements

Each of the environmental statutes mentioned above provides a criminal penalty for failure to comply with record-making and record-keeping requirements or for submitting false or misleading information on required records.

STANDARDS FOR CONVICTION

Criminal liability standards under environmental laws differ significantly from conventional standards of criminality. Conviction generally does not require proof of evil intent. The federal statutes use words such as "knowingly" or "negligently," but judicial interpretations often impute knowledge to the alleged wrongdoer based on his or her position or responsibilities. The state statutes do not expressly require any showing of knowledge or intent, and thus the state will argue that these statutes impose strict liability.

"Knowing" Violation of the Law

Each of the federal environmental statutes imposes criminal liability for a "knowing" violation. Courts have agreed that this does not require proof that the defendant knew his actions were illegal. Rather, knowledge may be inferred by the jury (or judge) in circumstances where the defendant should have known.

In *United States v. Johnson & Towers, Inc.*,[8] the corporation and two employees were charged with criminal violations of RCRA for dumping cleaning solvents from the company's engine overhauling operation into a tributary of the Delaware River. Although the Court held that the individual defendants could not be convicted unless they knew the company was required to have a permit and knew that it did not, it went on to hold that such knowledge could be inferred from their handling of hazardous wastes.

In *United States v. Hayes International Corp.*,[9] an airplane refurbishing company and the individual employee responsible for arranging for disposal of the company's hazardous waste were charged with criminal violations of RCRA for contracting for the disposal of hazardous wastes that were later found to have been dumped illegally. The Court held that the defendants could be convicted without knowledge of the permit status of the disposal facility and the transporter, if they knowingly failed to determine the permit status. Thus, the *Hayes* Court imposed an affirmative duty to

---

[6] 33 U.S.C. §1319(c).

[7] MD CODE, ENVIR. §9-343.

[8] 741 F.2d 662 (3rd Cir. 1984), *cert. denied*, 105 S. Ct. 1171 (1985).

[9] 786 F.2d 1499 (11th Cir. 1986).

determine the permit status of the facility to which the company was shipping its hazardous waste.

In *United States v. Weitzenhoff*,[10] two managers of a sewage treatment plant that operated under an EPA permit were convicted under the Clean Water Act. The managers argued that they lacked the requisite intent since they did not know that their conduct was in violation of the permit. The court rejected this argument and held that the government only needed to prove that the defendants knowingly engaged in the conduct that was prohibited. It did not need to prove that the defendant knew the conduct was prohibited.

In *United States v. Hansen*,[11] convictions of two corporate officers under RCRA's knowing endangerment provision were affirmed when the Eleventh Circuit found that the defendants had knowledge of the "general hazardous character" of the chemical and knew that the chemical had the "potential to be harmful" to others.

In *United States v. Wilson*,[12] the Fourth Circuit overturned the convictions of a Maryland developer and his development company who had been convicted of four felony counts of knowingly discharging fill material into wetlands without a permit under the Clean Water Act (CWA). Mr. Wilson had been sentenced to 21 months in prison and fined $1 million. In its reversal, the Court limited the jurisdiction of the U.S. Corps of Engineers over isolated wetlands and the types of activities regulated under Section 404 of the CWA.

Negligence Standard

Both the Clean Water Act and the Clean Air Act Amendments impose criminal liability for negligent violation of their provisions. The effect of these provisions is to impose a high standard of care to prevent violations. In *United States v. Frezzo Brothers, Inc.*,[13] two officers of a mushroom-growing company were convicted for discharging pollutants without a permit. The court held that the prosecution need only establish that the defendants negligently maintained the water pollution abatement facility that resulted in the discharge.

In *Apex Oil v. United States*,[14] a corporation was convicted for discharging oil into a river, even though none of the officers or directors of the corporation had knowledge of the violation. The decision suggests a company may be criminally liable for negligent supervision of its employees if the employees allow violations to occur.

The Supreme Court has held in a pair of decisions[15] that federal banking and gun registration statutes must contain a knowledge requirement to impose criminal liability. Lower courts, however, have distinguished environmental crimes from these cases on the ground that environmental crimes are public welfare offenses, which do not

---

10 35 F.3d 1275 (9th Cir. 1993), *cert. denied*, 115 S.Ct. 939 (1995).
11 263 F.3d 1217 (11th Cir. 2001).
12 133 F.3d 251 (4th Cir. 1997).
13 703 F.2d 62 (3rd Cir. 1983), *cert. denied*, 104 S.Ct. 106 (1983).
14 530 F.2d 1291 (8th Cir. 1976), *cert. denied*, 97 S.Ct. 84 (1976).
15 *Ratzlaf v. United States*, 114 S. Ct. 655 (1994); *Staples v. United States*, 114 S. Ct. 1793 (1994).

require proof of a criminal intent.[16] Courts are likely to continue to uphold convictions under criminal environmental statutes on the basis of negligence.

Ignorance as a Defense

Ignorance of the law rarely has succeeded as a defense in environmental prosecutions. While the *Johnson & Towers* case[17] held that the prosecution must prove the defendants' knowledge, the holding was qualified by the recognition that knowledge of the legal requirements could be inferred from the hazardousness of the substances, without direct evidence. The *Hayes* court went further, imposing an affirmative obligation on a company generating hazardous wastes to know the permit requirements and to determine the permit status of the disposal facility to which it transported its hazardous waste.[18]

Maryland Criminal Standards

The Maryland Controlled Hazardous Substances Act prescribes a felony fine of up to $250,000 per day or imprisonment for up to 15 years for knowing violations of its provisions that cause imminent danger of death or threat of serious bodily injury.[19] Violations committed negligently or accidentally are felonies incurring penalties of up to $100,000 in fines or five years' imprisonment. Other offenses draw anywhere from two to three years' imprisonment and up to $50,000 in fines.

"Knowing" violations of air pollution requirements are misdemeanors punishable by up to $25,000 per day in fines and one year of imprisonment for first offenses; double those amounts for repeat offenses.[20] Knowing falsification and tampering can result in fines up to $10,000 per day and six months' imprisonment.[21]

Violations of water pollution laws, regulations, or permits are misdemeanors carrying up to $25,000 per day in fines and one year of imprisonment for first offenses, with double those amounts for repeat offenses.[22] Falsifying documents or monitoring device tampering incurs up to $50,000 in fines per day and two years in jail.[23] However, the statute does not on its face require proof of "knowing" or "intentional" violations; therefore, the state will likely argue for strict criminal liability (i.e., liability without regard to fault).

Persons violating wetlands provisions may be penalized by up to $10,000 in fines per day for a first offense; $25,000 per day for repeat offenses.[24] However, in certain cases the court may order the defendant to restore the unlawfully disturbed wetlands area, a significantly burdensome and expensive process.[25]

---

16 *United States v. Weitzenhoff*, 35 F.3d 1275, 1280 (9th Cir. 1994).
17 741 F.2d 662 (3rd Cir. 1984), *cert. denied*, 105 S. Ct. 1171 (1985).
18 786 F.2d 1499 (11th Cir. 1986).
19 MD CODE, ENVIR. §7-265(d).
20 MD CODE, ENVIR. §2-609.l(b)
21 MD CODE, ENVIR. 2-609.1(c).
22 MD CODE, ENVIR. §9-343(a).
23 MD CODE, ENVIR. §9-343(b).
24 MD. CODE, ENV. §5-911(e)(1).
25 MD. CODE ANN., ENV. §5-91l(e)(2).

POTENTIALLY LIABLE PARTIES

Organizations

A corporation may be held criminally liable for the acts of any of its agents or employees if the environmental crime was committed within the scope of employment with intent to benefit the corporation.[26] The corporation may be criminally liable even if management was unaware of the conduct, did not participate, and took elaborate steps to ensure compliance with the law.[27]

Officers and Directors

Officers and other high-level corporate employees may be charged with responsibility for corporate violations. For instance, the Clean Air Act and the Clean Water Act both expressly include "any responsible corporate officer" among the persons subject to criminal liability.[28]

Corporate officer responsibility was essentially created in *U.S. v. Dotterweich*,[29] which arose under the Food, Drug and Cosmetics Act (FDCA). The court upheld convictions of corporate officers for criminal acts of the corporate employees, even when there was no evidence of personal knowledge or involvement on the part of the officer. The theory of liability is that the wrongdoing employees are agents of the corporation and its officers, both of whom bear ultimate responsibility.

Under the responsible corporate officer doctrine, a defendant may be liable for the illegal activities of the corporation if the defendant is an officer of the corporation, has direct responsibility for the activities alleged to be illegal, and has "knowledge" of the violation.[30] The standard of knowledge required in environmental criminal cases varies from statute to statute: for instance, the Clean Water Act imposes liability for negligent violations in some situations, while RCRA penalizes "knowing" violations.[31] "Knowledge" may be inferred from circumstantial evidence where appropriate.[32]

The Supreme Court has taken the view that persons in authority have a responsibility to seek out and remedy violations, as well as to implement measures within the corporate structure that will ensure that violations do not recur.[33] An officer or director exercising control over the company can be criminally responsible for failure to implement such measures.

---

26 *Apex Oil Co. v. United States*, 530 F.2d 1291 (8th Cir. 1976).

27 *Riss & Co. v. United States*, 262 F.2d 245 (8th Cir. 1958).

28 42 U.S.C. §7413(c)(6) (Clean Air Act); 33 U.S.C. §1319(c)(6) (Clean Water Act).

29 64 S.Ct. 134 (1947).

30 *U.S. v. MacDonald & Watson Waste Oil Co.*, 933 F.2d 35, 50 (1st Cir. 1991), *aff'd* by 980 F.2d 27 (1st Cir. 1992).

31 See 33 U.S.C. §1319(c)(I) (CWA); 42 U.S.C.§ 6928(d) (RCRA). In *United States v. Horg*. 242 F.3d 528 (4th Cir. 2001), the Fourth Circuit affirmed an expansive application of the responsible corporate officer doctrine under the Clean Water Act by convicting the sole shareholder on 13 counts of negligently violating pretreatment requirements.

32 See *MacDonald*, 933 F.2d at 55; *U.S. v. Brittain*, 931 F.2d 1413, (10th Cir. 1991). A showing of a person's position within a corporation or his level of official responsibility is not sufficient to conclusively prove knowledge, although it may be a factor. *MacDonald*, 933 F.2d at 55.

33 *United States v. Park*, 95 S. Ct. 1903 (1975).

Management Employees

The defendant need not be an officer or director having complete control over the organization. Mid-level management personnel may be held criminally liable if they have responsibility over the activity leading to the violation.[34]

Low-Level Employees

Even low-level employees of a company who do not exercise any degree of authority over the company's activities may be held criminally liable for their own conduct.[35] To be charged criminally, lower-level employees must have participated in the transaction.

ENVIRONMENTAL AUDITS

EPA encourages regulated entities to discover voluntarily, disclose, correct, and prevent violations of federal environmental law through its policy on self-policing.[36] If violations are found through voluntary environmental audits or efforts that reflect due diligence, and are promptly disclosed and corrected, EPA will not seek gravity-driven or non-economic benefit penalties and will not recommend criminal prosecution, generally.[37]

COLLATERAL CONSEQUENCES

An organization convicted of an environmental offense, particularly falsification of records and making false statements, may face debarment under the Federal Acquisition Regulations.[38] Debarment amounts to exclusion from government contracting or subcontracting. The Clean Water Act also prohibits federal agencies from entering into procurement contracts with organizations convicted of Clean Water Act violations, provided the violation occurred at the same facility where the contract is to be performed.[39] The Clean Air Act similarly prohibits federal procurement contracts with convicted Clean Air Act offenders.[40]

MITIGATING FACTORS

In practice, the Department of Justice considers certain mitigating factors in bringing a criminal prosecution for violation of an environmental statute. The factors include

---

[34] *United States v. Hayes International*, 786 F.2d 1499 (11th Cir. 1986).
[35] *United States v. Johnson & Towers, Inc.*, 741 F.2d 662 (3rd Cir. 1984), *cert. denied*, 105 S. Ct. 1171 (1985).
[36] 65 Fed. Reg. 19617 (April 11, 2000).
[37] See EPA's 1994 Investigative Discretion Memo.
[38] 48 C.F.R. §9.406-2.
[39] 33 U.S.C. §1368(a).
[40] 42 U.S.C. §7606(a).

voluntary disclosure of the violation, the degree of cooperation, the existence and scope of preventive noncompliance, the existence of effective internal disciplinary action, and any subsequent compliance efforts.[41]

The purpose of this policy is to promote and encourage self-auditing, self-policing, and voluntary disclosure by members of the regulated community, as well as to provide federal prosecutors discretion in granting leniency in certain cases.

TRENDS

State Enforcement Trends

Many of Maryland's environmental crime statutes contain broad language written at a time when environmental enforcement was limited at best. Now, with comprehensive regulations fleshing out a formidable environmental enforcement structure, such broad language can be used to further expand the state's environmental authority. Penalties have been broadened and increased in severity, and the statutory power of courts and administrators has been boldly asserted. It is becoming increasingly important for the regulated community to undertake affirmative measures to ensure compliance with state regulations.

On or before October 1 of each year, the Secretary of the Department of the Environment, in consultation with the Attorney General, is required to submit to the Legislative Policy Committee a report on the enforcement activities conducted by the Department during the previous fiscal year. The report must specifically include "criminal actions charged, convictions obtained, imprisonment time ordered, and criminal fines received."[42] This report is available to the public.[43]

Federal Enforcement Trends

EPA has a team of investigators with full federal criminal investigative powers to develop environmental crime cases in various regions across the country. The U.S. Sentencing Commission provides a 2018 Guidelines Manual for determining appropriate fines and criminal jail sentences for individuals and organizations convicted of environmental crimes.[44]

---

41 *Id.*
42 MD CODE ANN., ENVIR. §1-301(d)(3)(ii)7.
43 MD CODE ANN., ENVIR. §1-301(d)(1)(ii)2.
44 Available at https://perma.cc/5PUZ-3ZNL.

Chapter 11

Regulation of Underground Storage Tanks

TANKS

Extensive Maryland[1] and federal regulations govern the design, installation, operation, and closure of tanks used to store petroleum and other chemicals. Determining which regulations apply to any given storage tank depends on the substance stored in the tank and whether the tank is above or below ground. This chapter divides the discussion into four sections titled, "Underground Petroleum Tanks," "Aboveground Petroleum Tanks," "Underground Hazardous Substance Tanks," and "Hazardous Waste Tanks."

UNDERGROUND PETROLEUM TANKS

The Maryland Oil Control Program is the primary regulator of underground petroleum tanks in Maryland. Maryland's program has been authorized by the EPA to act as the implementing agency for the federally mandated underground storage tank program.[2] Thus, in Maryland, owners and operators of Underground Storage Tanks (USTs) may comply with the state regulations and not concern themselves (except in very rare instances where the UST is near surface waters) with slightly different federal regulations.

Responsible Parties

Under the Maryland regulations, persons responsible for complying with various tank regulations include tank owners; property owners; tank operators; owners of substances stored in tanks; persons in charge of the facility, vessel, or vehicle; and persons responsible for spills and discharges.[3] "Owner" means the present owner of a tank that is used or may be used to store regulated substances. If the tank has been

---

1 COMAR 26.10.02.01 *et seq.*
2 42 U.S.C. §6991.
3 COMAR 26.10.02.0lC.

abandoned, the owner is defined as the owner at the time of last use. The operator of a UST means any person having control of, or having responsibility for, the daily operation of the UST system.[4]

Banks and other persons with a security interest in a UST or real estate containing a UST may not be considered owners, and without some other basis, are exempt from RCRA Subtitle I requirements. Acts or omissions prior to the grant of a security interest will not be considered as participating in the management of the UST. The holder of a security interest may, without being considered an owner, require the borrower to fulfill any conditions, warranties, representations, or promises in the loan agreement. Also, a secured lender does not become an owner of a UST or a piece of property containing a UST if the lender obtained title to the property solely to protect its secured interest, provided the lender seeks to sell, re-lease or otherwise divest of the property in a reasonable manner.[5]

Petroleum Defined

Petroleum subject to Maryland tank regulations is defined broadly as oil of any kind and any liquid form, including petroleum and its by-products, fuel oil, sludge containing oil or oil residues, oil refuse, oil mixed with other waste, crude oils, aviation fuel, gasoline, kerosene, light and heavy fuel oils, diesel motor fuels, asphalt, and—regardless of specific gravity—every other nonedible, non-substituted liquid petroleum not specifically identified as a hazardous substance in CERCLA, 42 U.S.C. §9601 *et seq.*[6] Oil does not include liquefied propane, liquefied natural gas, or any edible oils.[7] Petroleum mixed with *de minimis* quantities of hazardous substances is considered petroleum for purposes of the tank rules.[8] Used oil is considered "petroleum" in Maryland.[9]

Underground Storage Tank Defined

"Underground storage tank" (UST) is defined to include all tanks or combinations of tanks used to contain regulated substances (petroleum or hazardous substances) with 10 percent or more of the volume of the tank beneath the surface of the ground.[10] As noted in the exclusions below, Maryland has exempted residential or farm heating fuel tanks of less than 1,100 gallon capacities used for noncommercial uses from the definition of UST.[11] Underground pipes connected to the tanks are part of the UST, and pipe volume is included as tank volume. Maryland defines "tank" broadly to include any stationary device, designed to contain an accumulation of regulated substances, that is constructed of non-earthen materials providing structural support.[12]

---

[4] COMAR 26.10.02.02.
[5] *Id.*
[6] MD. CODE, ENVIR. §4-401(h)(1).
[7] MD. CODE, ENVIR. §4-401(h)(2).
[8] 40 C.F.R. §280.12.
[9] COMAR 26.10.02.04B(46).
[10] COMAR 26.10.02.04B(64).
[11] *Id.*
[12] COMAR 26.1 0.02.04B(62).

The federal and Maryland programs exclude from regulation:

1. Farm or residential tanks of 1,100 gallons or less storing motor fuel and heating oil for non-commercial purposes (i.e., not for resale).
2. Septic tanks, both residential and commercial.
3. All pipeline facilities regulated under:
   (a) The Natural Gas Pipeline Safety Act of 1968;
   (b) The Hazardous Liquid Pipeline Safety Act of 1979; or
   (c) any state law similar to the above Acts.
4. Surface impoundments, pits, ponds, or lagoons.
5. Stormwater or wastewater collection systems.
6. Flow-through process tanks.
7. Liquid traps or associated gathering lines directly related to oil production.
8. Any storage tank in an underground area (e.g., basement, cellar, tunnel) if the tank is upon or above the surface of the floor.[13]

Certain Regulated Tanks Excused from Some Requirements

By regulation, Maryland has excluded the following tank systems from all technical requirements of these regulations (some are regulated elsewhere), although release reporting and corrective action requirements may still be in place:

1. USTs holding hazardous wastes or mixtures of hazardous wastes and other regulated substances.
2. Wastewater treatment tanks at facilities regulated under §§307(b) and 402 of the federal Clean Water Act.
3. Equipment or machinery containing regulated substances for operational purposes such as hydraulic lift tanks and electrical equipment.
4. UST systems containing *de minimis* concentrations of regulated substances.
5. Emergency spill or overflow containment UST systems expeditiously emptied after use.
6. Any farm or residential tank system of 1,100 gallons or less that is used to store heating oil for noncommercial purposes.[14]

Maryland has "deferred" regulation of wastewater treatment tank systems that do not store a regulated substance from all requirements except the release response and corrective action requirements. Emergency power generator UST systems (regardless of whether at nuclear power plants) are deferred for release detection requirements. UST storage systems that are used only for storage of heating oil only for consumptive uses are deferred for upgrade, release detection, and financial responsibilities.[15]

---

13 COMAR 26.10.02.04B(64).
14 COMAR 26.10.02.02B.
15 COMAR 26.10.02.02C.

Registration Requirements

All owners, operators, or persons in charge of regulated underground storage tanks located in Maryland are required to register their tanks with the Underground Storage Tank Division of the Maryland Department of the Environment.[16]

Owners of new or replacement USTs must notify within 30 days of the tanks' first use. A person who sells a tank for use as a UST must inform the purchaser of the registration obligations and must provide the purchaser a copy of the registration form.[17] The proper form, "Registration for Underground Storage Tanks," is available from MDE's Oil Control Program.

Permits

Underground storage tanks do not require individual state permits, since they are deemed to have "general permits" if the facility is in compliance with all applicable regulations and they allow access by MDE.[18]

New Tank Standards

New USTs are subject to numerous requirements for the prevention and prompt detection of releases.[19] To prevent releases, USTs must be engineered to prevent corrosion, to withstand structural failure, and to prevent spills and overfills. Release detection requirements include inventory control for metered systems, line leak detectors for pressurized piping, and 30-day release detection. The owner, operator, or person in charge of a UST system must notify the Administration three working days before the installation or replacement of a UST system.[20]

Technician and Remover Certification

Underground storage systems can only be installed, upgraded, repaired, or closed in the presence of a certified tank technician, who ensures that all applicable requirements are met. To be licensed, an installer must pass a certification test with a score of 90 percent or better, have two years or more UST experience, have had direct involvement in at least six UST installations, and pay a fee to MDE. These requirements may be waived by MDE for applicants with equivalent training or education.[21]

New Tank Construction Standards

New USTs must have cathodic protection or be constructed of non-corroding materials such as fiberglass-reinforced plastic or fiberglass-reinforced plastic-coated steel.

---

[16] MD. CODE, ENVIR. §4-411.1; COMAR 26.10.03.09.
[17] COMAR 26.10.03.09F.
[18] COMAR 26.10.02.05.
[19] COMAR 26.10.03.01.
[20] COMAR 26.10.03.0lC.
[21] COMAR 26.10.06.

Non-corroding tanks must be certified by the manufacturer as approved under American Society of Mechanical Engineer standards or listed by Underwriters Laboratories. A different industry standard is applicable to each type of UST system.[22]

All piping placed in contact with the ground must be installed in accordance with manufacturers' specifications and material standards established by MDE for each material type.[23] Fiberglass-reinforced plastic and flexible piping systems will not be used for direct fill lines or above grade vent lines. Pipes located below the ground surface must be placed on a six-inch bedding of approved backfill material, in accordance with clearance specifications.[24] All piping must rise one-eighth of an inch for every lateral foot from the tank to the piping end point. Flexible connectors must be used to connect piping carrying regulated substances to the tank and the dispensing unit at the end of the pipe.[25] Vent lines must be constructed in accordance with MDE specifications and must be separate from other non-storage system conduits, such as electrical conduits and water lines.[26]

Owners of piping systems associated with floating piers or docks must now submit plans for piping systems to MDE for approval. Approval by MDE is dependent on providing adequate protection to avoid the discharge of oil.[27]

Cathodic Protection

Cathodic protection is a technique that reverses the electrical forces that cause corrosion in steel tanks and piping. Two types of cathodic protection are acceptable: galvanic anode systems and impressed current systems.

Maryland requires an annual structure to soil potential test of cathodic protection systems. Maryland regulations require this test within six months of installation and then once a year for field installed systems, and every three years for factory installed systems.[28] Maryland requires impressed current systems to:

1. be inspected every 60 days; and
2. have a complete assessment performed by a corrosion expert when the system reaches five years of age and then every five years thereafter.[29]

Spill and Overfill Controls

Maryland requires installation of spill and overfill prevention devices on all new USTs. The devices required include spill prevention equipment to prevent the release of regulated substance into the environment by use of a spill catchment basin around

[22] COMAR 26.10.03.01.
[23] COMAR 26.10.03.02.
[24] COMAR 26.10.03.04.
[25] COMAR 26.10.03.06E.
[26] COMAR 26.10.03.06G, H.
[27] COMAR 26.10.03.07E.
[28] COMAR 26.10.04.02D.
[29] COMAR 26.10.04.02D, F.

the fill pipe with a minimum capacity of five gallons, and overfill prevention equipment, such as:

1. product-level sensors or automatic shut-off devices;
2. sensors that alert the operator when the tank is 90 percent full by restricting the flow into the tank or triggering a high-level alarm;
3. sensors that alert the operator with an alarm one minute before overfilling; or
4. alternative controls, as approved by the state.[30]

Maryland also requires the tank truck driver to be physically present at all times during filling of a UST. Each fill line for a UST must be clearly marked to indicate the size of the tank and the product stored. This marking can be done with tags next to the fill lines or by use of a color code posted in prominent locations.[31]

Monitoring Pipes

All new USTs subject to the Maryland regulations must have two vertical monitoring pipes located in opposing corners of the UST system excavation. These pipes are used in the event of a suspected release to determine if there is product in the tank pit. These pipes must extend to a minimum depth of two feet below the bottom of the tanks. They must be made of at least four-inch-diameter 40 PVC piping and be screened from the bottom to within two feet of the top, with the top two feet remaining solid PVC. The piping slot size must be between .020 inches and .025 inches. The piping must be backfilled with fine pea gravel or wrapped in filter cloth to prevent clogging, with a sealant used in the top eight inches to prevent surface water leakage. The wells must also be capped, protected from traffic, and clearly marked to avoid confusion with fill lines.[32] Keys or other locking tools must be kept on the tank site.

Excavation/Placement

New excavation standards have been developed for new USTs. Tanks must be at least five feet from the base of existing structures or property lines. All tanks must be placed on a 12-inch bedding of backfill that meets the state standards. All shoring must be removed from the tank excavation, unless there is at least 48 inches of clearance between the excavation and the UST. USTs must be anchored, if it is determined that movement of the tank is possible from high flood or groundwater flows.[33]

Vapor Recovery

Many gasoline tanks in Maryland are subject to Stage I and Stage II vapor recovery, required pursuant to the Clean Air Act. Stage I requirements—relating to vapor

---

[30] COMAR 26.10.03.03.
[31] COMAR 26.10.04.01N.
[32] COMAR 26.10.03.04B.
[33] COMAR 26.10.03.04.

generated in filling USTs—apply to most gasoline tanks with monthly throughput of 10,000 gallons or more.[34] Stage II requirements relate to vapors generated in dispensing gasoline to vehicles.[35] Whether Stage II requirements apply depends upon the location of the facility, its ownership, and the volume of gasoline dispensed.

Release Detection

Maryland law requires that all metered petroleum USTs take daily inventories, using a stick or electronic method.[36] Results of these daily tests must be reconciled with pump meter readings and receipt of product. This is sometimes called "daily inventory control." Records of these readings must be kept for five years.[37]

In addition to daily inventory control, tank systems must have 30-day monitoring using one of several release detection alternatives. These include:

1. Automatic in-tank monitoring that tests for the loss of regulated substances and conducts automatic inventory reconciliation.
2. Testing or monitoring for vapors within the soil gas of the excavation area.
3. Testing or monitoring to detect regulated substances on the groundwater in high groundwater areas.
4. Testing or monitoring for regulated substances using at least one monitoring well or device in the unsaturated zone between the UST system and an impermeable barrier in low groundwater areas.
5. Monitoring between the UST system and a secondary barrier immediately around it.
6. Statistical inventory control.
7. Precision tank testing.
8. Any other method of release detection that has been approved by MDE.[38]

Tanks with less than 600 gallons of capacity may comply with these requirements with weekly manual tank gauging as the sole method of release detection. Tanks between 601 and 2,000 gallons can also use manual tank gauging, but only in conjunction with precision tightness testing or hydrostatic testing conducted every five years.[39]

Combine Tank Gauging with Precision Testing

Release detection requirements for piping vary with reference to pipe type. Pressurized piping must be equipped with an automatic line leak detector, to be tested annually. Other requirements exist for pressurized pipes relating to warning to operators and sensitivity of the detectors. For suction piping, tightness tests must be conducted

---

[34] COMAR 26.11.13.04C.
[35] *See* COMAR 26.11.24.
[36] COMAR 26.10.04.01E.
[37] *Id.*
[38] COMAR 26.10.05.01 to .04, .06.
[39] COMAR 26.10.05.04C.

every two years with an approved test, or monthly in accordance with the regulations. Release detection is not required for suction piping under certain circumstances.[40]

Inventory Discrepancies

Inventory variations exceeding one-half of 1 percent of a metered quality of a regulated substance over a period of 30 days must be reported to the owner of the tank and investigated immediately.[41] Daily inventory showing seven straight days of losses totaling 80 gallons or more, regardless of percent, must be reported to the owner and investigated immediately. If the inventory variation is reconciled and there is no indication of a leak, the cause of the variation must be noted in the records. If the investigation indicates a loss of product, the owner or the person in charge must follow the release reporting requirements presented in another section of this chapter.

Precision Testing

A precision test is a test capable of detecting and quantifying leaks as small as 0.05 gallons in one hour from any portion of a tank system with a capacity of up to 12,500 gallons, while accounting for thermal expansion, concentration of the liquid, vapor pockets, tank deformation, evaporation, water, and any subsurface water contacting the UST.[42]

Pressurized piping without external release monitoring (e.g., vapor or groundwater monitoring) must be tested annually.[43] Systems that are not upgraded to new tank standards must also have periodic precision tests, regardless of whether piping is pressurized. Tanks that have alternative release detection (e.g., vapor monitoring) with suction piping that meets certain specifications, however, would never require testing. As a general rule, the more advanced the system, the less testing is required.

Any time a precision test is performed, the owner or person in charge of the storage system must record the commercial name of the test equipment, the name of the testing company, the name of the test operator, and some certification of his training for use of the test equipment, the data from the test, and whether the UST passed the test.[44] If a tank fails a precision test, the test operator must immediately notify the owner, the person in charge of the tank, and the MDE. The person in charge of the tank or the owner then must immediately empty the tank, investigate the location of the leak, and either repair, remove, or close the tank. If the tank is repaired, a precision test must be performed again after repairs have been made.[45]

Release Detection Schedule

All regulated UST systems are subject to release detection requirements, although they are more limited for heating oil USTs. As an interim measure—for 10 years after

[40] COMAR 26.10.05.02D.
[41] COMAR 26.10.04.01F.
[42] COMAR 26.10.02.04B(49).
[43] COMAR 26.10.05.02D.
[44] COMAR 26.10.08.03.
[45] COMAR 26.10.08.01 to .04.

the tank is otherwise upgraded by adding corrosion protection and spill and overfill controls—release detection on everything except pressurized piping may be accomplished by periodic tank testing and manual inventory control.[46] All pressurized piping, regardless of age, must have line leak detectors and either annual tightness testing or external release monitoring.[47] The frequency of the required testing is annual if the system has not been upgraded and every five years if it has been upgraded.

Corrosion Protection and Spill and Overfill Control for Existing USTs

Corrosion protection and spill and overfill controls were to be added to existing tank systems by December 22, 1998. If the interim method of release detection chosen for the system is daily inventory control, and if the system has suction piping, the upgraded tank system must only be tested every three or five years (depending upon where the check valve in the suction piping is located) instead of annually.[48]

Repairing Underground Storage Tanks

Tanks may be repaired and relined if several requirements are met. First, the repairs must be made in accordance with standards incorporated by reference into the regulation.[49] Repairs to fiberglass-reinforced plastic tanks shall be made to the manufacturer's specification. Metal pipes with sections or fittings that have released regulated substances as a result of corrosion or other damage must be replaced, while fiberglass pipes may be repaired in accordance with manufacturer's specifications. Repaired UST or piping must be precision tested before being placed back into service.[50] The owner must obtain and keep available a written certification from the repair contractor that all Maryland requirements were met.

Maryland also requires that all tank installations, upgrading, repairs, and closures be performed in the presence of a certified UST installer. The regulations specify the requirements necessary for certification.[51]

Responding to Releases

Suspected releases must be reported to MDE within two hours, and a precision tank test must be performed within 48 hours.[52] Under some circumstances, a preliminary site investigation is also required.[53] The regulations define suspected release to include:

1. discovery of released regulated substance at site or in surrounding area;
2. unusual operating conditions, unless explained;

---

[46] COMAR 26.10.03.08B.
[47] COMAR 26.10.05.02D.
[48] COMAR 26.10.03.03, 26.10.05.02.
[49] COMAR 26.10.04.04 and 26.10.02.06.
[50] COMAR 26.10.04.04E requires a precision test before operation.
[51] COMAR 26.10.06.01 to .09.
[52] COMAR 26.10.08.01–.03.
[53] COMAR 26.10.08.03.

3. sudden loss of the regulated substance from the system; or
4. release detection method monitoring results indicating a release has occurred.[54]

A site check is required if the regulated substance is found at the site or in surrounding areas and the tank system passes a tightness test, or if required by the MDE. Once a release is confirmed, that must also be reported, as described below.

Reporting Discovered Leaks

Any person discharging or permitting the discharge of petroleum must report the discharge to MDE immediately but not later than two hours after detection.[55] The report of the discharge must include:

1. time of discharge;
2. location of discharge;
3. type of facility involved;
4. type and quantity of substance spilled;
5. assistance required;
6. the name, address, and telephone number of the person making the report; and
7. any other pertinent information requested by the administration.

The person making the report must then remain available at the site until he or she is cleared to leave by the appropriate official. As discussed below, written reports are required later in the investigation.[56]

Remedial Action

Remedial action requirements are specific to the site and the incident. In most cases, they will depend upon the agreement reached between the regulators and the tank owner or operator. The responsible persons must stop further releases and recover free petroleum product promptly. The regulations also envision fairly prompt initial response actions to prevent migration of petroleum from saturated soils.[57]

Further treatment of vapors, soil, or groundwater are dependent upon the specific factors encountered at a site, as described in the site assessment, discussed below. Public participation in these decisions is also required.

Contaminated Soil

If contaminated soil is sent off-site for disposal or treatment, it must be sent to a permitted facility. MDE may require the development of a corrective action plan to ensure

[54] COMAR 26.10.08.01.
[55] COMAR 26.10.01.03; 26.10.08.01.
[56] COMAR 26.10.09.
[57] COMAR 26.10.09.02.

the protection of human health, safety, and the environment.[58] Excavated soils must be removed from the site within 50 days or treated in accordance with a corrective action plan approved by MDE.[59] An oil-contaminated soil storage facility may not receive soil with hazardous waste in it, and it must receive a certification statement from MDE or another authorized person that the soil is contaminated only by oil, and not used oil, oil refuse, or oil mixed with waste.[60]

Follow-Up Reports

The regulations require a short, written report within 20 days of release confirmation and a more detailed site assessment within 45 days of release confirmation.[61]

Public Participation

For each confirmed release requiring a corrective action plan, the responsible person in coordination with MDE must provide notice to the affected public.[62] Notice can be accomplished by publication in local newspapers, block advertisements, public service announcements, publications in the Maryland Register, individual letters, or personal contacts by field staff. MDE may also decide to hold public hearings and to provide additional information on the progress of the plan.

Closure of Petroleum USTs

Tanks containing regulated substances may be taken out of service for less than three months by complying with those regulations for in-service tanks. Additional restrictions apply to tanks out of service for over three months. Vent lines must be left open, and all other lines, pumps, manways, and ancillary equipment must be capped and secured.[63] Tanks temporarily closed for more than six months must be permanently closed if the performance standards for new or upgraded tanks are not met.[64]

If a UST system is taken out of service for longer than six months, it must be permanently closed regardless of compliance with new or upgraded tank performance standards. The regulations also allow changing a tank to unregulated status (i.e., to be used for the storage of unregulated substances). In those circumstances, an owner or operator must still empty and clean the tank and perform a site assessment.[65]

UST systems closed permanently must be removed from the ground, unless permission has been given by MDE to fill with a solid inert material. The MDE must be notified 30 days in advance of closure, with a confirmation of closure plans within 48

58 COMAR 26.10.09.07.
59 COMAR 26.10.09.03.
60 COMAR 26.10.13.07.
61 COMAR 26.10.09.03B, .04A.
62 COMAR 26.10.09.08.
63 COMAR 26.10.10.0lB.
64 COMAR 26.10.10.0lC.
65 COMAR 26.10.10.02.

hours of closure.[66] MDE requires that closure be conducted only by certified technicians, as described in a previous section of this chapter. An assessment of the tank system must also be performed to determine if there was a release. Any releases detected must be reported and cleaned up according to normal cleanup standards.

Financial responsibility is governed by federal standards incorporated by reference into the regulation.[67] Owners of regulated USTs (except heating oil tanks) must demonstrate the financial ability to respond to releases. They may demonstrate coverage by insurance, by a risk group, by satisfying a balance sheet test, or by satisfying another approved criterion. Maryland is unique in only imposing these requirements on tank owners rather than on both owners and operators. The levels of financial responsibility and the dates for demonstrating compliance depend upon the numbers of tanks owned, whether the owner is a petroleum marketing firm, the average throughput of the tanks, and the size of the company. For owners of tanks at petroleum marketing facilities or that have average monthly throughput of more than 10,000 gallons, the owner or operator must demonstrate financial ability to pay at least $1,000,000 per occurrence. All others must demonstrate coverage of $500,000 per occurrence. The aggregate responsibility level is $2,000,000 for owners of 101 or more tanks and $1,000,000 for all others.[68]

Demonstrating Financial Responsibility

There are many options for demonstrating financial responsibility, including: insurance; satisfying a financial test of self-insurance by demonstrating tangible net worth of at least 10 times the aggregate level; guarantees; risk retention groups; surety bonds; letters of credit; use of a state-required method; trust fund; or standby trust fund. The specific requirements for each of these methods are set out in the regulations.[69]

Maryland has not created a state fund to satisfy the financial responsibility requirements. Maryland does have a fund to expedite certain cleanups, the UST Site Cleanup Reimbursement Fund,[70] but it expressly does not meet the financial responsibility requirement.[71] Owners may be reimbursed for cleanup expenses incurred as a result of leaks from registered USTs. The remediation must be pursuant to an MDE-approved corrective action plan. The Fund is subject to deductibles, limitations, priorities, and allowances. Because this Fund does not meet the federal financial responsibility requirements, the federal regulations must still be followed.

An owner or operator of a registered underground oil storage tank system, including one storing heating oil for non-residential use,[72] can be reimbursed for some of the environmental cleanup costs associated with an oil-contaminated site. The program is subject to certain exclusions and the availability of funds.[73] The owner or operator seeking reimbursement from the Fund may apply to MDE for approval.

---

66 *Id.*
67 COMAR 26.10.11.01.
68 40 C.F.R. §280.92.
69 40 C.F.R. §§280.95–280.103.
70 *See* COMAR 26.10.14.01–.11.
71 MD. CODE, ENVIR. §4-703(B).
72 COMAR 26.10.14.01.
73 COMAR 26.10.14.02.

The Department also enumerates reimbursement limits for eligible sites depending on whether the application was approved before or after July 1, 1996.

Heating Oil USTs

Regulated heating oil USTs installed prior to March 15, 1985, must:

1. have the tank gauged before filling and the reading recorded;
2. have a precision test at age 15 and then once every five years;
3. have the fill line marked on the pipes; and
4. follow the closure requirements, which only require the tank to be emptied and capped.

Regulated heating oil USTs installed after March 15, 1985, must:

1. have corrosion protection;
2. be installed by a certified installer if installed after February 4, 1991;
3. have a precision test before first use, at age 15, and then once every five years;
4. have two monitoring pipes in the backfill;
5. have the fill line marked on the pipes; and
6. follow the closure requirements, which only require the tank to be emptied and capped.

There are more limited requirements for the removal of heating oil tanks from a residential property when the use of heating oil as fuel is permanently abandoned. The owner of the heating oil tank must comply with the following requirements:

1. All flammable and combustible liquids must be removed from the tank itself and all pipes.
2. The tank and piping must be removed from the property if they are not in operable condition, or if located underground, they must be filled with dirt, sand, or some similar matter.
3. The tank must be secured from any accidental filling.[74]

If the abandonment was a result of converting to another heating fuel, the new heating system must be inspected.

ABOVEGROUND PETROLEUM TANKS

Aboveground petroleum tanks in Maryland are regulated by the Maryland Oil Pollution Program,[75] the federal Clean Water Act (CWA), and the federal Oil Pollution

---

[74] MD. CODE ANN., ENVIR. §4-420.
[75] COMAR 26.10.01.

Act (OPA).[76] The Maryland Oil Pollution Program and the CWA have overlapping requirements for aboveground petroleum storage.

The CWA regulates only those tanks that, due to their location, could reasonably be expected to release oil in harmful quantities into the navigable waters of the United States or adjoining shorelines.[77] This section will discuss the Maryland requirements for aboveground petroleum tanks and CWA requirements for those tanks near navigable waters.

"Regulated aboveground petroleum tanks," defined by the Clean Water Act provisions regarding oil pollution prevention, do not apply to:

1. Facilities not subject to CWA jurisdiction of the Environmental Protection Agency based on the contents of the tank (i.e., not oil) or the tank's location.
2. Facilities otherwise subject to CWA jurisdiction because of their location when two requirements are met:
   (a) the complete buried storage capacity of the facility is 42,000 gallons or less of oil, and
   (b) the aggregate aboveground storage capacity of the facility is 1,320 gallons or less of oil.[78]

Compliance

Maryland regulations place compliance responsibility on the owner of the tank, the owner of the stored substance, the person in charge of the facility, and the person responsible for any spill or discharge.[79] Owners and operators of the storage tank are responsible for CWA compliance.[80]

Design and Installation Requirements

All aboveground storage tanks, venting, piping, and metering devices installed must meet certain industry standards, as listed at COMAR 26.10.01.12A, and they must comply with other applicable Maryland regulations. These industry standards are regulatory requirements and are enforceable as such.

Secondary Containment Requirements

Aboveground oil storage facilities with a capacity of 10,000 gallons or more must be surrounded with a continuous dike or wall capable of holding the total volume of the largest storage tank in the enclosed area.[81] The construction of this emergency holding area must prevent movement of the oil into surface water or groundwater. The nature

---

[76] 33 U.S.C. §1321; 33 U.S.C. §2701.
[77] 40 C.F.R. §112.1.
[78] *Id.*; the aggregate aboveground storage capacity of a facility excludes oil containers with a capacity of less than 55 gallons, as well as containers that are "permanently closed" as defined by §112.2.
[79] COMAR 26.10.01.
[80] 40 C.F.R. §112.1.
[81] COMAR 26.10.01.12B(1).

of the soil and groundwater conditions at the site must be considered in the design and location of the emergency holding area. Valves used to drain diked areas must be locked closed when not draining trapped water; flapper-type valves may not be used. MDE may require secondary containment at facilities of less than 10,000-gallon capacity if the facility is in a location likely to pollute Maryland waters.

Any facility can be exempt from the diking requirements if it provides adequate alternative procedures for oil spill control. Requests for exemptions must be submitted to MDE in writing.

All aboveground petroleum tanks must have a high liquid level gauge, an alarm system, or a pump cut-off device to prevent overflows when filling tanks. Additionally, personnel must supervise the filling of tanks.[82]

Permits

Maryland regulations require the following facilities to obtain "Oil Operations Permits" from MDE:

1. Oil delivery and transfer facilities, and other oil storage facilities involving the storage of oil in quantities of 10,000 gallons or more.
2. Facilities for the handling, reuse, processing, reprocessing, or disposal of used oil and having storage capacity of 1,000 gallons or more.

The following facilities generally do not require an Oil Operations Permit, but they are still subject to other relevant Maryland regulations:

1. Facilities under 10,000 gallons.
2. Tanks at single-family residences and for personal use regardless of storage capacity.[83]

Procedure

The person in charge of a facility requiring a permit must submit a written application to the MDE. The application must be submitted at least 60 days before the date of intended operation. Included must be a copy of the facility's containment and cleanup plan. Permits are effective for five years.[84]

Containment and Cleanup Plan

Permitted facilities are required to have containment and cleanup plans to be followed in the event of a spill. The plan must be kept on the premises at all times, and a copy must be submitted for approval with the Oil Operations Permit application. The minimum requirements for the plan are as follows:

---

[82] COMAR 26.10.01.12B(8).
[83] COMAR 26.10.01.09A.
[84] COMAR 26.10.01.10, .11.

1. List of persons, including addresses and telephone numbers, to be notified in the event of a spill.
2. Provisions for quick control of an oil spill, including personnel, location, and procedures necessary to obtain equipment available for the containment and cleanup operations.
3. Communication facilities available for use in control and clean-up operations.
4. List of qualified contractors, equipment, and facilities available for oil spill cleanup operations.

The permit application includes a form that may be used for the plan.

An Oil Operations Permit is required for all aboveground tanks meeting the facility type and capacity-level specifications discussed in the underground storage tank section above. All application requirements including containment and cleanup plans applicable to USTs also apply to aboveground tanks.

Construction of aboveground oil tanks within tidal wetlands or within the 100-year floodplain is prohibited unless a State Wetlands License, Wetlands Permit, or Waterway Construction Permit is first obtained.[85] Requirements for these permits are strict. Where there is doubt about whether a tank may be subject to these permits, counsel familiar with these regulations should be consulted.

SPCC Plans

If a tank can reasonably be expected to discharge oil into a waterway in the event of a spill and it exceeds minimum gallonage requirements, certain CWA requirements must be met.[86] A Spill Prevention Control and Countermeasure Plan (SPCC) is required for these facilities.[87] An SPCC plan required by the federal regulation may be submitted with the Oil Operations Permit application in lieu of the less comprehensive containment and cleanup plan required by Maryland regulations. The SPCC plan must be prepared within six months after the facility begins operating, and it must be reviewed and certified by a registered professional engineer.

The SPCC plan must include a description or discussion of the following:

1. The physical layout of the facility, including containers, container contents, discharge prevention measures, and discharge or drainage controls, including secondary containment.
2. Countermeasures for responding to spills, including methods of disposal of recovered materials.
3. Analysis of likely direction, rate, and quantity of oil that could be discharged in a major equipment failure.

---

[85] Tidal wetlands are defined as lands bordering or beneath tidal waters, which are subject to regular or periodic tidal action and which support aquatic growth. COMAR 08.05.07.01. The 100-year floodplain is the area subject to a 100-year frequency flood event as defined by flood insurance studies. COMAR 08.05.03.03C.

[86] 40 C.F.R. §112.7.

[87] *Id.*

4. Containment structures or equipment to prevent discharged oil from reaching water.
5. Security around oil storage facilities.
6. Personnel training.
7. Integrity testing.
8. Tank car/tank truck loading and unloading area containment.[88]

Operating Requirements

The requirements for operation of aboveground petroleum tanks involve periodic inspections and some inventory control. All aboveground tanks installed after April 21, 1978, must have some way to measure the content level of the tank. Before filling any tank installed after this date, the liquid level must be gauged and the measurement recorded. These gauging records must be kept for 30 days and made available for reasonable inspection. Additionally, MDE has requirements for marine oil transfer facilities to have high-level alarms or automatic shutdown systems to prevent overfilling.[89] Seams, rivets, nozzle connections, valves, pumps, and pipelines directly connected to aboveground storage tanks must be visually examined for leaks at least once a month.[90]

Release Reporting and Cleanup

If a leak is discovered from an aboveground petroleum tank, it must be reported to MDE within two hours after detection. The details of this reporting requirement are the same as those for underground petroleum tanks outlined above.

Maryland law allocates the initial task of implementing cleanup procedures to the persons responsible for the spills as defined in MD Code, Environment Article 4-401. Most owners prefer this because cleanup may then be accomplished with greater efficiency and less cost than if the government intervened. Discharges from improperly abandoned storage systems are the responsibility of the current landowner and any person who owned, leased, or was otherwise responsible for a system at the time it was abandoned.[91] The procedure for removal designates the manner in which the responsible parties should remove a spill. As in the case of USTs, the MDE reserves the right to assume control of any cleanup operation where officials conclude that the conditions constituting the hazard have not been corrected.[92]

In addition, in the event of a spill, certain provisions of the Oil Pollution Act (OPA) (1990) may come into play. OPA establishes liability rules for parties responsible for oil spills in navigable waters and authorizes the President to use the Oil Spill Liability

[88] These guidelines of the SPCC plan requirements are in summary form. Those preparing plans should consult the more detailed requirements of 40 C.F.R. §112.7.
[89] COMAR 26.10.01.22
[90] COMAR 26.10.0l.12B(5).
[91] COMAR 26.10.01.04.
[92] *Id.*

Trust Fund within a national contingency plan to facilitate state or federal cleanup actions.[93]

OPA assigns the liabilities for damages consequent to the responsible party's oil spillage. Liabilities include damages to natural resources, damages to personal property, lost profits, lost earning capacity, loss of public services, and removal costs, all to be determined by the federal government.[94]

UNDERGROUND HAZARDOUS SUBSTANCE TANKS

Underground storage of hazardous substances is regulated by Subtitle I of RCRA and the implementing Maryland regulations.[95] Those regulations are essentially the same as the regulations for underground petroleum storage, with a few additional requirements. As with petroleum tanks, these regulations are administered by the Oil Control Program.

Hazardous Substance Defined

Hazardous substances within the meaning of these regulations are those designated as hazardous under the Comprehensive Environmental Response, Compensation, and Liability Act, except for RCRA hazardous wastes.[96] There are separate regulations for underground tanks containing RCRA hazardous wastes (called controlled hazardous substances in Maryland), which are discussed in the next section. "Hazardous substances" do not include petroleum, although petroleum tanks are regulated under overlapping regulations described earlier in this chapter.

Hazardous Substance Tank Defined

Underground tanks for storing hazardous substances are defined the same as those underground tanks storing petroleum, discussed above. Essentially, the regulations apply to all tanks or combinations of tanks used to contain hazardous substances with 10 percent or more of the volume of the tank beneath the surface of the ground. Certain tanks are exempted from these regulations. The exemptions are the same as those exemptions from the petroleum tank regulations listed above.

Compliance

Owners and operators of UST systems are responsible for compliance with most regulatory requirements. "Owner" means the present owner of a tank that is used or may be used to store regulated substances. If the tank has been abandoned, the owner is defined as the owner at the time of last use. The operator of an underground hazardous

---

[93] See 33 U.S.C. §2701, *et seq.*
[94] 33 U.S.C. §2702.
[95] COMAR 26.10.02, *et seq.*
[96] 42 U.S.C. §6991(2)(A), incorporating 42 U.S.C. §6901(14) and implementing regulations by reference, COMAR 26.10.02.04(26).

substance tank is any person having control of or having responsibility for the daily operation of the UST system. Persons other than owners and operators may also be responsible for responding to releases.[97]

Registration Requirements

Owners of new or replacement tanks must register within 30 days of first use.[98] The proper form and filing address are the same as those for underground petroleum tanks.

Operating Requirements

Spill and overfill controls for hazardous substance USTs are the same as those for petroleum USTs.[99] Hazardous substance USTs may be repaired, subject to the same conditions that apply to repair of petroleum USTs. These conditions are detailed above.

New Tank Installation Standards

The regulations concerning new tank and piping installation essentially transform industry standards into mandatory requirements. A different industry standard is applicable to each type of UST system and piping type. New hazardous substance USTs are also required to have secondary containment. The secondary containment requirement can be met by using a double-walled UST or a secondary liner or vault around the UST system.[100] Detailed requirements are set out in the regulations.

New hazardous substance USTs must have "interstitial monitoring" as a release detection method. This method entails surveillance of the space between a tank and a secondary containment structure for a change in steady state conditions. In a double-walled tank, this change may be indicated by a loss of vacuum, a decrease in pressure, a drop in the fluid level in a visible reservoir, or the detection of the stored substance in the interstitial space. In a secondary barrier system or vault, the surveillance consists of 30-day monitoring of the space between the UST and the liner to detect the presence of the stored substance in the space.[101]

Release Reporting, Corrective Action, and Closure Requirements

The requirements for responding to a suspected release from a hazardous substance UST are the same as for a petroleum UST, except that any spill or overfill of a hazardous substance that exceeds its CERCLA reportable quantity is reportable.

After reporting, the above suspected release must be investigated to confirm that a release has either occurred or been disproved.[102] The requirements for corrective

---

[97] COMAR 26.10.02.0lC, COMAR 26.10.09.01.

[98] The Maryland regulation does not provide a time limit, but the equivalent federal regulation requires notification within 30 days.

[99] COMAR 26.10.04.01.

[100] COMAR 26.10.05.03.

[101] COMAR 26.10.05.04.

[102] COMAR 26.10.09.

action are the same as those for petroleum USTs.[103] Likewise, restrictions on abandonment of hazardous substance USTs are the same as those controlling abandonment of petroleum USTs.

HAZARDOUS WASTE TANKS

Subtitle C of RCRA regulates the management of hazardous wastes. Pursuant to Subtitle C, BPA has promulgated regulations governing tank storage of these wastes. MDE, which calls hazardous wastes "controlled hazardous substances," has adopted the most recent amendments to these regulations.[104]

Hazardous Waste Defined

Hazardous wastes subject to the Maryland storage tank regulations are basically all substances defined as such by the EPA, plus some additions under Maryland law.

Regulated Tanks

Hazardous waste tanks subject to regulation are all those tanks (both aboveground and underground) used to store or treat hazardous waste. A tank is defined as any stationary device used to contain an accumulation of hazardous wastes. This definition includes sumps, although many sumps are likely to qualify for one of the existing exemptions from these rules. Exempted from the secondary containment requirement of these regulations are tanks storing waste that contain no free liquids and are situated inside a building with an impermeable floor.[105]

Compliance

Persons responsible for compliance with these regulations are owners and operators of facilities using tanks for hazardous waste storage or treatment. "Owner" means any person owning all or part of the facility. "Operator" means the person responsible for the overall operation of the facility.[106]

Operating Requirements

Restrictions on hazardous waste tank operation require periodic inspections of tanks and associated equipment. Formal written assessments are also required for those tanks without secondary containment. Additional restrictions apply to tank storage of certain hazardous waste defined as ignitable, reactive, or incompatible.

---

103 *Id.*
104 COMAR 26.13.05.10.1–.7.
105 COMAR 26.13.05.10A(22).
106 COMAR 26.13.01.03B(58), (59).

Periodic Inspections

The Maryland regulations require the following daily inspections:

1. Overfill controls must be inspected according to a schedule and procedures developed by the owner or operator that will ensure good working order.
2. Aboveground portions of a tank system must be inspected at least once each operating day to detect corrosion and releases of waste.
3. Data gathered from monitoring and leak detection equipment must be reviewed at least once each operating day to ensure that the tank system is being operated according to design.
4. The construction materials and the area immediately surrounding the externally accessible portion of the tank, including the secondary containment system, must be inspected each operating day to detect corrosion, erosion, or signs of releases.
5. Cathodic protection systems must be inspected within six months after installation and then annually thereafter. Impressed current sources for these systems must be inspected or tested at least every other month.[107]

Written Assessments

All existing hazardous waste tanks that do not have secondary containment meeting present standards (discussed above) must be assessed to determine that the system is not leaking or unfit for use. This assessment should be conducted, reviewed, and certified by an independent, qualified, registered, professional engineer.[108] Tanks storing materials that are subsequently regulated as hazardous wastes must be assessed within one year after the materials being handled therein become regulated as hazardous wastes.

The assessment must determine that the tank system will not collapse, rupture, or fail under intended use.[109]

Leaking Tank Systems

The owner and operator of any tank system or secondary containment system from which there has been a leak or that has been found unfit for use must follow these steps:

1. The system must be removed from service immediately.
2. The owner or operator must remove enough waste from the system such that further releases are prevented. This removal must be performed within 24 hours if possible or the earliest practicable time if not possible.
3. Migration of the waste through soil or water must then be prevented and any visibly contaminated soil or water must be removed and properly disposed of.

---

107 COMAR 26.13.05.lOD.
108 COMAR 26.13.05.10-2B.
109 COMAR 26.13.05.10C(1).

4. Any release must be reported to MDE within 24 hours, unless the release is less than one pound and cleaned up immediately.
5. Within 30 days of a release, a written report must be submitted to MDE containing the following information:
   (a) Likely route of migration of the release;
   (b) Characteristics of the surrounding soil;
   (c) Results of any monitoring or sampling connected with the release;
   (d) Proximity to downgradient drinking water, surface water, and population areas; and
   (e) Description of response actions taken or planned.[110]

Returning to Service

If the cause of a release is not related to tank system integrity or if the system has secondary containment, then it may be put back into service after repairs have been made. If the source of the release had no secondary containment, this must be installed before putting the system back into service. This secondary containment requirement does not apply to tanks or components that are aboveground and can be inspected visually. All major repairs (e.g., new liner; ruptured primary or secondary containment) must be certified by an independent, qualified, registered, professional engineer.[111]

Ignitable or Reactive Hazardous Wastes

Those wastes defined as ignitable or reactive may be stored in tanks only if precautions are taken to prevent ignition or reaction or if the tank system is used only for emergencies. These tanks must also maintain protective distances from any public thoroughfares or adjoining property lines as required in Tables 2-1 through 2-6 of the National Fire Protection Association "Flammable and Combustible Liquids Code" (1990).[112]

Incompatible Wastes

Incompatible materials may not be mixed unless precautions are taken to prevent reactions that generate extreme heat or pressure or violent reactions; produce uncontrolled toxic mists, fumes, or gases; produce uncontrolled flammable fumes or gases; damage the structural integrity of the storage system; or threaten human health or the environment.[113]

New and Existing Tank Design and Construction Standards

All new hazardous waste tanks must have a written assessment reviewed and certified by an independent, qualified, registered, professional engineer attesting that the tank

---

[110] COMAR 26.13.05.10-6A.
[111] COMAR 26.13.05.10-6A(7)–(8).
[112] COMAR 26.13.05.10-l; COMAR 26.13.0l.05A(3).
[113] COMAR 26.13.05.10-lB.

system has sufficient structural strength, compatibility with the wastes to be stored, and corrosion protection to ensure that it will not collapse, rupture, or fail.[114] The engineer must also inspect the tank system after installation, to ensure that no damage has occurred, and check the backfill substance and support. The entire tank system must also be tested for tightness prior to use.

Secondary Containment with Interstitial Monitoring

Secondary containment with interstitial monitoring is required for all new tank systems before they are put in service. Secondary containment requirements are phased in for existing tank systems. Most existing tank systems must have had secondary containment by January 12, 1995, but timing requirements vary depending upon age, contents, and physical characteristics of the tank.[115]

Types of Secondary Containment

Acceptable secondary containment systems are external liners, vaults, or double-walled tanks. Each of these system types has separate construction and interstitial monitoring criteria that must be followed.[116] The construction criteria ensure that no waste will enter the soil, groundwater, or surface water in the event of a spill.

Spill and Overfill Controls

Maryland regulations require that owners or operators use appropriate controls and practices to prevent spills and overflows from all hazardous waste tanks (new or existing).[117] These controls must include, at a minimum:

1. Spill prevention controls check valves, dry disconnect couplings.
2. Overfill prevention controls (e.g., level-sensing devices, high-level alarms, automatic feed cutoffs).
3. Maintenance of sufficient freeboard in uncovered tanks to prevent overtopping by waves, wind, or precipitation.

SITE STATUS LETTERS

Notice of Compliance Letter

A person who has received from MDE a notice of a violation may request a notice of compliance letter, but only after the MDE is satisfied that the violation has been corrected.[118]

---

[114] COMAR 26.13.05.10-3.
[115] COMAR 26.13.05.10-4A.
[116] COMAR 26.13.05.10-4B.
[117] COMAR 26.13.05.10C(2).
[118] COMAR 26.10.01.05B.

Site Condition Letter

Upon request, a site condition letter can be issued stating that the site requires remedial action or that it complies with the regulations.[119]

Cleanup Suspension Letter

Upon request, the MDE can issue a cleanup suspension letter if no further treatment of the soil or groundwater is needed for the discharge to be removed. However, the person responsible for the discharge or the person responsible for the cleanup must monitor the site continually.[120]

Final Closure Letter

When MDE determines that a site is in compliance, it will issue a final closure letter releasing the party responsible for the spill or the party responsible for the cleanup from any further remedial action. However, there are some exceptions to this, which include a fraudulently obtained letter or a site that continues to threaten the environment and public health.[121]

Innocent Purchaser Recognition

A person who purchases an oil-contaminated piece of property does not become responsible for the discharge, unless the person would otherwise be held responsible for the discharge.[122]

[119] COMAR 26.10.01.05C.
[120] COMAR 26.10.01.05D.
[121] COMAR 26.10.01.05E.
[122] COMAR 26.10.01.05G.

Chapter 12

Maryland Environmental Common Law

Although environmental legislation dominates the environmental law arena, common law doctrines continue to be important. In the environmental context, Maryland courts have recognized the applicability of nuisance, trespass, negligence, and strict liability for "abnormally dangerous activities." An action for waste may also be available in appropriate circumstances. Common law theories have broader applicability than statutory claims and sometimes provide damage remedies when statutes do not.

NUISANCE

Definition

Maryland has adopted the definition of "nuisance" set out in the *Restatement (Second) of Torts*, §821D: "a non-trespassory invasion of another's interest in the private use and enjoyment of land."[1] The interference must be unreasonable and substantial. An injunction to stop a nuisance will be granted "where it is shown that the injury is of such a character as to materially diminish the value of [the] property and seriously interfere with the ordinary comfort and enjoyment of it."[2]

Case Law

Among the activities that have been held to constitute nuisances in Maryland are blasting;[3] storing large quantities of highly flammable and explosive oils;[4] loud noise,[5] emissions of smoke, soot, or other substances that settle on the plaintiff's property or constitute offensive odors;[6] and leaking underground storage tanks.[7]

---

1 See *Exxon v. Yarema,* 69 Md. App. 124, 147 (1987).
2 *Leatherbury v. Gaylord Fuel Corp.,* 276 Md. 367, 377 (1975).
3 *Scott v. Bay,* 3 Md. 431 (1853); *Green v. T.A. Shoemaker & Co.,* 111 Md. 69 (1909).
4 *Hendrickson v. Standard Oil Company,* 126 Md. 577 (1915).
5 *Meadowbrook Swimming Club, Inc. v. Albert,* 173 Md. 641 (1938); *Gorman v. Sabo,* 210 Md. 155 (1956).
6 See *Hart v. Wagner,* 184 Md. 40 (1944); *Fox v. Ewers,* 195 Md. 650 (1950); *Jackson v. Shawinigan Electro Products Co.,* 132 Md. 128 (1918).
7 *Yommer v. McKenzie,* 255 Md. 220, 257 A.2d 138 (1969); *Exxon v. Yarema,* 69 Md. App. 124 (1986).

The Maryland Court of Special Appeals upheld a landowner's right to a nuisance in a case concerning a scrap metal operation.[8] In this case the court held that neither successive property ownership nor periodic complaints interrupted the prescriptive use. The court rejected the argument that "the passage of regulations controlling air pollution in 1980 tolled the prescriptive period."[9]

In *Exxon v. Yarema*, an underground storage tank case, the court held that "harm to property should be construed broadly to include tangible tortious interferences of plaintiffs' use and enjoyment of their properties."[10] Consequently, defendants were liable under nuisance to property owners whose land was not actually contaminated but who were adjacent to contaminated properties. In *Exxon* the Baltimore County Health Department forbade plaintiffs from using their groundwater, building houses, or selling their land. This, according to the court, was sufficient to sustain a nuisance action.[11]

In *WSSC v. CAE-Link Corp.*, the Maryland Court of Appeals suggested that interference with the plaintiff's reasonable enjoyment of property would be sufficient to constitute a nuisance, without regard to: (1) whether the conduct underlying the interference was unreasonable or negligent in nature, or (2) whether the defendant was complying with a court order. The impact of the activity complained of is the focus, not the nature of that activity. However, a defendant not considered an owner or occupier for the purpose of exercising control of the property is not subject to this strict liability standard.[12]

In *State of Maryland, Department of Natural Resources v. Amerada Hess Corporation*,[13] the United States District Court was faced with the question of whether a single oil spill on the surface waters of the Baltimore Harbor constituted a common law nuisance. The court found that this single act did not qualify as a nuisance because it lacked the continuance of evasion that is characteristic of nuisances.[14] The Maryland Court of Appeals has also recognized that "nuisance necessarily involves the idea of continuance."[15]

A "public" nuisance must be differentiated from a "private" nuisance. A public nuisance is an interference with the rights of the community at large and is punishable by the state. However, a person may bring a claim of "private" nuisance if the individual can demonstrate an injury that is distinct from those suffered by the general public. In *Liller v. State Highway Administration*,[16] a public nuisance was found when a pile of waste material, excavated during the construction of a highway, was dumped above another highway and landslides of the material blocked the public highway. The court granted an injunction prohibiting the defendant from maintaining the waste pile "in its present state."[17]

---

[8] *Hoffman v. United Iron & Metal Co.*, 108 Md. App. 117 (1996).
[9] *Id.* at 139.
[10] *Exxon*, 69 Md. App. at 152.
[11] *Id.* at 153.
[12] *Toy v. Atlantic Gulf & Pacific Co.*, 176 Md. 197 (1939).
[13] 350 F. Supp. 1060 (D. Md. 1972).
[14] *Id.* at 1068.
[15] *Wynkoop v. Mayor and Council of Hagerstown*, 159 Md. 194, 202 (1930), followed in *Burley v. Annapolis*, 182 Md. 307, 313 (1943).
[16] 25 Md. App. 276 (1975).
[17] *Id.* at 284.

In order to enjoin a citizen against the accumulation of trash or rubbish on his property, as a public nuisance, it must be demonstrated that the trash imposes an immediate threat to health or public safety.[18] In Maryland, a junkyard is not a nuisance *per se*; a threat to public health or safety must be demonstrated.[19]

Remedies

Property owners may obtain injunctive relief and/or damages for nuisance actions in Maryland.

In *Gault v. Transcontinental Gas Pipe Line Corporation*,[20] plaintiffs complained that the defendant's booster station's noise, smoke, soot, and odors interfered with the reasonable enjoyment of their property. The court stated that an injunction was appropriate where this could be remedied or avoided by reasonable efforts by the defendant.[21]

Under Maryland law, permanent damages—past, present, and prospective—for diminution in market value caused by a nuisance can only be recovered if the nuisance is permanent.[22] This is based on the premise that a nuisance will continue to cause damage and a permanent reduction in the market value of the property results.

In order for punitive damages to be awarded, there must be a finding of actual malice. In *Exxon v. Yarema*, the Court of Special Appeals held that punitive damages may be awarded in nuisance cases where *implied* malice is found. Punitive damages were appropriate in this case, according to the court, due to the defendant's delay in remediating the site.[23] However, *Exxon*'s holding as to punitive damages was expressly overruled six years later by the Court of Appeals in *Owens-Illinois, Inc. v. Zenobia*.[24] In *Owens*, the Court ruled that punitive damages could be awarded only on a showing, by clear and convincing evidence, that the defendant was guilty of *actual* malice.[25]

TRESPASS

Definition

Trespass is defined by the *Restatement* as an invasion of one's exclusive possession of land—an unprivileged intentional or negligent intrusion on land in the possession of another.[26] According to some commentators, Maryland law may include in trespass unintentional, non-negligent intrusions upon one's exclusive possession of land.[27]

---

[18] *Leet v. Montgomery County*, 264 Md. 606, 612 (1972).
[19] Of course, there are ordinances, separate from common law actions, that regulate these activities.
[20] 102 F. Supp. 187 (D. Md. 1952).
[21] *Id.* at 193.
[22] *Goldstein v. Potomac Electric Power Co.*, 285 Md. 673, 682 (1979).
[23] *Exxon*, 69 Md. App. at 163.
[24] 325 Md. 420, 457, 460 (1992).
[25] *Id.* at 460.
[26] *Restatement (Second) of Torts*, §§157, 158 (1965).
[27] *Restatement*, Appendix, §166 pp. 181–183; *Nissan Motor Corp. v. Maryland Shipbuilding & Drydock Co.*, 544 F. Supp. 1104, *aff'd* 742 F.2d 1449 (D. Md. 1982).

Maryland courts have not yet addressed this definitional issue squarely, and the one case that highlighted it involved admiralty law considerations.[28]

Case Law

In *Exxon v. Yarema*, those plaintiffs that could show no actual physical invasion of their property had their claims dismissed at summary judgment proceedings.[29] As a result, an action for trespass did not lie because trespass requires an actual physical invasion onto the property of another.

Owners of a prescriptive right do have a "privilege" that precludes legal action for any torts arising out of that prescriptive right. In *Hoffman v. United Iron and Metal Co.*,[30] the court discarded claims filed for trespass, strict liability, and nuisance where these claims arose from the same type of acts that supported the prescriptive right.

In *Nissan Motor Corp. v. Maryland Shipbuilding and Drydock Co.*,[31] however, smoke emanating from the shipbuilding company's property, which allegedly damaged an automobile company's vehicles on an adjacent property, did *not* amount to a trespass since there was no interference with the automobile company's possession of the property. "[T]he invasion of Nissan's property by soot and ash did not amount to an interference with Nissan's exclusive possessory interest. Rather, the smoke and particulate fallout has interfered with Nissan's use and enjoyment of its property."[32] It is important to note that in *Nissan*, the court found that admiralty law controlled.

Remedies

In an action for trespass, damages may be measured by either (1) loss of value that results from the harm, or (2) cost of restoration, subject to the limitation that if cost of restoration is disproportionate to diminution in value, then the loss of value is the appropriate standard.[33]

NEGLIGENCE

Definition

A victim of environmental damage may seek relief in negligence if the damage was caused or threatened by the defendant's negligence. In Maryland, in order to prove liability for negligence, generally, a plaintiff must demonstrate that the defendant

---

[28] See *Nissan Motor Corp. v. Maryland Shipbuilders & Drydock Co.*, 544 F. Supp. 1104, *aff'd* 742 F.2d 1449 (D. Md. 1982).

[29] *Exxon*, 69 Md. App. at 130, 146.

[30] 108 Md. App. 117 (1996).

[31] 544 F. Supp. 1104, *aff'd* 742 F.2d 1449 (D. Md. 1982) (applying admiralty law, but also discussing Maryland law).

[32] *Id.* at 1116.

[33] *Regal Construction Co. v. West Lanham Hills Citizen's Ass'n.*, 256 Md. 302 (1970).

owed them a duty, that the duty was breached by unreasonable conduct, and that the breach caused damage to the plaintiff.[34]

The "unreasonable conduct" standard may be difficult to meet. In Maryland, however, violation of a statute or ordinance can be evidence of negligence.[35] Therefore, if a violation of an environmental regulation can be demonstrated, such as a violation of the new regulations governing underground storage tank care and maintenance, negligence may be proven.

Case Law

In *Exxon*[36] the plaintiffs sought damages for the contamination of their drinking water well. According to the court, the leaking underground storage tanks on the adjacent service station property, and the tardiness of the remediation at the site, constituted a "breach of [the defendant's] duty to its neighboring landowners not to impair their ownership rights through water contamination."[37]

In *State of Maryland, Department of Natural Resources v. Amerada Hess Corporation*,[38] Maryland sought to recover damages as a result of an oil spill into the Baltimore Harbor. The state claimed that the defendant's actions were "improper, negligent, and reckless."[39] The court determined that the state could maintain a common law action, in the absence of legislation, in order to prohibit pollution.[40]

Remedies

The appropriate relief for injured plaintiffs in negligence cases generally is damages, although injunctions may be sought where the environmentally damaging activity is continuous.[41]

STRICT LIABILITY

Definition

Maryland has adopted the rule of strict liability found in the *Restatement (Second) of Torts*, §519. An activity is "abnormally dangerous" if it involves a high degree of risk of harm to the person or land of others, the risk cannot be eliminated by the exercise of reasonable care, and the activity is inappropriate to the place in which it is being

---

[34] See *Lamb v. Hopkins*, 303 Md. 236, 241 (1985).

[35] *Pahanish v. Western Trails, Inc.*, 69 Md. App. 342, 362 (1986) (violation of a statutory duty may be evidence of negligence if (1) the plaintiff is a member of the class of persons the statute was designed to protect; (2) the injury suffered is the type the statute was designed to protect; and (3) the statutory violation is the proximate cause of injury).

[36] 69 Md. App. 124, 516 A.2d 990 (1986).

[37] *Id.* at 153.

[38] 350 F. Supp. 1060 (D. Md. 1972).

[39] *Id.* at 1065.

[40] *Id.*

[41] See *Amerada Hess*, 350 F. Supp. 1060 (D. Md. 1972); *Exxon v. Yarema*, 69 Md. App. 124, 516 A.2d 990 (1986).

conducted.[42] Most environmental statutes impose strict liability—one is liable for violation of the statute, whether negligent or not.

Case Law

In *Yommer v. McKenzie*, the Maryland Court of Appeals adopted the *Restatement* version of strict liability for abnormally dangerous activities and applied it to certain leaking underground gasoline tanks. The court determined that strict liability was applicable but emphasized the importance of the appropriateness of the activity to the particular area of concern. In *Yommer*, the storage tanks were "immediately adjacent" to private residences using well water for drinking purposes. This, according to the court, was an abnormally dangerous activity for which strict liability was appropriate. The McKenzies were awarded $3,500.

In *Exxon v. Yarema*, the court simply stated that "placement of large underground gasoline tanks in close proximity to private residences and drinking wells constitutes an abnormality." In *Kelly v. R.G. Industries, Inc.*,[43] the court asserted that the abnormally dangerous activity doctrine in §519 of the *Restatement* only imposes strict liability upon alleged tortfeasors who are owners or occupiers of land.[44]

Remedies

A strict liability action lies in tort. Plaintiffs are entitled to the damages that are the natural consequence of the tortious conduct. The Court made clear in *Exxon* that physical impact to the property is not required in order to recover damages. "[P]laintiffs may recover for economic injuries that defendant's pollution caused, even though there was no physical damage to plaintiffs' property."[45]

WASTE

Definition

According to *Black's Law Dictionary,* waste is the "destruction or material alteration or deterioration of the freehold, or the improvements forming a material part thereof, by any person rightfully in possession, but who has not the fee title for the full estate." In Maryland, tenants who commit waste are liable for the actual damages suffered by the property, provided the actions precipitating the waste are unauthorized.[46]

---

42 *Restatement (Second) of Torts,* §520.
43 304 Md. 124, 497 A.2d 1143 (1985). Negative treatment
44 See also *Toy*, 176 Md. at 213, 4 A.2d at 765 (1939).
45 *Yarema,* 69 Md. App. at 155.
46 MD. REAL PROP. CODE ANN. §14-102(a).

Case Law

While waste as it relates to environmental concerns has not been addressed in Maryland courts, in *Beesley v. Hanish*[47] the court restated the fundamental Maryland statutory waste law found in the Annotated Code of Maryland.[48]

Remedies

In Maryland, any person who commits waste shall be liable for the actual damages suffered by the property, even if that person grants or assigns his interest in the property.[49] Furthermore, an injured party may seek an injunction to stay waste; if a person commits waste after the injunction, a court may levy a fine equal to or double the ascertained damages.[50]

LIMITATIONS PERIOD

Maryland has a three-year statute of limitations applicable to tort actions.[51] In *Poffenberger v. Risser*,[52] Maryland adopted the discovery rule, which states that a cause of action accrues "when the claimant in fact knew or reasonably should have known of the wrong."[53] As a result, plaintiffs must bring any common law environmental claims within three years from the date that they had reason to know of the tortious conduct.

In *Goldstein v. Potomac Electric Power Co.*,[54] the court stated that in nuisance cases, where the nuisance is permanent in nature, the statute of limitations begins to run when the permanency of the conditions causing the plaintiff's damages becomes manifest. Actions for past, current, and future damages brought more than three years after the statute starts to run are barred. In cases of temporary nuisance, successive actions for damages may be brought for each invasion of the plaintiff's land until the 20-year prescriptive rights period has lapsed.[55]

BUYER BEWARE

The Maryland Court of Appeals has held that a person who purchases or leases a piece of commercial property in Maryland that has been polluted by a prior owner is barred from bringing an action in negligence, nuisance, trespass, or strict liability against that earlier owner.[56] The underlying rationale for this rule is that a buyer or lessee has the

---

[47] 70 Md. App. 482, 521 A.2d 1235 (1987).
[48] MD. REAL PROP. CODE §14-102.
[49] MD. REAL PROP. CODE §14-102(a).
[50] *Id.* §14-102(b).
[51] MD. CTS. & JUD. PRO. CODE §5-101.
[52] 290 Md. 631 (1981).
[53] *Id.* at 636.
[54] 285 Md. 673 (1979).
[55] *Id.* at 1072, n. 4.
[56] *Roseblatt v. Exxon,* 335 Md. 58 (1993).

opportunity to investigate and conduct environmental assessments before deciding to buy or lease the property. Additionally, such a rule increases the chances of an adjacent owner being able to recover if the contamination damages his/her property.

Owners or lessees of property adjacent to contaminated sites, however, are not barred from recovery even if they knew at the time of purchase that there was contamination or threat of contamination from a nearby leaking underground storage tank. In *JBG/Twinbrook Metro Limited Partnership v. Wheeler*,[57] the trial court found that the leaking gasoline from the defendant's underground storage tanks constituted a trespass, but that the plaintiff was barred from recovery because he assumed the risk when he bought the property with knowledge of prior contamination. On appeal, the Maryland Court of Appeals held that although assumption of the risk may be applicable to negligence claims, it is not a defense to trespass.[58] Therefore, the plaintiff was allowed to recover under a trespass theory, even though he had knowledge of the contamination when he purchased the property.

---

[57] 346 Md. 601 (1997).
[58] *Id.* at 619.

Index

About the Author

Theda Braddock has been an environmental and securities attorney for more than 20 years. She is author of *California Environmental Law and Natural Resources Handbook*, 13th edition; *Washington Environmental Law Handbook*, 5th edition; and *Wetlands: An Introduction*, 3rd edition. Braddock is admitted to practice before the state and federal courts in California, Maryland, Massachusetts, and Washington State. She is also admitted to practice before the U.S. Court of Federal Claims and the U.S. Supreme Court. Braddock attended the Great Books Program at St. John's College in Annapolis, Maryland, and received her B.A. from Mills College in Oakland, California. She received her J.D. from Golden Gate University in San Francisco, California.

www.ingramcontent.com/pod-product-compliance
Ingram Content Group UK Ltd.
Pitfield, Milton Keynes, MK11 3LW, UK
UKHW051417150926
475561UK00005B/218